T0210882

Lecture Notes in Computer Science   11345

Commenced Publication in 1973
Founding and Former Series Editors:
Gerhard Goos, Juris Hartmanis, and Jan van Leeuwen

More information about this series at http://www.springer.com/series/8277

Zhigeng Pan · Adrian David Cheok ·
Wolfgang Müller · Mingmin Zhang ·
Abdennour El Rhalibi · Kashif Kifayat (Eds.)

Transactions on Edutainment XV

Editors-in-Chief
Zhigeng Pan
Hangzhou Normal University
Hangzhou, China

Adrian David Cheok
Imagineering Institute
Nusajaya, Malaysia

Wolfgang Müller
University of Education
Weingarten, Germany

Guest Editors
Mingmin Zhang
Zhejiang University
Hangzhou, China

Abdennour El Rhalibi
John Moores University
Liverpool, UK

Kashif Kifayat
Air University
Islamabad, Pakistan

ISSN 0302-9743   ISSN 1611-3349 (electronic)
Lecture Notes in Computer Science
ISSN 1867-7207   ISSN 1867-7754 (electronic)
Transactions on Edutainment
ISBN 978-3-662-59350-9   ISBN 978-3-662-59351-6   (eBook)
https://doi.org/10.1007/978-3-662-59351-6

This Springer imprint is published by the registered company Springer-Verlag GmbH, DE
part of Springer Nature
The registered company address is: Heidelberger Platz 3, 14197 Berlin, Germany

Editorial

In this issue, we have four sections on different topics. In the first section on multimedia, there are four papers. In the first paper by Chunbao Pei et al., the authors propose a speech recognition algorithm called "Tibetan Hidden Markov Model." They have experimentally shown that the hidden Markov model in noisy environments for Tibetan better voice recognition. In the second paper, Guopeng Qiu et al. present a style-transfer generated against networks based on Markov random fields to generate high-quality style transition images in a short time. In the third paper by Zehua Jiao et al., the authors describe a point cloud registration algorithm based on 3D-SIFT features to deal with the problem of the traditional ICP algorithm being inefficient and incorrect if the correct initial point set is not obtained. In the fourth paper, Mei-li Zhu et al. introduce an algorithm based on the model of lip deep learning. They projected the binary image of the lip contour motion sequence onto the spatio-temporal energy, and employed the dynamic grayscale of the lip to reduce the noise interference in the recognition process.

The second section on simulation includes four papers. In the first paper, Xiuchun Xiao et al., in order to solve the problem of estimating the parameters of the decaying DC component in the process of fault current denoising, propose a special neural network, and then an adaptive learning algorithm based on the improved Levenberg–Marquardt algorithm is deduced. In the second paper by Jiang-lin Luo et al., the authors describe a facial expression recognition method based on a mixed feature fusion of nine types of personality. The method calculates the coordinate difference between the expression key points of the expression frame and the neutral frame in the image sequence, and extracts the geometric deformation characteristics. In the third paper, Haiying Zhao et al. put forward a method based on interactive choice mechanisms and establishment color constraint rules in order to create Xinjiang carpet patterns. In the fourth paper by Guopeng Qiu et al., the authors propose the structure–behavior coalescence process algebra, which is based on a systems unified view.

In the third section on cybersecurity, there are four papers. In the first paper by Djedjiga Mouheb et al., the authors present an overview and comparison of existing curriculum design approaches for cybersecurity education. The survey can help researchers and educators to have an overview of the existing approaches for the purpose of developing a suitable and more effective cybersecurity curriculum in their future endeavors. In the second paper, Patricia A.H Williams et al. research an innovative tactile learning activity developed through the European project with tertiary education students, that was designed to provide students with experience in real-world modeling of complex information security scenarios. In the third paper by Abdullahi Arabo et al., the authors improve student motivation, engagement, and interest in cybersecurity by contextualizing teaching material with current real-world scenarios. In the fourth paper, Chitra Balakrishna aims to develop a holistic cyber-security training environment that enables a change in learners' behavior by making them security conscious for every action they perform in the real-world environment.

The fourth section on e-learning comprises four papers. In the first paper by Tom Chothia et al., the authors develop a method for adding competition and story-telling to an introductory cybersecurity course. In the second paper, Nuria Benjuma et al. introduce the ICS-SES framework for helping developers in designing secure control systems by enabling them to reuse secure design patterns and improve their security knowledge. In the third paper by Jens Haag et al., the authors first give a full account of their earlier work on a distributed virtual computer lab for cybersecurity education. Then, this virtual lab is extended with educational enhancements, such as an intelligent tutoring system, which resulted in a prototype for a virtual classroom for cybersecurity education. In the fourth paper, Beaumont et al. explain and critically evaluate innovative approaches that address both the supply of competent graduates and SME infosec problems.

April 2019

Mingmin Zhang
Abdennour El Rhalibi
Kashif Kifayat

Transactions on Edutainment

This journal subline serves as a forum for stimulating and disseminating innovative research ideas, theories, emerging technologies, empirical investigations, state-of-the-art methods, and tools in all the different genres of edutainment, such as game-based learning and serious games, interactive storytelling, virtual learning environments, VR-based education, and related fields. It covers aspects from educational and game theories, human–computer interaction, computer graphics, artificial intelligence, and systems design.

Contents

Multimedia

Wearable Sensors and Equipment in VR Games: A Review

Mingliang Cao[1,2(✉)], Tianhua Xie[3], and Zebin Chen[3]

[1] Guangdong Academy of Research on VR Industry,
Foshan University, Foshan 528000, China
merlin.cao@connect.polyu.hk
[2] VR Research Institute, NINEDVR Corp, Guangzhou 310036, China
[3] Automation College, Foshan University, Foshan 528000, China

Abstract. Virtual Reality (VR) has been developed dramatically in recent years due to its benefits of providing an engaging and immersive environment. The objective of this study was to collect and critically analyze wearable sensors and equipment used in VR games, aiming at classifying wearable sensors according to the player's key needs and the characteristics of the VR game. The review is organized according to three perspectives: the player's needs, the player mode and the functional sensor modularization in a VR game. Our review work is useful for both researchers and educators to develop/integrate wearable sensors and equipment for improving a VR game player's performance.

Keywords: Virtual Reality · Wearable sensors and equipment · VR game

1 Introduction

Economic and technological changes have spurred dramatic shifts in human lives, including entertainment. Many breakthrough sciences and technologies have opened access to new trends in the past three decades [1]. The Virtual Reality (VR) technology will be a bellwether for the next generation of technological revolution, and it will completely affect people's lifestyles, including entertainment [2, 3]. The aim of current VR systems is mainly to immerse users in virtual environments with special VR equipment or 3D visual setting. However, this is achieved at the expense of usability, since users are inherently obstructed from viewing and interacting with physical objects. This poses many limitations to state-of-the-art VR devices, which typically do not provide a well-integrated interaction way to complement the high-standard immersive experience they offer. Wearable sensors and equipment are most important in VR games and there will be a huge trend for their use to rise in the near future [4]. Ever since the emergence of many mature wearable VR devices on the market (see Fig. 1), VR equipment seems to have potential to enrich people's lives. Technology developers (including hardware and software) from around the world have been trying to work with big brand marketers to build more tangible and auditory VR solutions to match clients' requirements and objectives.

Wearable sensors have received a considerable amount of research and development attention within the past two decades [5]. However, the traditional research

© Springer-Verlag GmbH Germany, part of Springer Nature 2019
Z. Pan et al. (Eds.): Transactions on Edutainment XV, LNCS 11345, pp. 3–12, 2019.
https://doi.org/10.1007/978-3-662-59351-6_1

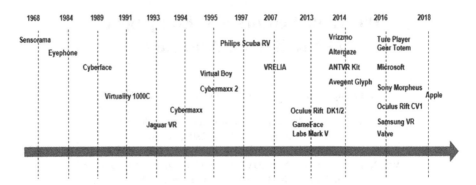

Fig. 1. The development of VR equipment.

methods in VR game field have tended to follow old conventions, which means that all kinds of sensors are integrated into the VR game equipment according to individual functions. It is time to make some changes. From the entertainment perspective, the top mission of VR game equipment is to meet player's fundamental needs by using wearable sensors and equipment. Likewise, the entertainment-related characteristics of the VR game can provide us more clues to resolve what kind of wearable sensors and equipment best reflect players' fundamental needs. The purpose of this study was to provide a critical review of the wearable sensors and equipment in the VR game field from three perspectives: player's needs, player mode and functional sensor modularization in a VR game.

2   Perspective on VR Game Player's Needs

One of the key perspectives of this paper is to develop wearable sensors and equipment for VR games based on Maslow's Theory of Needs [6]. According to Maslow's theory, the key needs associated with VR games can cover three levels: safety, society and esteem. First, at the "safety" level, the wearable sensors and equipment should ensure players safety when they are playing a VR game, it is beyond doubt. Second, at the "society" level, they should encourage players to interact with each other. Normally, multiplayer VR games add an element of group way that leads to experience that can be more fun than relying on a single player experience crafted in advance. VR inputs are ideally suited for social interactions. Third, at the "esteem" level, player should allow for their personality in the VR game. For example, you can create an avatar according to your physiological information in the VR game. There are a lot of sensors which can be classified according to the VR game player's needs (see Table 1).

Table 1. VR game needs for wearable sensors and equipment.

Maslow's needs	Player's needs	Wearable sensors and equipment
Safety	To keep player safety when playing VR game	E.g. heart rate sensors [7], temperature sensors [8], respiration sensors [9], acceleration sensor [10], gyroscope [11], tilt sensor [12], HMD, digital glove [13], wearable motion capture equipment [14], digital garment [15].
Society	To make players interact with each other in VR game	E.g. HMD, digital glove, sound sensor [16], heart rate sensor, temperature sensors, force feedback equipment [17]
Esteem	To show player's personality in VR game	E.g. physiological sensors [18], customized VR equipment

3 Perspective on VR Game Player's Mode

Another perspective of this paper is the development of wearable sensors and equipment in VR games according to three player modes (see Fig. 2): single-player, multi-player, and team players. First, for a single-player VR game, the wearable sensors should meet needs such as movement and the collection of information for the player. Second, for multi-players, the wearable sensors should meet needs such as sound communication, and should force feedback between game players. Third, for team players, the wearable sensors should meet needs such as character assignment using the physiological information among game players. A study shows that the multi-player VR game is more immersive and interactive than the single-player game [19, 20]. More importantly, VR game equipment has made a great progress in contributing to teamwork, and should be the trend of future VR game, such as in the example of Virtual Battlegrounds [21].

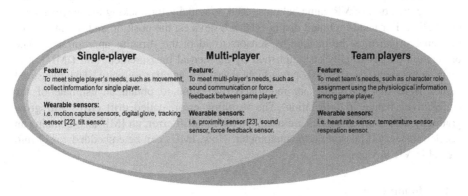

Fig. 2. Features of single-player, multi-player and team players in VR game.

4 Perspective on Functional Sensor Modularization in VR Game

There is a number of widget sensors integrated as one functional module in a VR game, for example, the acceleration sensor, the gyroscope and the geomagnetic sensor are integrated as an inertial sensor module to collect information about the user's head movement. The wearable sensors in a VR game are like a speech transmitter that communicates between the player and the VR game environment, to enable the game to receive data and take some action in order to meet the player's requirements. The other perspective of this paper is the development of VR game equipment through four kinds of functional sensor modularization (see Table 2): IMU [24], motion capture [14], physiological monitoring [25] and environmental monitoring [26].

Table 2. Summary of functional sensor modularization in VR games.

Modularization	Types	Key function
Inertial measurement unit (IMU)	E.g. gyroscope; acceleration sensor; geomagnetic sensor [27]	To capture head movement and track player's head distance
Motion capture	E.g. infrared sensor [28]; FOV sensor [29]; electromagnetic sensor [30]	To capture player's motion of their body
Physiological monitoring	E.g. temperature sensor; respiration sensor; galvanic skin response [31]; pulse oximeter [32]; skin electrodes [33]	To analyze and evaluate their psychological state in the VR game
Environmental monitoring	E.g. temperature sensor; humidity sensor [34]; light intensity sensor [35]	To collect the information of real world

4.1 Inertial Measurement Unit

The inertial measurement unit is one of the important authoring technologies for the current generation of VR game helmets, used principally for tracking the player's head orientation. For head-mounted display (HMD) devices, the position and orientation of the sense organ must be tracked by sensors to adapt the stimulus appropriately. The orientation part is usually accomplished by an inertial measurement unit (IMU). The main component is a gyroscope, which measures angular velocity. The measured values from the gyroscope are integrated over time to obtain an estimate of the cumulative change in orientation. The resulting error, called drift error, will grow gradually unless other sensors are used. To reduce drift error, an IMU also contains an accelerometer and possibly a magnetometer. Now, IMUs can be embedded easily into wearable VR devices.

4.2 Motion Capture

Motion capture (MOCAP) is an important technology for the VR game industry, as it can capture the motions of real actors into a virtual world for virtual games or animations. Generally it is used in the process of capturing the large-scale body movements of a subject at some resolution, as well as the overall tracking of a player by using wearable sensors, such as infrared sensors, FOV sensors or electromagnetic sensors. There are five kinds of popular technologies in motion capture (see Table 3).

Table 3. Summary of motion capture technology.

Technology	Essential	Advantage	Disadvantage
Mechanical motion capture [36]	Mechanical devices	High accuracy; real-time	Cumbersome; movement restriction
Acoustic motion capture [37]	Acoustic units	Low cost	Noise jamming
Electromagnetic motion capture [38]	Electromagnetic effect	Good robustness	No metal objects; limits to large extent
Optical motion capture [39]	Specific points of light	High-speed processing; addible	Expensive; incapacity for big data
Inertial navigation motion capture [40, 41]	Attitude heading reference (AHR) and IMUs	High integration; high accuracy	Expensive

4.3   Physiological Monitoring

The physiological data collection is generally for the purpose of learning about human physical conditions. The market products and research about VR wearable sensors and equipment have failed to make full use of VR game players' physiological data. In this paper, we propose creating a virtual player in the VR game, which is related closely to the actual players based on their physiological data. On one hand, this can make the game more interesting. On the other hand, it can make the players learn more about their own real physical situations during the game. There are some kinds of physiological sensors which can be used for VR game players (see Table 4).

Table 4. Summary of physiological monitoring sensors.

Type of bio-signal	Type of sensors	Description of physiological data
Skin temperature [42]	Temperature sensor	A measure of the body's ability to generate and get rid of heat when game playing
Respiration rate [43]	Respiration sensors	Number of movement indicative and breathing rate
Electromyogram [44]	Skin electrodes	Electrical activity of the skeletal muscles
Perspiration (sweating) or skin conductivity [33]	Galvanic skin response	Electrical conductance of the skin in associated with the activity of the sweat glands
Oxygen saturation [32]	Pulse oximeter	Indicates the oxygen is being "carried" in blood

4.4 Environmental Monitoring

In this review, we consider the environmental information into the VR game in oder to increase the sense of realic immersion for players. On one hand, the collection of environmental information is mainly for the purpose of learning about the real environmental details. On the other hand, it is to provide players with a connection between the real environment and the virtual environment, thus providing a more satisfactory game experience, which is also an important purpose of VR game development [45, 46]. Up to now, there are a few wearable sensors and equipment in VR games that take environmental information into account. Developers ignore the influence of environmental information on players, such as light intensity, humidity, temperature and smell. There are many kinds of environmental information which have potential effects on VR game players. Of course, the collected environmental information should be related to the fundamental needs of the VR game player, which can be used to inform the future development of wearable sensors and equipment. There are some kinds of environmental monitoring sensors which can be used in VR games (see Table 5) [47].

Table 5. Summary of environmental monitoring sensors.

Type of environment information	Type of sensors	Description of environmental data
Light intensity in environment	Light intensity sensor [35]	Light intensity is related to the sun
Humidity in environmental air	Humidity sensor [34]	Humidity is related to the weather
Temperature in environmental air	Temperature sensor [8]	Temperature is related to the weather
Smell in the environment	Smell sensor [48, 49]	Smell is related to the environment

5 Conclusion

The paper has reviewed the reported literature on wearable sensors and equipment in VR game. The wearable sensors are needed more and more in future markets because they have a few distinct advantages compared with the unwearable ones [50, 51]. These remarkable features include: they can be placed optionally and moved effectively as the user wishes; they can be turned on or off only when there is a need to collect or chip data; they can be designed to fit a player's body size comfortably; and they can create a dynamic system by linking whole sensors to the VR game equipment. Therefore, the wearable sensor must be an important trend in technology development. Most VR game equipment is dependent on the individual function of sensors, which has hitherto limited the development of VR games in the market. Obviously, if the wearable sensor systems are focused on customer needs, they should start with four points: they should be based on or supported by sensor network technology; they should aim to provide intelligent entertainment services; the system should always be human-centered; and, the system should be subjected to collecting physiological parameters with non-invasive monitoring.

Technology is still very important, but it is not the only issue that should be considered in the future development of VR game equipment [52]. In addition to visual sensory, other sensations, motor or sensorimotor interfaces will evolve slowly, as is the case in the quarter century. For example, the manipulation of a virtual object is easily accomplished in the VR game. On the other hand, if a player wants to manipulate with fingers, creating a realistic tactile sensation, the difficulties in mechatronics to realize such a glove with tactile feedback and realistic efforts on all fingers, are enormous. No matter how the technology develops, it may never be possible to make such a perfect glove. And the technical compromises must always be made. Moreover, even if tactile stimuli are approximate and impractical, tactile gloves that only provide mechanical touch feedback and possible thermal changes are readily conceivable and effective. They have to find a larger number of economic markets, which is not obvious because their practical use in VR games is limited. Olfactory interfaces have also been developed, but there are no major commercial developments because they are rarely used in VR games. In addition, they are very difficult to manage because they need to store the odor chemicals. Brain-Machine Interface (BMI) is another example of providing a spectacular effect to move virtually or to manipulate virtual objects by thinking. But in addition to this surprising effect, BMI is of little use to VR game applications because they can cause inappropriate and ineffective cognitive overload on the user.

The future developmental trends in VR game equipment look to be more related to artificial intelligence (AI), multimodal technology and so on. Fundamental to the foundation of every system is the collection and analysis of data. Therefore, future research should pay more attention to the means of data collection and the kinds of equipment that are more suitable for players. On one hand, wearable sensors will be one of the greatest things in VR game equipment development, because the future of the chip will lead to more wearable device miniaturization and integration. Customization of future mainstream chips can be based on chip platforms, the integration of individual characters, and open sources. As well, players can be enabled to understand the information about their own bodies by using wearable physiological monitoring sensors or equipment. In conclusion, wearable sensors and equipment in VR game can be developed according to player's needs, player mode and the modularization of functional sensors.

Acknowledgments. We would like to acknowledge the support of the Guangzhou Innovation and Entrepreneurship Leading Team Project under grant CXLJTD-201609.

References

1. Zyda, M.: From visual simulation to virtual reality to games. IEEE Comput. **38**(9), 25–32 (2005)
2. State, A., Hirota, G., Chen, D.T., et al.: Superior augmented reality registration by integrating landmark tracking and magnetic tracking. In: Conference on Computer Graphics and Interactive Techniques, pp. 429–438. ACM (1996)
3. Gaitatzes, A., Papaioannou, G., Christopoulos, D.: Virtual reality systems and applications. In: Symposium on Virtual Reality Software and Technology, p. 384. ACM (2006)

4. Tyson, A.M., Duma, S.M., Rowson, S., et al.: Laboratory evaluation of low-cost wearable sensors for measuring head impacts in sports. J. Appl. Biomech. **34**(4), 320–326 (2018)
5. Lara, O.D., Labrador, M.A.: A survey on human activity recognition using wearable sensors. IEEE Commun. Surv. Tut. **15**(3), 1192–1209 (2013)
6. Gawel, J.E.: Herzberg's theory of motivation and Maslow's hierarchy of needs. ERIC. AE Dig., p. 4, July 1997
7. Chittaro, L., Sioni, R.: Affective computing vs. affective placebo: study of a biofeedback-controlled game for relaxation training. Int. J. Hum Comput Stud. **72**(8-9), 663–673 (2014)
8. Chen, P., Chen, C.C., Tsai, C.C., et al.: A time-to-digital-converter-based CMOS smart temperature sensor. IEEE J. Solid-State Circuits **40**(8), 1642–1648 (2005)
9. Higashikaturagi, K., Nakahata, Y., Matsunami, I., et al.: Non-invasive respiration monitoring sensor using UWB-IR. In: IEEE International Conference on Ultra-Wideband, pp. 101–104 (2008)
10. Jones, P.E.: Three-dimensional input device with six degrees of freedom. IEEE ASME. Trans. Mechatron. **9**(7), 717–729 (1999)
11. Dai, R., Stein, R.B., Andrews, B.J., et al.: Application of tilt sensors in functional electrical stimulation. IEEE Trans. Rehabil. Eng. **4**(2), 63–72 (1996)
12. Goo, J.J., et al.: Effects of guided and unguided style learning on user attention in a virtual environment. In: Pan, Z., Aylett, R., Diener, H., Jin, X., Göbel, S., Li, L. (eds.) Edutainment 2006. LNCS, vol. 3942, pp. 1208–1222. Springer, Heidelberg (2006). https://doi.org/10.1007/11736639_151
13. Kushida, T., Takefuta, H., Muramatsu, H.: Acceleration sensor: US, US5005412 (1991)
14. Cui, Z.G., Ai-Hua, L.I., Yan-Zhao, S.U., et al.: Collaborative object tracking algorithm in large FOV with binocular active vision sensors. J. Optoelectron. Laser **25**(4), 784–791 (2014)
15. Le Thanh, T., Gagalowicz, A.: Virtual garment pre-positioning. In: Gagalowicz, A., Philips, W. (eds.) CAIP 2005. LNCS, vol. 3691, pp. 837–845. Springer, Heidelberg (2005). https://doi.org/10.1007/11556121_103
16. Kim, W., Mechitov, K., Choi, J.Y., et al.: On target tracking with binary proximity sensors. In: International Symposium on Information Processing in Sensor Networks, p. 40. IEEE (2005)
17. Ferreira, A., Cassier, C., Hirai, S.: Automatic microassembly system assisted by vision servoing and virtual reality. IEEE-ASME Trans. Mechatron. **9**(2), 321–333 (1960)
18. Friedl, K.E.: Military applications of soldier physiological monitoring. J. Sci. Med. Sport. **21**(11), 1147–1153 (2018)
19. Jain, N., Wydra, A., Wen, H., et al.: Time-scaled interactive object-driven multi-party VR. Vis. Comput. **34**(9), 1–11 (2018)
20. Menin, A., Torchelsen, R., Nedel, L.: An analysis of VR technology used in immersive simulations with a serious game perspective. IEEE Comput. Graph. Appl. **38**(2), 57–73 (2018)
21. Crawford, E.: Virtual battlegrounds: direct participation in cyber warfare. SSEP (2013)
22. Eom, D.S., Kim, T., Jee, H., et al.: A multi-player arcade video game platform with a wireless tangible user interface. IEEE Trans. Consum. Electron. **54**(4), 1819–1824 (2008)
23. Annie, G., Guyot-Mbodji, A., Demeure, I.: Gaming on the move: urban experience as a new paradigm for mobile pervasive game design. Multimed. Syst. **16**(1), 43–55 (2010)
24. Mousa, M., Sharma, K., Claudel, C.G., et al.: Inertial measurement units-based probe vehicles: automatic calibration, trajectory estimation, and context detection. IEEE Trans. Intell. Transp. Syst. **19**(10), 3133–3143 (2018)

25. Navarro, E., Gonzalez, P., Lopezjaquero, V., et al.: Adaptive, multisensorial, physiological and social: the next generation of telerehabilitation systems. Front. Neuroinform. **12**, 43 (2018)
26. Haghi, M., Stoll, R., Thurow, K., et al.: A low-cost, standalone, and multi-tasking watch for personalized environmental monitoring. IEEE Trans. Biomed. Circuits Syst. **12**(5), 1144–1154 (2018)
27. Zhai, J., Dong, S., Xing, Z., et al.: Geomagnetic sensor based on giant magnetoelectric effect. Appl. Phys. Lett. **91**(12), 405 (2007)
28. Berger, K., Ruhl, K., Schroeder, Y., et al.: Markerless motion capture using multiple color-depth sensors. In: VMV, pp. 317–324 (2011)
29. Kasapakis, V., Gavalas, D.: Occlusion handling in outdoors augmented reality games. Multimed. Tools. Appl. **76**, 1–26 (2016)
30. Hastenteufel, M., Vetter, M., Meinzer, H.P., et al.: Effect of 3D ultrasound probes on the accuracy of electromagnetic tracking systems. Ultrasound Med. Biol. **32**(9), 1359–1368 (2006)
31. Larradet, F., Barresi, G., Mattos, L.S.: Effects of galvanic skin response feedback on user experience in gaze-controlled gaming: a pilot study. In: International Conference of the IEEE Engineering in Medicine & Biology Society, p. 2458 (2017)
32. Kahol, K.: Integrative gaming: a framework for sustainable game-based diabetes management. J. Diabetes Sci. Technol. **5**(5), 293–300 (2011)
33. Liao, L.D., Chen, C.Y., Wang, I.J., et al.: Gaming control using a wearable and wireless EEG-based brain-computer interface device with novel dry foam-based sensors. J. Neuroeng. Rehabil. **9**(1), 1–12 (2012)
34. Chen, Z., Lu, C.: Humidity sensors: a review of materials and mechanisms. Sens. Lett. **3**(4), 274–295 (2005)
35. Chiang, C.T., Chang, C.M., Chang, C.C.: Design of an ultraviolet light intensity monitor for personally wearable devices digital object identifier inserted by IEEE. IEEE Sens. J. **PP**(99), 1 (2018)
36. Miller, E., Kaufman, K., Kingsbury, T., et al.: Mechanical testing for three-dimensional motion analysis reliability. Gait Posture **50**, 116–119 (2016)
37. Vlasic, D., Adelsberger, R., Vannucci, G., et al.: Practical motion capture in everyday surroundings. ACM Trans. Graphics **26**(3), 35 (2007)
38. Schnabel, U.H., Hegenloh, M., Müller, H.J., et al.: Electromagnetic tracking of motion in the proximity of computer generated graphical stimuli: a tutorial. Behav. Res. Methods **45**(3), 696–701 (2013)
39. Aurand, A.M., Dufour, J.S., Marras, W.S.: Accuracy map of an optical motion capture system with 42 or 21 cameras in a large measurement volume. J. Biomech. **58**, 237–240 (2017)
40. Kok, M., Jeroen, D.H., Thomas, B.S.: An optimization-based approach to human body motion capture using inertial sensors. IFAC Proc. Vol. **47**(3), 79–85 (2014)
41. Wang, X., Xiao, L.: Gyroscope-reduced inertial navigation system for flight vehicle motion estimation. Adv. Space Res. **59**(1), 413–424 (2017)
42. Chudecka, M., Lubkowska, A.: Temperature changes of selected body's surfaces of handball players in the course of training estimated by thermovision, and the study of the impact of physiological and morphological factors on the skin temperature. J. Therm. Biol **35**(8), 379–385 (2010)
43. Darzi, A., Gorsic, M., Novak, D.: Difficulty adaptation in a competitive arm rehabilitation game using real-time control of arm electromyogram and respiration. In: International Conference on Rehabilitation Robotics, pp. 857–862 (2017)

44. Watanabe, M., Yamamoto, T., Kambara, H., et al.: Evaluation of a game controller using human stiffness estimated from electromyogram. In: International Conference of the IEEE Engineering in Medicine and Biology Society, pp. 4626–4631 (2001)
45. Jennett, C., Cox, A.L., Cairns, P.A., et al.: Measuring and defining the experience of immersion in games. Int. J. Hum. Comput. Stud. **66**(9), 641–661 (2008)
46. Wilcoxnetepczuk, D.: Immersion and realism in video games - the confused moniker of video game engrossment. In: International Conference on Computer Games, pp. 92–95 (2013)
47. Lara, O.D., Labrador, M.A.: A survey on human activity recognition using wearable sensors. IEEE Commun. Surv. Tutor. **15**(3), 1192–1209 (2013)
48. Chalmers, A., Debattista, K., Ramic-Brkic, B.: Towards high-fidelity multi-sensory virtual environments. Vis. Comput. **25**(12), 1101–1108 (2009)
49. Groen, F.C.A., Pavlin, G., Winterboer, A., et al.: A hybrid approach to decision making and information fusion: combining humans and artificial agents. Robot. Auton. Syst. **90**(C), 71–85 (2017)
50. Lee, S., Mase, K.: Activity and location recognition using wearable sensors. IEEE Pervasive Comput. **1**(3), 24–32 (2002)
51. Mukhopadhyay, S.C.: Wearable sensors for human activity monitoring: a review. IEEE Sens. J. **15**(3), 1321–1330 (2015)
52. Fuchs, P.: Théorie de la réalité virtuelle. Les véritables usages (A Theory of Virtual Reality: The Real Uses). Presses des Mines (2018)

A Style Image Confrontation Generation Network Based on Markov Random Field

Guopeng Qiu[1], Jianwen Song[2(⊠)], and Lilong Chen[1]

[1] Strait Animation Institute of Sanming University, Sanming 365004, China
{qgp, smxyl102}@fjsmu.edu.cn
[2] China Academy of Art, Hangzhou 310024, China
songjw888@126.com

Abstract. A style-transfer generates against network based on Markov random field is proposed in this paper. Based on the original image, a new image is generated by generate network, and then the error between the original image and the style image is calculated using the discriminant network and backward propagation to the generate network, high-quality style transfer images are generated through the continuous confrontation of the two networks. In the quantification of style loss and content loss, we have introduced Markov random field, which uses its limitation on the spatial layout to reduce the distorted distortion of the generated image and improve the quality of the generated image. Experiments show that the network can quickly generate high-quality style transition images in a short time.

Keywords: Fast style migration ·
Deep convolution countermeasure generation network · Markov random field ·
Perceived loss

1 Introduction

In recent years, with the deep network in the computer vision field has achieved breakthrough results, some researchers began to turn their attention to artistic creation, style transfer is one of the more successful attempt [1]. Style transfer is the fusion of classic art and artificial intelligence technology, regardless of the field of art or technology has great influence. Not only that, as the core technology to transfer the product style in a short period of time to attract a large number of users also proved its broad application scenarios. Based on the migration algorithm based on style, the perceptual loss rather than pixel loss to reduce the time cost, and using Markov Random Field (MRF) Loss to calculate the image loss, both using the extraction ability of CNN abstract features, but also can make use of space layout constraints MRF, improve the quality of image. In the generation of the migration images combined with Generative Adversarial Network (GAN) generated against network thought, migration generated by the image and the original image of the original image and style against the "content" and "style" style map to generate images, generate high quality image style transfer.

© Springer-Verlag GmbH Germany, part of Springer Nature 2019
Z. Pan et al. (Eds.): Transactions on Edutainment XV, LNCS 11345, pp. 13–23, 2019.
https://doi.org/10.1007/978-3-662-59351-6_2

2   Style Transfer

The image style transfer process from the specified style image (Style Image) feature extraction, without destroying the image (content image) structure under the premise of using features extracted from the style conversion of the image content, the output image obtained is perfect image and style of image fusion.

As shown in Fig. 1, the contents of the above picture is an ordinary photography style image below is the post impressionist painter Van Gogh's masterpiece "starry night", on the right side of the image (result image) is a novel image, which obviously retains the structure and shape of the information content of images but also image style the texture and color.

Fig. 1. Left figure (content image), the content of the picture in Middle figure is Van Gogh's "Star" style (style image) as a picture, Right figure is the output in the pictures on left one with middle one as the style of image style after the migration

2.1   Traditional Style Transfer

Style transfer is not a new concept, related research also has twenty years of history, but from the perspective of neural network to solve the problem is to transfer the style in recent years. Before using the neural network to solve the problem of image style migration, the consensus in both academia and industry is that if you want to migrate a style image, the first task is to create a mathematical model or statistical model for the style image, and then make changes to the content image. It can better conform to the established model [4, 5]. This method practical application effect is good, but the problem is that this method to achieve the program portability is poor, basically can only be used for processing a style or a specific scene, need to adjust the model to replace the style picture, picture of the modeling process of the content is trouble. So the application scenarios products based on the development of the traditional style of migration is very limited.

2.2   Style Transfer Neural Network

Although the traditional style transfer algorithm can achieve good results, but there is a fundamental flaw: the traditional algorithm migration process using only the style of image characteristics of shallow application in target image in style [8]. In fact, the style transfer algorithm should be able to extract semantic information effectively from the style in the image and the target image fusion structure with [10] reconstruction. How will the natural picture of the content and style of separation is still a challenging problem. In recent years, with the development of deep convolutional neural network, has produced a lot of specialized computer vision system used to extract high-level semantic information from natural images.

Recent studies by Gatys et al. used the powerful feature extraction capabilities of convolutional nerves, and for the first time used deep learning to learn styles of art and achieved great success. The author believes that the problem of image style transfer can be achieved by two operations: maintaining the content of the original image and incorporating the underlying visual features of the style image. The quantified mathematical formulas are used to describe the "style" and "content" of art paintings, and a style similarity evaluation method based on depth characteristics is proposed. The method starts with a random noise map and minimizes the total loss (i.e., the weighted average of style loss and content loss) by iteratively updating the pixels in the noise map so that the stylized image can simultaneously render the content image. The content matches the style of the style image. This method automatically extracts texture, color, and other features in the picture through the neural network and defines the "style" and "content" of the image based on these features. Compared with the traditional algorithm, it has greatly improved, but there are also many problems. Firstly, this method uses a pixel-by-pixel difference loss function. This loss function can't catch the gap between the input and output images. For example, consider two identical images, only a one-pixel offset, although the two images are exactly the same in perception, but they are very different when measured pixel-by-pixel. Secondly, this method requires retraining every time the image is generated, which is costly to calculate and therefore slower, making it difficult to make real-time applications.

2.3   Perceptual Loss

Gats et al.'s style transfer algorithm has strong portability, and the actual output effect is very good. However, due to slow performance, real-time results cannot be produced, which greatly limits the application scenario of the algorithm. The style transfer algorithm finds an image with both content and style from a white noise image. By adjusting the pixel points to minimize the total loss, the generated image is approximated by the original image's content features and style image's style features. Recent work has shown that high-quality images can be calculated by establishing a perceptual loss function, i.e., not based on a pixel-by-pixel gap, instead of extracting high-level image features from pre-trained CNNs to calculate perceptual loss. The perceptual loss function is generated to minimize. Based on the perceptual loss method, the generation problem is regarded as a transformation problem. The generated image is directly obtained from the content image, and the generated image, original image and style map are put into a pre-trained convolutional neural network, and the volume is compared. The high-level feature layer of the neural network calculates the loss function, and then reverse-adjusts the generation network. The method of using perceptual loss does not require retraining of the convolutional neural network. It requires only a one-time calculation to obtain the output, and the time cost is reduced by two orders of magnitude, which fully satisfies the needs of the real-time system.

3   Generative Adversarial Network

Generative Adversarial Network (GAN) is an unsupervised learning methods, learning by making two neural network game between the way. The method proposed by Ian Goodfellow et al. in 2014.

Generative Adversarial Network consists of a network with a discrimination network composition. The network generated from potential space in random sampling as input, the output results need to imitate the real samples in the training set. The input of the network output for distinguishing real samples and generation of the network, the purpose of which is to generate network output from real samples as far as possible out. The network is to generate as much as possible to deceive the discrimination network. Two network confrontation [2, 3, 10], constantly adjusting the parameters, the ultimate goal is to make the discrimination network unable to determine whether the results of real output generation network. The calculation process and structure formation against the network as shown in the figure (Fig. 2):

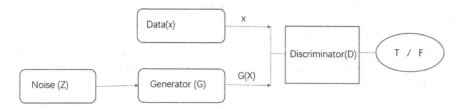

Fig. 2. This graph is D and G differential function which represents the discriminator and the generator, their input respectively x data and random variable z. G (z) is generated to obey samples of real data distribution. If the arbiter input from the X data, labeled as 1. if the input sample is G, mark 0. here is the goal of D is to realize the data source two classification: true (distribution derived from real data of X (G) or pseudo data from the generator (z)), and the goal of G is to make G pseudo data generation (z) in D (on the table now G (z)) and x data in D on the performance of D (x), the two against each other and iterative optimization process so that the performance of D and G increase, when the final D enhance discriminant ability to a certain extent, and cannot distinguish the data source, can think of this generator G has learn the distribution of real data.

3.1   Depth Convolution Generative Adversarial Network

Generative Adversarial Network does not need specific loss function can be in the process of learning to well said, but generated against cyber training is very unstable, often makes no sense generator output. The depth against the network will generate convolution neural network supervised learning and unsupervised learning in the generation of network confrontation together. The specific implementation would be generated G model and discriminant model with two D convolutional neural network instead of [4, 9], and the structure of the convolutional neural network makes a change, in order to improve the quality and speed of convergence of the sample, these changes have:

(1) Cancel all pooling layer. Generation of the network using the transpose of the convolution of the sampling, identification by adding stride convolutional network instead of pooling.
(2) Batch normalization is used both in the discrimination network and in the generation.
(3) Remove all connection layer, the network becomes the convolutional network.
(4) Using ReLU as the activation function of G network, the last layer using tanh.
(5) Using LeakyReLU as the activation function of D network.

Generation of the network structure depth against network convolution generated as shown in Fig. 3:

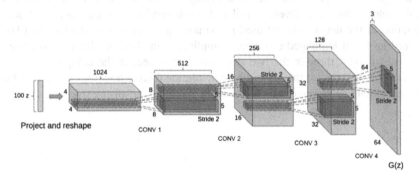

Fig. 3. The picture shows the structure graph of the network, the network input (100 dimensional random noise) is projected to a convolutional network, through 4 micro amplitude convolution (convolution transpose) feature maps into high level 64 * 64 pixel RGB three channel image.

4   Generate Adversarial Style Transfer Network

Inspired by the depth of the convolution of the generating network confrontation, algorithm design added generation against the migration of ideas in the image style, style for the migration of generation against network construction. As shown in Fig. 4, in the input, we will enter the original network instead of random noise generation. The original conversion in the generation model of G using a deep residual network, through a nonlinear transformation in the original generation is based on a new image [3, 7], ensure the generation capacity of generating model. Convolutional neural network model represented by VGG can be a very good time of the formation of image feature extraction and effective characterization of the image, and achieved excellent performance in large-scale image classification, image segmentation and image target detection on multiple tasks. So we use a discriminant model of part in the large training set on the pre trained VGG-16 convolutional neural networks, high-level feature extraction ability to extract images using its powerful feature comparison.

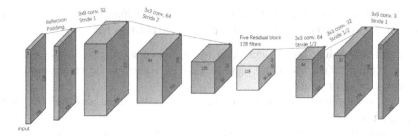

Fig. 4. Blue is the five residual blocks are 128 * 80 * 80, Activation, Size, 128 * 76 * 76, 128 * 72 * 72, 128 * 68 * 68 and 128 * 64 * 64. (Color figure online)

4.1 Generate Network

The design idea of generating network belongs to the whole residual network, the overall architecture has 3 layers, 5 roll and 3 roll residual block laminated structure. Generation of the network is not used in the pooling method, including second layers and third layers of laminated roll under sampling, at the back of the three volumes of laminated samples, through the two step operation to reduce the computational complexity of the network, at the same time convolutional layer down sampling will bring increased efficiency of regional. On behalf of the blue part of the five residual block,

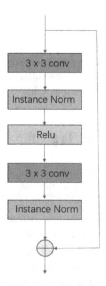

Fig. 5. In Fig. 5, we use Instance Normalization instead of Batch Normalization, is one of the goals is to consider the migration process style image (Style Image) contrast to also need a new picture of the neglect of the contrast of the picture content. Although the Batch in the picture, video classification task of Normalization Instance is better than Normalization, but Gan and Style Transfer in tasks such as the generative class in Instance Normalization is better. (Color figure online)

residual block interior details, see Fig. 5. The residual block using the same number (128) of the filter, each residual block has two volumes (3 × 3 conv), laminated layer convolution without the use of 0 filling (0 padding). As shown in Fig. 4, generating network in the initial image input part joined the reflection filled [5], ensure the input and output image sizes, avoiding the 0 filling (0 padding) image edge artifact problems.

4.2 Discrimination Network

Determine the input for the network image generation network generated image R and image C (original) content and style of the image S, calculated by the discriminant network image content and R content of C image and image style and image loss R S style loss. Different from the traditional generation against the network is that the output of our discrimination network is not a two classification, but from the extraction characteristics of relu VGG-19 layer, through the comparison of several types of image features to calculate the losses we need to generate network back propagation to the front, straight to the total loss calculated image formation of R network formed in the discrimination network reaches a minimum spanning network [9], this adjustment is good batch can generate high quality image style transfer. The network structure as shown in Fig. 6 discrimination network:

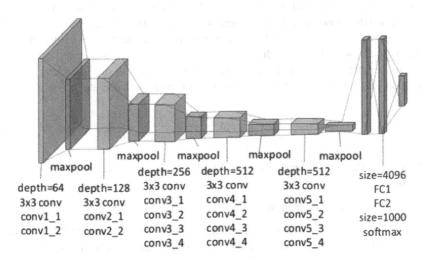

Fig. 6. As shown in Fig. 6, we use the pre-trained discrimination network convolutional neural network VGG-19, with its ImageNet large-scale data sets for training, have powerful ability of feature extraction. In the CNN network layer, the currently accepted view is closer to the underlying characteristics of traditional low-level features (such as visual texture, color), and high-level features is more abstract description of image content, so naturally we will think through the calculation method of two images of CNN high-level feature similarity to evaluate the similarity of [8] with the characteristics of the underlying, relative to the image similarity evaluation style. In practice, we use relu3_1 and relu4_1 layer feature map through Marr, with the airport style loss calculation with relu4_2 content loss characteristics.

4.3 Loss Function Calculation

In the calculation of the loss function, we use Maldives, random algorithm, using the spatial layout of the limitations of the original image to improve image fidelity. MRF algorithm, with the entire Markoff Airport [1], with the character of Markoff random field limit. Is the so-called Markov property, any random variable Markov with the airport in a given field, all other variables under the variable distribution, distribution of the variable neighbor nodes equal to that given in the field variables. The application of MRF in image generation, will use the nearest neighbor algorithm to find the most similar patch to generate [7].

(1) Style loss function

We use 3 * 3 relu3_1 and relu4_1 from the convolution feature map in step 1 intensive extraction patch. By comparing the generated image R and image style S to calculate the loss function style:

$$Loss_s(F(R), F(S)) = \sum_{i=1}^{n} \|Pt_i(F(R)) - Pt_i(F(S))\|^2 \tag{1}$$

In the formula R images, S style image, $F(R)$ to generate images in the feature map network discriminant extraction, $F(S)$ the style of image in the feature map network discriminant extraction, Pt_i said the features extracted from the I batches. By the formula, to be generated in the image of MRF Loss is composed of various batches of loss value add up. Each patch loss value is patch A in the Euclidean distance and style in the image closest to A patch, the loss is based on feature_map, and use the Euclidean distance calculation [11]. The judge is the closest distance formula to calculate the Near (I):

$$Near(i) = \arg_{j=i,\dots,n_s} \min \frac{Pt_i(F(R)) \cdot Pt_j(F(S))}{|Pt_i(F(R))| \cdot |Pt_j(F(S))|} \tag{2}$$

Where j is the S style image batches, two batches of distance by cosine similarity calculation.

(2) The content of loss function

The content of loss, we use the traditional Euclidean distance to calculate the image content and R image C differences in the convolutional networks high level features of the [2], the specific calculation function:

$$Loss_c(F(R), F(C)) = \|F(R) - F(C)\|^2 \tag{3}$$

Fig. 7. The three pictures on the left side of the Fig. 7 in figure A is Van Gogh's most famous masterpiece "starry night", "mulberry" figure B is Van Gogh in Saint Remy during the creation of one of the representative figure C, "Guernica" (Guernica) is the government of the Republic of Spain Picasso was commissioned to create masterpieces in 1937.

(3) The regularization term

In order to achieve in the style of the migration process, without losing the true details of the image, we add square gradient regularization to punish migration process in the image distortion loss function:

$$r(R) = \sum_{i,j} \left((R_{i,j+1} - R_{i,j})^2 + (R_{i+1,j} - R_{i,j})^2 \right)$$

The total weighted average loss in front of a few:

$$Loss = a \cdot Loss_s(F(R), F(S)) + (1 - a) \cdot Loss_c(F(R), F(C)) + \theta \cdot r(R) \qquad (4)$$

We adjust the weight of a to balance the style and content of the proportion of loss loss, especially when the a hours, and the original generation network will generate very similar images, especially when a is large, the network will generate and generate the original color texture similar but different image content.

5 Conclusion

Style algorithm can quickly generate a variety of different transfer pictures, can be used in films such as post processing, poster design, artistic creation and concept design direction. Style transfer algorithm of scene processing compared to the traditional method reduces the cost and time cost, but also brings new ideas for the workers in the field. Fast style transfer algorithm means that the application system based on the style of migration can be deployed in the cloud and mobile terminal, business prospects are bright. In the future, will focus on the application in video stream transfer style.

Acknowledgments. We thank the Fujian Science and Technology Agency for funding support of this research through Soft Science Project with project codes 2017R01010181. We would like to thank the support of the Fujian Young and Middle-aged Teacher Education Research Project with project codes JAT160472.

References

1. Gatys, L.A., Ecker, A.S., Bethge, M.: Image style transfer using convolutional neural networks. In: Computer Vision and Pattern Recognition, pp. 2414–2423. IEEE (2016)
2. Johnson, J., Alahi, A., Fei-Fei, L.: Perceptual losses for real-time style transfer and super-resolution. In: Leibe, B., Matas, J., Sebe, N., Welling, M. (eds.) ECCV 2016. LNCS, vol. 9906, pp. 694–711. Springer, Cham (2016). https://doi.org/10.1007/978-3-319-46475-6_43
3. Luan, F., Paris, S., Shechtman, E., et al.: Deep photo style transfer, 6997–7005 (2017)
4. Ioffe, S., Szegedy, C.: Batch normalization: accelerating deep network training by reducing internal covariate shift. In: International Conference on Machine Learning, pp. 448–456. JMLR.org (2015)
5. Li, M., Zuo, W., Zhang, D.: Deep identity-aware transfer of facial attributes (2016)

6. Gatys, L.A., Ecker, A.S., Bethge, M.: A neural algorithm of artistic style. Comput. Sci. (2015)
7. Ignatov, A., Kobyshev, N., Vanhoey, K., et al.: DSLR-quality photos on mobile devices with deep convolutional networks, 3297–3305 (2017)
8. Combining Markov Random Fields and Convolutional Neural Networks for Image Synthesis
9. Radford, A., Metz, L., Chintala, S.: Unsupervised representation learning with deep convolutional generative adversarial networks. Comput. Sci. (2015)
10. Goodfellow, I.J., Pouget-Abadie, J., Mirza, M., et al.: Generative adversarial networks. In: Advances in Neural Information Processing Systems, vol. 3, pp. 2672–2680 (2014)
11. Denton, E.L., Chintala, S., Szlam, A., Fergus, R.: Deep generative image models using a laplacian pyramid of adversarial networks. In: International Conference on Neural Information Processing Systems, pp. 1486–1494. MIT Press (2015)
12. Jing, Y., Yang, Y., Feng, Z., et al.: Neural style transfer: a review (2017)

A Point Cloud Registration
Algorithm Based on 3D-SIFT

Zehua Jiao, Rui Liu[✉], Pengfei Yi, and Dongsheng Zhou

Key Laboratory of Advanced Design and Intelligent Computing
(Dalian University), Ministry of Education, Dalian 116622, China
liurui@dlu.edu.cn

Abstract. Point cloud registration is a key technology in reverse engineering. The registration process of point cloud is divided into coarse registration and fine registration. For fine registration process, ICP (Iterative Close Point) is a classic algorithm. The traditional ICP algorithm is inefficient and incorrect if the correct initial point set is not obtained. In this paper, a point cloud registration algorithm based on 3D-SIFT features is proposed. In this method, the 3D-SIFT algorithm is used to extract key points. At the same time, the 3D-feature descriptor is used as a constraint on the initial set of points in the ICP algorithm. The results show that the method improves the efficiency and precision of the ICP algorithm, and achieves better results of point cloud registration.

Keywords: Registration · Point cloud · 3D-SIFT · ICP

1 Introduction

Reverse engineering is a process that uses measurement technology to measure the object itself or model, and then reconstructs the CAD model of the object by a three dimensional reconstruction method. In this process, due to the limitation of the measurement conditions, the surface of the scanned object needs to be measured many times. In multiple measurements, the relative changes in the space position between the measuring equipment and the measured object cannot be estimated effectively. Therefore, it is necessary to use the algorithm to integrate and register the 3D point cloud obtained by scanning in order to get a complete image of the object point cloud. This is the registration process of the point cloud data. Point cloud data registration is a key step in reverse engineering. The point cloud registration looks for the conversion between two independent point cloud coordinate systems, making the source cloud coincide with the target cloud maximally under this transformation.

The traditional algorithm of point cloud registration is generally divided into coarse registration and fine registration. Coarse registration is used to reduce rotation and misalignment error between point clouds. It provides good initial value for accurate registration, so the efficiency of registration is improved. Fine registration is the process of making the registration error of two point clouds minimum which on the basis of coarse registration.

© Springer-Verlag GmbH Germany, part of Springer Nature 2019
Z. Pan et al. (Eds.): Transactions on Edutainment XV, LNCS 11345, pp. 24–31, 2019.
https://doi.org/10.1007/978-3-662-59351-6_3

With the development of the computer measurement technology, especially the three-dimensional scanning technology, the point cloud registration has become an important research direction. At present, point cloud registration technology has made great progress. But due to the huge amount of point cloud data and the influence of noise data, it is easy to lead to large data matching error and low matching efficiency. Therefore, the research of point cloud data registration is still facing many challenges.

2 Related Works

At present, the method of point cloud coarse registration has been developed well, but there is still a certain development space in this field [1]. Most of the coarse registration algorithms extract feature descriptors for locating and describing key points form point cloud data. The efficiency of the coarse registration process is improved by the characteristic descriptors that are invariant in the process of rotation and translation and are robust to noise. Rusu et al. [2] presents a fast feature point histogram algorithm (FPFH). This algorithm, using key points under multi-scale histogram of the point cloud, greatly reduces the time of point cloud registration. Liu [3] proposed a general object recognition method based on two-dimensional and three-dimensional invariant feature transform descriptors. By training support vector machine (SVM) to classify the multi-dimensional features, a good registration result is achieved. Elbaz et al. [4] use the deep neural network based on automatic encoder to extract the low dimensional descriptors of point cloud, and realizes the coarse registration between close scan point cloud and large point cloud.

For fine registration, most of the research is carried out on the basis of the ICP (Iterative Closest Points) algorithm and its improved type. Besl and Chen [5, 6] propose an iterative reduction algorithm based on the initial point pair convergence to the global minimum, which is the ICP algorithm. The ICP algorithm is the pioneering work of point cloud registration, which provides a theoretical basis for the development of the subsequent iterative registration algorithm. Chang [7] proposes a method of combining the computing computed closer point (CCP) with the ICP algorithm, which improves the success rate and accuracy of point cloud registration applied to robot vision. Zheng et al. [8] obtain the feature points of the picture by extracting the two-dimensional correspondence point of the laser radar point cloud and the SIFT (Scale-invariant feature transform) algorithm. Then the three-dimensional corresponding points are obtained as the starting points of the ICP algorithm through the transformation of the coordinate system. Thus, the robustness of the registration of laser radar point cloud data is improved. Yang [9] proposed a ICP algorithm based on adaptive optimal threshold. In his theory, first, coarse registration is done by principal component analysis (PCA). Then, KD-tree nearest neighbor search is used to improve the speed of corresponding point search. Finally, the ICP algorithm is implemented on the two models by using optimal threshold algorithm, so the accuracy of ICP has been improved. Makadia et al. [10] use the correlation of the extended Gauss image in the Fourier domain to propose a fine registration method. Although it is an alternative to the ICP algorithm, it still needs to rely on the ICP algorithm for the iteration in the final stage. The present registration method can achieve high matching accuracy. But in the process of registration, data preprocessing and iteration need to be done. These processes affect the efficiency of registration. In this paper, a point cloud registration algorithm based on 3D-SIFT features is proposed. In the case of ensuring a certain degree of accuracy, the efficiency of the registration process is improved.

3   Method

3.1   Traditional ICP Algorithm

The basic principle of traditional ICP algorithm is: In the target point cloud P and the source point cloud Q, the nearest neighbor pair (p_i, q_i) is found according to certain constraints. The least square method is used to calculate the optimal matching parameters and the error function (1) is minimized.

$$E(R, t) = \frac{1}{n} \sum_{i=1}^{n} \| q_i - (Rp_i + t) \|^2 \tag{1}$$

In which, n is the number of nearest neighbor pairs, p_i is a point in target point cloud P, q_i is the nearest point of the source point Q corresponding to the p_i. R is a rotation matrix, and t is a translation vector.

The ICP algorithm is an optimal matching algorithm based on the least square method. The steps of this algorithm can be summarized as follows:

Step1:   Sampling in the source point set.
Step2:   Setting the target point set to form the corresponding point set;
Step3:   Removing the wrong corresponding points;
Step4:   Solving of coordinate transformation;
Step5:   Constructing the error evaluation function;
Step6:   Judging whether the error evaluation function meets the requirement of accuracy.

The traditional ICP algorithm uses straight line search to select the nearest two points in the matching point cloud as the corresponding point. Although this calculation is simple and intuitive, it is easy to produce a large number of error corresponding points, resulting in the iterative calculation is not convergent. The accuracy and efficiency of the traditional ICP algorithm depend on the selection of initial corresponding points. Strictly speaking, the traditional ICP algorithm for the establishment of corresponding points is impossible to really get the "correct" correspondence. In order to solve this problem, this paper proposes a method based on 3D-SIFT features. The nearest point is determined according to the degree of feature similarity based on two feature descriptors.

3.2   3D-SIFT Feature

The scale invariant feature transform algorithm (SIFT) is a computer vision algorithm used to find and describe the local features of the high dimension in the image. It finds the extreme points from the scale space, calculates the information of the location, scale and rotation invariants of the target, and finally obtains the SIFT feature description. The SIFT feature is based on the interest points of some local appearance on the object and is independent of the size and rotation of the image. The tolerance for light, noise, and angle of view is also very high.

In this paper, the 3D-SIFT algorithm is used to extract the feature descriptor of point cloud data. The extraction process can be divided into the following steps.

Step1. Creates a scale space that is like the scale space created by 2D-SIFT, and the definition of scale space by 3D-SIFT is:

$$L(x, y, z, \sigma) = G(x, y, z, \sigma) * P(x, y, z) \tag{2}$$

Among them, $G(x, y, z, \sigma) = \frac{1}{(\sqrt{2\pi}\sigma)^3} e^{-(x^2 + y^2 + z^2)/2\sigma^2}$ is the 3D-SIFT Gauss kernel function, and $P(x, y, z)$ is the three-dimensional coordinate of the point cloud.

Step2. Use Gauss function to construct point cloud Gauss Pyramid and obtains Gauss differential scale space (DOG Scale-Space), to detect key points in scale space effectively. Here we set up each group of Gauss Pyramid inside the number of S, set $k^s = 2$. The calculation formula of DOG is as follows:

$$DOG(x, y, z, k^i\sigma) = P(x, y, z) * (G(x, y, z, k^{i+1}\sigma) - G(x, y, z, k^i\sigma)) \tag{3}$$

Step3. The extreme points of the Gauss difference space as the extreme point of the DOG function are calculated. These extreme points are approximately equal to the key points.

Step4. Calculate the direction of the key point. Like 2D-SIFT, once all the key points in the three-dimensional space are determined, a direction based on the local properties must be assigned. The establishment of this direction realizes the rotation invariance of three dimensional objects [11]. The calculation formula of the key point descriptor direction is as follows:

$$\begin{cases} m(x, y, z) = \sqrt{(x - x_c)^2 + (y - y_c)^2 + (z - z_c)^2} \\ \theta(x, y, z) = \tan^{-1}((y - y_c)/(x - x_c)) \\ \phi(x, y, z) = \sin^{-1}((z - z_c)/m(x, y, z)) \end{cases} \tag{4}$$

There $m(x, y, z)$ is the vector size of the key point direction. $\theta(x, y, z)$ is the azimuth of each point (x, y, z) to their center (x_c, y_c, z_c). $\phi(x, y, z)$ is the elevation angle.

Step5. The location and scale of the key points are accurately determined by fitting the two - dimensional function. To remove the key points of low contrast and unstable edge response points, an approximate Harris Corner detector is used. In this way, the stability and improvement of the matching and the ability to resist noise are enhanced. In this way, we get the key points that describe the location, the scale, and the direction.

3.3   Point Cloud Registration Based on 3D-SIFT Features

The feature descriptor obtained by 3D-SIFT algorithm has the characteristics of scale invariance. In this paper, a point cloud registration algorithm based on 3D-SIFT feature is proposed. The specific steps of the algorithm are as follows:

Step1. The initial set of points are Obtained. Through the 3D-SIFT feature extraction, we get a set of new initial points, D and B. They are obtained by the original point sets P and Q.

Step2. According to the initial point set D and B, the point set geometry center is determined as:

$$\mu_d = \frac{1}{m}\sum_{i=1}^{m} d_1, \mu_b = \frac{1}{m}\sum_{i=1}^{m} b_i \tag{5}$$

Step3. The optimal objective function (1) can be converted to:

$$E = \sum_{i=1}^{N} |(\mu_d + d_i) - [R(\mu_b + b_i) + t]| \tag{6}$$

In which R is the rotation matrix obtained by registration, and t is the translation vector obtained by registration.

Step4. The covariance matrix of the set of structural points is as follows:

$$COV_{d,b} = \sum_{i=1} [(d_i - \mu_d) \cdot (b_i - \mu_b)^T] \tag{7}$$

Step5. The singular value decomposition of covariance matrix can be obtained:

$$COV_{d,b} = U \cdot D \cdot V^T \tag{8}$$

The matrix D is diagonal matrix, $D = diag(d_i), d_1 \geq d_2 \geq d_3 \geq d_3$.

Step6. If $rank(COV_{d,b}) \geq 2$, then the rotation matrix R for rigid transformation:

$$R = U * A * V^T \tag{9}$$

The matrix A is:

$$A = \begin{cases} I_3 & \det(U) \cdot \det(V) \geq 0 \\ diag(1,1,-1) & \det(U) \cdot \det(V) \leq 0 \end{cases} \tag{10}$$

In which, $\det(U)$ and $\det(V)$ represent the values of the determinant of U and V respectively.

Step7. The translation vector t can be calculated as follow:

$$t = \mu_d - R \cdot \mu_b \tag{11}$$

Through the above steps, the rotation matrix R and the transition matrix t, which make the error function (1) minimum, are obtained. The rotation matrix R and the transition vector t are applied to the registration point cloud, thus the registration of the point cloud data is realized.

4 Experiments

The experimental environment used in this paper is the Windows7 64-bit operating system, and the CPU is Intel Core i3-4160, the main frequency is 3.60 GHz, and the memory is 4G. The main compiling environment is Microsoft Visual Studio 2010, and the compiler library is PCL-1.7.1. Finally, the registration effect is analyzed with Geomagic.

a. effect of traditional ICP algorithm   b. effect of 3D-SIFT+ICP algorithm

Fig. 1. Surface contrast graph of traditional ICP algorithm and 3D-SIFT+ICP algorithm

In order to prove the validity of the proposed method, the traditional ICP algorithm and the 3D-SIFT+ICP algorithm are used to register the David's point cloud respectively. The surface reconstruction of the point cloud data after registration is carried out by Geomagic, and the experimental results are compared.

As seen in Fig. 1. The effect of the point cloud reconstruction after the registration of the traditional ICP algorithm is not ideal, and there are many holes. A relatively complete model is obtained after the 3D-SIFT+ICP algorithm is used to reconstruct the point cloud.

The specific reconstruction effect of the 3D-SIFT+ICP algorithm is given in Fig. 2.

Figure 2 shows the comparison chromatogram which is processed by Geomagic. It shows the comparison between 3D-SIFT+ICP algorithm and software splicing. Most of the data are mostly yellow or green, which means that the registration effect is much better. The average deviation of the 3D-SIFT+ICP algorithm is 0.1332 mm, and the average deviation of the traditional ICP algorithm is 0.558 mm.

Fig. 2. 3D-SIFT+ICP registration effect diagram under Geomagic (Color figure online)

In order to verify the running efficiency of the 3D-SIFT algorithm, a contrast experiment of the total running time has been done between the traditional ICP algorithm and the 3D-SIFT+ICP algorithm on the MATLAB. The results are shown in Table 1.

Table 1. Comparison of the total running time between the traditional ICP algorithm and the 3D-SIFT+ICP algorithm

Point cloud model	Running time (s)	
	Traditional ICP	3D-SIFT+ICP
Horse	64.527524	0.745236
Rabbit	46.502741	0.433519
Duck	20.995025	0.401742

As the number of subsequent iterations of the ICP algorithm is affected by the selection of the initial point pair. The original corresponding point of the traditional ICP algorithm is based on the search of an error measure, which takes longer time and has more noise. So, the running time of the traditional ICP algorithm is long. The 3D-SIFT feature matching ICP algorithm extracts the feature of point cloud as the constraint of the initial point set which reduces the time of ICP algorithm in the initial point selection, and reduces the number of ICP iterations. Experiments show that the efficiency of the ICP algorithm based on 3D-SIFT features is greatly improved.

5   Conclusion

Based on the classical ICP algorithm, a point cloud registration algorithm based on 3D-SIFT feature has been proposed. First, the key points are extracted by introducing the 3D-SIFT feature descriptor with scale invariant property, which effectively reduces the complexity of subsequent algorithm. Then, the point clouds are matched according to a constraint method of 3D-SIFT feature descriptor. Compared with the traditional ICP algorithm, the mismatch rate is reduced, and the convergence speed and registration accuracy of the algorithm are improved.

Although the proposed algorithm has a good improvement in some aspects compared with the traditional ICP algorithm, there are still some shortcomings. For example, for the relatively smooth surface of the point cloud data, the efficiency of registration is slow, and the accuracy is reduced because it is difficult to extract the 3D-SIFT features. Therefore, in the next step, we will use the deep learning method to extract the feature of point cloud data as a general registration matching standard to improve the applicability of the algorithm.

Acknowledgment. We thank the anonymous reviewers for the insightful and constructive comments. This work is in part supported by the Liaoning Province Doctor Startup Fund (No. 201601302).

References

1. Tam, G.K.L., et al.: Registration of 3D point clouds and meshes: a survey from rigid to nonrigid. IEEE Trans. Visual Comput. Graphics **19**(7), 1199–1217 (2013)
2. Rusu, R.B., Blodow, N., Beetz, M.: Fast Point Feature Histograms (FPFH) for 3D registration. In: IEEE International Conference on Robotics and Automation, ICRA 2009, pp. 3212–3217 (2009)
3. Liu, M., Li, X., Dezert, J., Luo, C.: Generic object recognition based on the fusion of 2D and 3D SIFT descriptors. In: 2015 18th International Conference on Information Fusion, pp. 1085–1092 (2015)
4. Elbaz, G., Avraham, T., Fischer, A.: 3D point cloud registration for localization using a deep neural network auto-encoder. In: IEEE Conference on Computer Vision and Pattern Recognition, pp. 2472–2481 (2017)
5. Besl, P.J., Mckay, N.D.: A method for registration of 3D shapes. IEEE Trans. Pattern Anal. Mach. Intell. **14**(2), 239–256 (1992)
6. Chen, Y., Medioni, G.: Object modeling by registration of multiple range image. Image Vis. Comput. **10**, 145–155 (1992)
7. Chang, W.C., Wu, C.H.: Eye-in-hand vision-based robotic bin-picking with active laser projection. Int. J. Adv. Manuf. Technol. **85**(9–12), 2873–2885 (2016)
8. Zheng, Z., Li, Y., Jun, W.: LiDAR point cloud registration based on improved ICP method and SIFT feature. In: Proceedings of the 2015 International Conference on Progress in Informatics and Computing, Nanjing, 18–20 December 2015, pp. 588–592. IEEE Computer Society, Washington (2015)
9. Yang, J., Zhang, Y., Huang, L.: Research on 3D model registration by improved ICP algorithm. J. Front. Comput. Sci. Technol. **12**(1), 153–162 (2018)
10. Makadia, A., Patterson, A., Daniilidis, K.: Fully automatic registration of 3D point clouds. In: 2006 IEEE Computer Society Conference on Computer Vision and Pattern Recognition (CVPR 2006), vol. 1, pp. 1297–1304 (2006)
11. Chen, H., Zhao, J., Luo, Q., Hou, Y.: Distributed randomized singular value decomposition using count sketch. In: International Conference on Security, Pattern Analysis, and Cybernetics (SPAC), pp. 187–191 (2017)

Lip-Reading Based on Deep Learning Model

Mei-li Zhu[1(✉)], Qing-qing Wang[2], and Jiang-lin Luo[1]

[1] Science and Technology Innovation Center, Jilin Animation Institute,
Changchun 130000, China
zhumeilizhu@163.com
[2] College of Optical and Electronic Information,
ChangChun University of Science and Technology, Changchun 130000, China

Abstract. With the rapid development of computer computing power, deep learning plays a more and more important role in the fields of automatic driving, medical research, industrial automation and so on. In order to improve the accuracy of lip-reading recognition, an algorithm based on the model of lip deep learning was proposed in this paper. Binary image of the lip contour motion sequence was projected to the spatio-temporal energy, lip dynamic grayscale was used to reduce noise interference in the recognition process and then lip-reading recognition result was improved by using the excellent characteristics of deep learning ability. The experimental results show that deep learning can obtain the effective characteristics of lip dynamic change from the lip dynamic gray scale and get better recognition results.

Keywords: Lip-reading recognition · Deep learning · Sparse coding

1 Introduction

Lip reading (lip - reading/speech - Reading) was contents recognition of speaker from mouth moving [5]. Lip reading technology came from the learning and understanding skill of weak hearing and hearing impaired. The lip reading technology studied in this paper was using computer technology and artificial intelligence technology to understand the speaker's lip movement. The study of lip reading involved many fields, such as artificial intelligence, knowledge engineering, pattern recognition, image processing, natural language understanding and so on. It had important research value and application prospect. For example, lip reading could be an auxiliary method for improving the speech recognition rate (noisy environment), a language ability recovery training for handicapped people, a high security detection method for identification, a new human-computer interaction method (such as lip reading input method). An animation making method, and also could be reliable legal evidence and counter-terrorism means.

The key links of lip reading technology included lip detection and localization, lip movement feature extraction, lip recognition model training and recognition. At present, lip detection and location included the following methods: (1) Determining the lip position according to the physiological structure of the face, such as Yao proposed to detect the position of the eyes, and then segmented the lip images according to the relative positions of the eyes and the mouth [6], this method could well locate left and

© Springer-Verlag GmbH Germany, part of Springer Nature 2019
Z. Pan et al. (Eds.): Transactions on Edutainment XV, LNCS 11345, pp. 32–43, 2019.
https://doi.org/10.1007/978-3-662-59351-6_4

right position of the mouth, but the upper and lower positions were inaccurate. (2) Based on gray information or color space change and skin color model. Such as Rao extracts the edge of the face image, and then calculates the gray value of rows and columns to determine the lip area [7]. This method was susceptible to light, shadow, whiskers and other factors. Jun et al. proposed an adaptive lip location algorithm based on chroma contrast [8]. This method was influenced by the color of the speaker and the change of illumination. (3) Using the moving target to detect the mouth. Pao et al. proposed a lip region detection method based on motion information [9]. Da Silveira et al. proposed a method based on inter frame difference and mathematical morphology [10]. This method could effectively avoid the problem of different speakers and different skin color. However, when the contrast of the gray image sequence was low, the threshold was difficult to choose because of the range of the adjacent frames was too small, this affected the segmentation effect seriously.

Although lip region detection and localization technology was relatively mature, but there were many worthy of continued research and improvement. For example, the problem of light change in the actual environment, the problem of speaker detection in motion, different angles and different head pose detection problems, and the problem of reducing redundant information and improving processing speed.

Lip movement feature selection was the key link of lip reading recognition. Effective and robust feature affected the recognition rate directly. At present, the lip feature extraction methods were mostly the development on traditional function to adopt visual feature extraction method. The main methods are as follows: (1) Based on texture features, taking the transformed results of lip's gray image as feature vector [11, 12]. (2) based on the shape feature, taking the lip shape as the feature vector [13, 14]. (3) hybrid method, using statistical model and global texture model to get feature vectors [15, 16]. (4) based on motion analysis, extracting lip movement parameters and analyzing motion rules [17, 18].

In recent years, with the powerful ability of computers in data processing and computation, Deep learning played a more and more important role in all walks of life, such as aviation, defense, medical research, industrial automation, and so on. Especially in the learning classification task of image, text and sound, depth learning had achieved the most advanced accuracy. Therefore, this paper applied the deep learning method to lip recognition, and improved the accuracy of lip recognition by the powerful ability of deep learning for image recognition. The main features of this method were: (1) Transformed visual information into a gray energy feature map that contained lip movement features, and realized lip recognition through the classification of gray energy features (2) Used depth learning to transform layer by layer, automatic feature learning, obtaining effective features and improving recognition accuracy.

2 Correlative Theories

2.1 Deep Learning

Deep learning was a branch of machine learning. It was the development of neural network. Different from the neural network, the depth learning system model was a multi-layer network structure composed of the input layer, the hidden layer (multilayer) and the output layer, which was closer to the structure of the human brain. A deep learning model with multiple hidden layers was shown in Fig. 1.

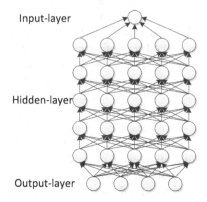

Fig. 1. A deep learning model with multiple hidden layers

In the deep learning model, the hidden layer can be up to hundreds. The essence of deep learning is to train a large number of data that had been labeled by constructing these hidden layers, and use big data to automatically learn features, then improve the accuracy of classification or prediction. The training process of deep learning included two parts: unsupervised learning from bottom to up, and supervised learning from top to bottom.

2.2   Deep Learning Models

(1) Automatic encoder (AutoEncoder)

AutoEncoder [19] was a neural network that restores the input signal as much as possible. It included two parts: encoder and decoder. Input data reduced by neural network, and a coding was obtained. Then another neural network was decoded to get the generated data that were similar to the input data. Then, the encoder and decoder parameters were trained by minimizing the difference between the input data and the generated data. Finally, the characteristics that could represent the input data were obtained. Finally, the supervised training method was used to complete the classification in the top coding layer.

(2) Restricted Boltzmann Machine (RBM)

The RBM model [20] was a bipartite graph. The first level was the visual layer which was the input data layer (V). The second level was the hidden layer (H), and all nodes were random two-valued variable, and the full probability distribution P (V, H) satisfied the Boltzmann distribution. When you inputted V, you could got the hidden layer h through P (h|v). After you got h, you could also got the visual layer (V1) through P (v|h). Therefore, the visible layer V1 obtained from the hidden layer is consistent with the input V by adjusting the parameters, then the hidden layer could be used as the feature of input data.

(3) Deep Belief Networks (DBNs)

DBNs consists of a number of restricted Boltzmann planes that were regarded as a visible layer and a hidden layer. There was a connection between each layer, and the inner layer was unconnected. The hidden layer was trained to capture the correlation of high-order data in the visual layer. The weights of the production model were obtained by using the unsupervised greedy layer by layer training method. Then the weight were connected to the memory content at the top level. Finally, the BP algorithm was used to classify.

(4) Convolutional Neural Networks (CNNs)

CNNs was a multi-layer neural network, each layer had a number of two-dimensional plan, and each plane was made up of a number of independent neurons. The feature of CNN convolution got feature by learning of input data. The two dimensional volume layer was used, and this framework was very suitable for processing two-dimensional data, such as images.

3 Lip Reading Method Based on Sparse Coding Depth Learning

In recent years, the deep learning model had made a breakthrough in image classification and recognition. The recognition rate of deep learning model was even higher than human brain. Inspired by this, this paper attempted to transform the lip recognition problem into image classification and recognition. In order to improve the recognition rate of lip words, the deep learning model was used to extract and recognize the features.

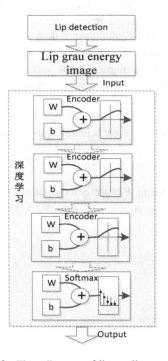

Fig. 2. Flow diagram of lip reading method

The process of lip reading based on the deep learning model was shown in Fig. 2. First, in order to get two-dimensional image information that can reflect lip movement, the two valued image of the lip contour motion sequence was projected into the space-time energy diagram. Then using lip gray energy as input of deep neural network for feature learning and classification. The deep learning model adopts the sparse encoder model, which was composed of three hidden layers and one classification layer.

3.1   Lip Detection and Location

The purpose of lip detection and location is to extracted changes in lip contour movement. In this paper, the active shape model (ASM) [21] method was adopted. The geometry of the lip was represented by the coordinates of 18 key points in a shape vector. ASM lip detection algorithm process was as follows:

Training process:

(1) Collecting N training samples;
(2) Recording the K key points in each training sample (lip geometric contour). The K value was 18, which was the key points of lip contour;
(3) Constructing the shape vector of training set, making up a shape vector by the K key feature points in a picture.

$$a_i = (x_1^i, y_1^i, x_2^i, y_2^i, \cdots, x_k^i, y_k^i), i = 1, 2, \cdots n \tag{1}$$

where: (x_j^i, y_j^i) represented the coordinates of the j characteristic point on the i training sample. N represented the number of training samples.

(4) Shape normalization, Procrustes method was used to align point distribution models. First, all lip models in the training set were aligned to the first lip model, and the average lip model was calculated $\bar{a}$, then all lip models were aligned to the average lip model $\bar{a}$. Repeat the above process until convergence.
(5) PCA was processed after the aligned shape vector.
(6) Constructing local features for each feature point.

Search process:

(1) calculating the new location of each feature point, and the initial model was:

$$X = M(s, \theta)[a_i] + X_c \tag{2}$$

Where: s represented scaling, θ represented rotation, X_c represented displacement, then selecting the feature points with minimum Mahalanobis distance as new positions.

(2) Updating the parameters and parameters b in affine changes until the number of iterations reaches the threshold.

$$X_c = X_c + w_t dX_c, Y_c = Y_c + w_t dY_c, \theta = \theta + w_\theta d\theta, s = s(1 + w_s ds), b = b + w_b db \tag{3}$$

Where: w_t, w_θ, w_s, w_b represented the weight that controls the change of the parameter. The effect of lip detection as shown below (Fig. 3):

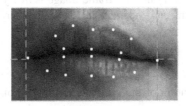

Fig. 3. Lip detection

3.2 Lip Gray Energy Image

After lip detection, the lip image was extracted from the face image sequence and the lip movement sequence image was obtained. The lip gray energy map was calculated according to the lip movement sequence images of each pronunciation. The specific methods were as follows:

First, the gray image of the lip color image was obtained. The formula is:

$$Gray = (R * 77 + G * 151 + B * 28)/256 \tag{4}$$

Where: $Gray$ represented gray pixel value, R, G, represented B the pixel values of red, green and blue channels respectively.

Then lip gray energy Image (LGEI) was calculated. The method was to calculate the average gray scale [20] of the gray lip sequence. The formula is:

$$LGEI(x, y) = \frac{1}{N} \sum_{i=1}^{N} I(x, y, i) \tag{5}$$

Where: $I(x, y, i)$ was the gray value of the pixel point (x, y) in the i frame image, N represented the number of training samples (Fig. 4).

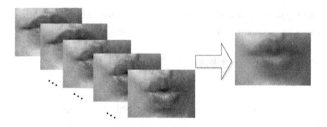

Fig. 4. Labial grayscale energy map

The noise of the point (x, y) in the i frame image is $n(x, y, i)$. Assuming that noise and signals are independent and independent of each other, the noisy image signal could be expressed as:

$$I'(x, y, i) = I(x, y, i) + n(x, y, i) \tag{6}$$

The mean and the equation of the gray energy of the noisy image were:

$$
\begin{aligned}
E(LGEI'(x,y)) &= E(\frac{1}{N}\sum_{i=1}^{N}[I(x,y,i) + n(x,y,i)]) \\
&= E(\frac{1}{N}\sum_{i=1}^{N}I(x,y,i) + \frac{1}{N}\sum_{i=1}^{N}n(x,y,i)) \\
&= \bar{I}(x,y) + \bar{n}(x,y)
\end{aligned} \tag{7}
$$

$$
\begin{aligned}
\sigma^2_{LGEI'(X,Y)} &= E([LGEI'(x,y) - E(LGEI'(x,y))]^2 \\
&= E(\{\frac{1}{N}\sum_{i=1}^{N}[I(x,y,i) + n(x,y,i)] - [\bar{I}(x,y) + \bar{n}(x,y)]\}^2) \\
&= E(\{[\frac{1}{N}\sum_{i=1}^{N}I(x,y,i) - \bar{I}(x,y)] + \frac{1}{N}\sum_{i=1}^{N}[n(x,y,i) - \bar{n}(x,y)]\}^2) \\
&= \sigma^2_{LGEI(x,y)} + \frac{1}{N}\sigma^2_{n(x,y)} \\
&= \frac{1}{N}\sigma^2_{I(x,y)} + \frac{1}{N}\sigma^2_{n(x,y)}
\end{aligned} \tag{8}
$$

By formula (6) and (8), the mean value of the lip gray energy map with noise was the same as that of a single noise image, variance was $1/N$ points of a single noisy image. In the process of image analysis and processing, noise were often overlaid. Therefore, the projection of lip motion sequence images into spatiotemporal energy space could achieve the effect of smoothing noise and improved the noise immunity of the algorithm.

3.3   Construction of Deep Neural Network

Deep learning could automatically learn the features, so the deep neural network containing three hidden layers was used to extract the features. Each hidden layer is a sparse AutoEncoder, and training a hidden layer at a time. The AutoEncoder model was shown in Fig. 5.

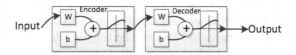

Fig. 5. AutoEncoder model

As shown in the figure above, AutoEncoder consists of two parts: encoder and decoder, the encoder mapped or hidden the input data, and the decoder attempted to reverse the mapping to reconstruct the original input. Each neuron in the encoder had a weight vector associated with it, which will be adjusted to respond to specific visual features. An expression that was obtained by the encoder was a representation of input data, that was the feature. The features of the labial grayscale energy map were shown in Fig. 6.

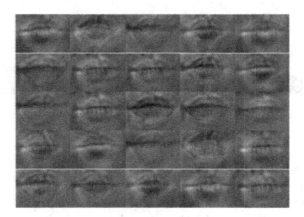

Fig. 6. The features from AutoEncoder1

As shown in the figure above, the features obtained by AutoEncoder represent the curl and edge features in the lip gray energy map. The code obtained by the first level AutoEncoder would be the input signal of the second level AutoEncoder. Training the second and the third level in the same way. The code obtained by the third layer was the final feature.

After training the three level of AutoEncoder, the features of the input signal were obtained. Then add classifier to the top level for supervised training. After the completion of supervision training, the top level network could be classified. The problem was the multi classification, so the softmax classifier was selected in the classification layer. Finally, stacking the first level AutoEncoder, the second level AutoEncoder, the third AutoEncoder and the classifier into a deep neural network.

4   Experiment

At present, there was no standard and open lip language database at home and abroad, the data used by research institutions are usually recorded by themselves. The public video data was limited, this paper had built two lip language databases. The database 1 was the pronunciation of 0 to 9, which was recorded by 25 people, 20 times per person, 5000 videos in all. The video resolution was 1280 × 800, the frame rate was 25 frames per second. The samples was shown in Fig. 7. Database 2 was 50 common Chinese single word pronunciation, which was recorded by 15 people, 20 times per person, 15000 videos in all. The common words are shown in Table 1.

Fig. 7. The database 1 samples

Table 1. The database 2

ban	chu	ci	diu	duo	fa	guo	hao	qing	ti
ji	kan	lai	mai	neng	peng	piao	qu	ren	xin
re	shang	suan	cao	cong	gao	hai	hei	rang	xiang
hong	geng	gui	lan	lv	ku	luo	gai	ke	yun
gan	luan	ma	kuo	leng	lian	shen	qi	tian	yin

Experiment 1: In order to verify the feasibility of the proposed method, the data in database 1 were tested. Learning and classification of lip motion features using sparse coding. After searching the lip area, the lip regions were aligned in order to facilitate map the temporal and spatial energy, each lip image was 100 * 65. The first hidden layer was set to 900, the second hidden layer was set to 200, and the third hidden layer was set to 80. There were ten sets of figures from 0 to 9, each containing 500 samples. The identification results were shown in Table 2.

Table 2. Experimental results

Category Result	0	1	2	3	4	5	6	7	8	9
0	471	9	5	3	2	1	2	2	3	1
1	11	476	4	4	3	2	4	2	2	0
2	0	0	475	3	0	0	4	2	5	0
3	5	2	3	478	7	5	2	3	2	1
4	5	7	1	2	480	0	4	4	0	4
5	0	0	0	0	0	485	0	1	3	5
6	3	0	0	5	3	4	478	2	2	1
7	5	6	6	3	4	0	2	482	0	4
8	0	0	6	2	0	0	1	0	481	1
9	0	0	0	0	1	3	3	2	2	483
Correct rate	94.2%	95.2%	95%	95.6%	96%	97%	95.6%	96.4%	96.2%	96.6%

It could be seen from Table 2 that in the case of enough data, the depth neural network could got better recognition rate identify for lip-reading.

Experiment 2: Contrast experiment. The method was compared with the gray energy map using DCT and PCA to extract lip features, and HMM to classify. Select 20 videos in database 2, and the sample data amount to 6000. The results of were shown in Table 3.

Table 3. Experimental results

Method	Correct	Incorrect	Correct rate
DCT + PCA + HMM	4057	1943	67.62%
AutoEncoder	4984	1016	83.07%

Contrast experiments show that deep learning has excellent feature learning ability, the abstract features obtained can better depict the essence of data, so that recognition rate was higher.

5 Conclusion

A method of lip reading recognition based on deep learning was proposed in this paper. In this method, the two value image of the lip contour motion sequence was projected into the space-time energy map, and then the lip dynamic gray energy map was used as the input of the deep neural network. Automatic learning of features were achieved through three layers of hidden network structure, and hidden layer neural network structure was sparse encoder, the classification layer is softmax. Experimental results shown that deep learning had excellent feature learning ability and could improve the recognition results effectively. But this method needed enough sample data, and the experimental data were recorded by ourselves, that impacted on the experimental results.

In the next work, we will standardize the sample data in the lip language database, and improve the algorithm, do sentence recognition.

Acknowledgments. This work was supported by The Education Department of Jilin Province. I would like to thank those who took care of me, encouraged me and helped me when I am finishing this paper.

References

1. Baldonado, M., Chang, C.-C.K., Gravano, L., Paepcke, A.: The stanford digital library metadata architecture. Int. J. Digit. Libr. **1**, 108–121 (1997)
2. Bruce, K.B., Cardelli, L., Pierce, B.C.: Comparing object encodings. In: Abadi, M., Ito, T. (eds.) Theoretical Aspects of Computer Software. LNCS, vol. 1281, pp. 415–438. Springer, Heidelberg (1997). https://doi.org/10.1007/BFb0014561
3. van Leeuwen, J. (ed.): Computer Science Today. Recent Trends and Developments. Lecture Notes in Computer Science, vol. 1000. Springer, Heidelberg (1995). https://doi.org/10.1007/BFb0015232
4. Michalewicz, Z.: Genetic Algorithms + Data Structures = Evolution Programs, 3rd edn. Springer, Heidelberg (1996). https://doi.org/10.1007/978-3-662-03315-9
5. Yao, H., Gao, W., Wang, R.: A survey of lipreading-one of visual languages. Acta Electronica Sinica **2**, 239–246 (2001)
6. Yao, W., Liang, Y., Du, M.: A real-time lip localization and tacking for lipreading. In: Proceedings of the 3rd International Conference on Advanced Computer Theory and Engineering, pp. 363–366. IEEE, Chengdu (2010)
7. Rao, R.A., Russell, R.M.: Lip modeling for visual speech recognition. In: Proceeding of 28th Annual Asilomar Conference on Signals Systems and Computers, Pacific Grove: [s.n.] (1994)
8. Jun, H., Hua, Z:. A real time lip detection method in lipreading. In: 2007 Chinese Control Conference, CCC 2007, 31 June–26 July 2007, pp. 516–520 (2007)

9. Pao, T.L., Liao, W.Y.: A motion feature approach for audio-visual recognition. In: Proceedings of 48th Midwest Symposium on Circuits and Systems, vol. 1, pp. 421–424 (2005)

10. Da Silveira, L.G., Facon, J., Borges, D.L.: Visual speech recognition: a solution from feature extraction to words classification. In: Proceedings of 16th Brazilian Symposium on Computer Graphics and Image Processing, pp. 399–405 (2003)

11. Hong, X., Yao, H., Liu, Q., Chen, R.: An information acquiring channel — lip movement. In: Tao, J., Tan, T., Picard, R.W. (eds.) ACII 2005. LNCS, vol. 3784, pp. 232–238. Springer, Heidelberg (2005). https://doi.org/10.1007/11573548_30

12. Leszczynski, M., Skarbek, W.: Viseme recognition - a comparative study. In: AVSS-Advanced Video and Signal Based Surveillance, pp. 287–292 (2005)

13. Kaynak, M.N., Zhi, Q., Cheok, A.D., et al.: Analysis of lip geometric features for audio—visual speech recognition. IEEE Trans. Syst. Man Cybern. Part A: Syst. Hum. 34(4), 564–570 (2004)

14. Seguier, R., Cladel, N.: Multiobjectives genetic snakes: application on audio-visual speech recognition. In: Proceedings of Fourth EURASIP Conference Focused on Video/Image Processing and Multimedia Communications, vol. 2, pp. 625–630 (2003)

15. Matthews, I., Cootes, T.F., Bangham, J.A., et al.: Extraction of visual features for lipreading. IEEE Trans. Pattern Anal. Mach. Intell. 24(2), 198–213 (2002)

16. Wang, W., Cosker, D., Hicks, Y., Saneit, S., Chambers, J.: Video assisted speech source separation. In: 2005 Proceedings of International Conference on Acoustics, Speech, and Signal Processing, (ICASSP 2005), pp. 425–428. IEEE (2005)

17. Cootes, T.F., Walker, K.N., Taylor, C.J.: View-based active appearance models. In: Proceedings of International Conference on Face and Gesture Recognition, pp. 227–232 (2000)

18. Bourlard, H., Kamp, Y.: Auto-association by multilayer perceptrons and singular value decomposition. Biol. Cybern. 59(4), 291–294 (1988)

19. Hinton, G.E.: A practical guide to training restricted Boltzmann machines. Momentum 9(1), 599–619 (2012)

20. Cootes, T.F., Hill, A., Taylor, C.J., et al.: The use of active shape models for locating structures in medical images. Image Vis. Comput. 12(6), 355–366 (1994)

21. Li, G., Wang, M., Lin, L.: Improving Chinese lip-reading recognizing rate by unsymmetrical lip contour model. Optics Precis. Eng. (3), 473–477 (2006)

Simulation

Parameter Estimation of Decaying DC Component via Improved Levenberg-Marquardt Algorithm

Xiuchun Xiao[1], Baitao Chen[2(✉)], and Jingwen Yan[3(✉)]

[1] College of Electronics and Information Engineering,
Guangdong Ocean University, Zhanjiang 524088, China
[2] Department of Planning and Regulation, Guangdong Ocean University,
Zhanjiang 524088, China
chenbt@163.com
[3] College of Engineering, Shantou University, Shantou 515063, China
jwyan@stu.edu.cn

Abstract. Fault current usually contain a decaying DC component and some kinds of noise. This DC component and noise decrease the accuracy and speed of the operation of digital relay protection. In order to remove the decaying DC component and noise in current signals for power system, parameters of decaying DC component should be estimated firstly. To solve this parameter estimation problem, a specific neural network is proposed, and then an adaptive learning algorithm based on improved Levenberg-Marquardt algorithm is derived to iteratively resolve its weights by optimizing the pre-defined objective function. From weights of the trained neural network, all parameters of decaying DC components can be well calculated. Profiting from good nature in fault tolerance of neural network, the proposed algorithm possess a good performance in resistance to noise. Simulation experimental results indicate that our algorithm can achieve a high accuracy with acceptable time consumption for parameters estimating in noise.

Keywords: Smart grid · Decaying DC estimation · Time constant · Neural network model · Levenberg-Marquardt algorithm

1 Introduction

Nowadays, electricity becomes a very important energy and people's livelihood seriously depends on a safe and stable electricity power system [1–4]. However, issue of power quality is on the rise in recent years with the application of power electronics in industry for production needs, energy saving and new energy access [5–7]. These changes in power system result in more and more different faults that may have a great impact on its safe and stable operation [8].

In general, when a fault occurs in power system, besides fundamental component, the fault current may also contain decaying DC component and a lot of harmonic components [3, 9–12]. However, the current relay protection system is generally used only fundamental signal for fault discrimination. Other components and noise are

Z. Pan et al. (Eds.): Transactions on Edutainment XV, LNCS 11345, pp. 47–58, 2019.
https://doi.org/10.1007/978-3-662-59351-6_5

obstacles in extracting the fundamental component from the current's waveform [5]. In practical relay protection schemes, the decaying DC component is usually removed from the power signal [9–12]. Therefore, effective detection and analysis of all different components in power system is the premise of taking corresponding protective measures in power system [1, 5].

Discrete Fourier Transform (DFT), which can be efficiently calculated using Fast Fourier Transform (FFT), is widely used to extract the fundamental component from power current signals. It can effectively suppress the influence of harmonics and has a relatively fast response time for the fundamental component calculation, but it can cause undesired error results for decaying DC component [5, 13–15]. That is to say, the existence of decaying DC component will make the system unable to extract the fundamental component accurately.

At present, there are many methods to estimate and eliminate the decaying DC component in power signals. These methods can be mainly categorized into two types. One is the decaying DC offset removal scheme, which extracts fundamental component without a DC component computation [5, 13]. Benmouyal proposed a mimic filter to remove the decaying DC component. This decaying DC removal method can be used under circumstances over a broad range of time constants as encountered on real power systems [13]. In [14], an adaptive compensation method has been presented by combining adaptive Fourier filtering technique and a fault detector. The filtering technique takes the advantage of recursive computing and variable window size to adaptively speed up its transient response under various systems under fault conditions. The other method is the DC estimation scheme, which estimates the parameters of DC component and subtracts it from the original signal to obtain the fundamental component only. Sidhu et al. proposed a method of using DFT to estimate the phase complex vector, which can effectively eliminate the decaying DC component [16]. Based on weighted least squares (WLES) technique, Rosolowski proposed an adaptive estimation method with phase complex vector; it can effectively limit the effects of decaying DC component [17]. However, one drawback of this approach is the calculation process based on complex computing might need great time consumption. In a word, these methods start with estimating the difference between fundamental wave and harmonics. If there is noise or other signal in the current signal, this difference will not only contain the DC component, but also include noise and other components.

Cho et al. put forward a method to directly estimate the decaying DC component by integrating one cycle of the fault current with decaying DC component [5]. This method takes advantage of all the fundamental component and harmonics in a cycle must equal to 0, therefore, the actual integrating process will be equivalent to integrate to the decaying DC component in a fundamental period. By using this property, only two fundamental periods with a certain interval of time are needed to be integrated respectively, and the parameters of the decaying DC component can be easily estimated by using the two integral results. Although the algorithm is very clever, it has two drawbacks. Firstly, in the case of small scale of sampling signal, the integral error is relatively large, this may result in the estimation accuracy is not good enough. On the other hand, it demands fundamental period to be stable and needs to determine the size of a fundamental period in advance, so the method will fail when the fundamental frequency is abnormal.

In the recent years, neural networks have received wide attention due to its parallel processing, distributed storage, self-learning, adaptive, and good fault tolerance. In power system signal detection, Marei et al. put forward a method which apply ADALINE neural network for power system harmonic detection, and achieved very high detection accuracy [19]. But for the detection of fault current signal with decaying DC component, it seems difficult to construct this kind of neural network model since the fault current signal contains exponential and trigonometric functions.

In this paper, we construct a specific neural network model to estimate decaying DC component, and then an adaptive learning algorithm based on improved Levenberg-Marquardt algorithm is derived. Since the neural network model is consistent with the mathematical model of the fault current signal, parameters of the decaying DC component can be directly calculated after obtaining the converged weights of the neural network. Simulation results and comparative analysis validate that the proposed algorithm possess a good nature in resistance to noise, a higher accuracy and acceptable time consumption.

The rest of this paper is organized as follows. In Sect. 2, we introduce the problem formulation and the proposed neural network for parameter estimation of fault current with decaying DC component. As to the proposed neural network model, we divide it into two main parts: one is how to construct the specific topology and the other is to derive the improved Levenberg–Marquardt algorithm to train it. Section 3 reports experimental results of parameter estimation of fault current with decaying DC component. Finally, we conclude our paper in Sect. 4.

2   The Proposed Algorithm

In this section, we will discuss the proposed scheme in detail. Firstly, we present the mathematical formulation of practical problem of parameter estimation of decaying DC component, and then a specific topology neural network is constructed according to this formulation. In order to effectively calculate its weights, an adaptive learning algorithm based on improved Levenberg-Marquardt is derived. Finally, the parameters of decaying DC component are directly calculated using converged weights of the neural network.

2.1   Problem Formulation

Generally, fault current flowing through the primary circuit might be considered as combination of some sinusoidal components and an exponentially decaying DC component. We can represent the sinusoidal components by their unknown amplitudes, angular frequencies and initial phases. Meanwhile, the exponentially decaying DC component can be denoted by an exponential function with an initial magnitude and an unknown damping factor or time constant. The discrete current signal with uniformly sampling interval time can be recorded as following [5],

$$i(t) = I_0 e^{-t/\tau} + \sum_{k=1}^{n} I_k \sin(2\pi k f_1 t + \varphi_k), \tag{1}$$

where, I_0 is the magnitude of the exponentially decaying DC component, τ is the time constant of the decaying DC component, n is the maximum harmonic order, k is the harmonic order, I_k and φ_k are the magnitude and phase of the k-th harmonic component, f_1 is the fundamental angular frequency, and $i(t)$ denotes the signal sampled at time t.

By using the identity trigonometric given by the following well-known equation to the second item of the right part in Eq. (1),

$$\sin(\alpha + \beta) = \sin(\alpha)\cos(\beta) + \cos(\alpha)\sin(\beta),$$

then, Eq. (1) can be rewritten as follows,

$$i(t) = v e^{\omega t} + \sum_{k=1}^{n} v_k \sin(w_k t) + \sum_{k=1}^{n} v'_k \cos(w_k t), \tag{2}$$

where, $v = I_0$, $\omega = -\frac{1}{\tau}$, $v_k = I_k \cos(\varphi_k)$, $w_k = 2\pi k f_1$, $v'_k = I_k \sin(\varphi_k)$.

Obviously, all the parameters in Eq. (1) can be directly calculated from the parameters in Eq. (2) as follows,

$$\begin{aligned}
I_0 &= v, \\
\tau &= -\frac{1}{\omega}, \\
f_1 &= \frac{w_k}{2k\pi}, \\
I_k &= \sqrt{v_k^2 + (v'_k)^2}, \ k = 1, 2, \cdots, n, \\
\varphi_k &= \arctan(v'_k / v_k), \ k = 1, 2, \cdots, n.
\end{aligned} \tag{3}$$

From the above analysis, we can know that it is only necessary to obtain the parameters v, ω, v_k, w_k, v'_k, $k = 1, 2, \cdots, n$, and the parameters I_0, τ, f_1, I_k, φ_k, $k = 1, 2, \cdots, n$ can be calculated using Eq. (3).

2.2 Neural Network Structure

In order to adapt to the power system decaying DC component detection shown in (2), we can construct a specific topology structure of neural network model, as illustrated in Fig. 1. The neural network has a three layer feed-forward structure. The hidden layer has $3n + 2$ neurons which use exponential function and trigonometric functions (sine and cosine) as their active functions, corresponding to the exponentially decaying DC component, the fundamental component and harmonics in the power system signal. The input of the neural network is signal sampling time t and output is $\hat{y}(t)$. In addition, the connection weight vectors between the input layer and hidden layer, and the connection weight vectors between the hidden layer and output layer are defined as follows,

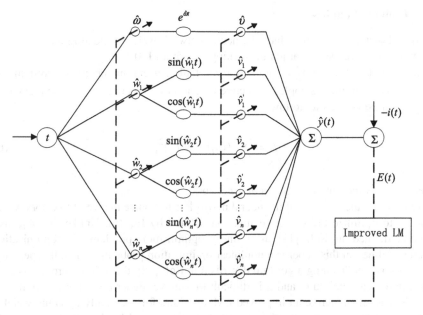

Fig. 1. Specific neural network for parameter estimation of decaying DC.

$$w := \begin{bmatrix} \hat{\omega} & \hat{w}_1 & \cdots & \hat{w}_n \end{bmatrix} \in \mathbf{R}^{1 \times (n+1)},$$
$$v := \begin{bmatrix} \hat{v} & \hat{v}_1 & \cdots & \hat{v}_n & \hat{v}_1' & \cdots & \hat{v}_n' \end{bmatrix} \in \mathbf{R}^{1 \times (2n+1)}.$$

Obviously, the mathematical relation between the input and output denoted by the neural network shown in Fig. 1 can be expressed as follows,

$$\hat{y}(t) = \hat{v}e^{\hat{\omega}t} + \sum_{k=1}^{n} \hat{v}_k \sin(\hat{w}_k t) + \sum_{k=1}^{n} \hat{v}_k' \cos(\hat{w}_k t). \tag{4}$$

After comparison between Eqs. (2) and (4), we can know that the mathematical model of a certain fault signal in the power system is consistent with the neural network model expressed in Eq. (4) in mathematical sense.

Suppose the actual current signal as shown in Eq. (5),

$$\{(t_j, i(t_j)\}, j = 1, 2, \cdots, m, \tag{5}$$

where, t_j is sampling time, $i(t_j)$ is current value of time t_j, and $m(m \gg n)$ is the sampling size.

2.3 Problem Solution

In this subsection, we will deduce the neural network weights updating method based on improved Levenberg-Marquardt learning algorithm [20–23].

If the data $\{(t_j, i(t_j))\}_{j=1}^{m}$ sampled from fault current in the power system are regarded as the training samples, objective function of the neural network expressed in Eq. (4) can be defined as follows,

$$E = \sum_{j=1}^{m} (i(t_j) - \hat{y}(t_j))^2, \tag{6}$$

where, $\hat{y}(t_j)$ is the output of the neural network.

Obviously, the learning of the neural network is to update the weight vectors **w** and **v**, so as to optimize the objective function defined by Eq. (6). Unlike the objective function defined in Ref. [18] as a linear optimization problem, the optimization problem defined in this paper is a nonlinear optimization problem. Generally speaking, if we still use the learning algorithm described in Ref. [18], the training process is easy to fall into local minimum, and it is difficult to achieve higher precision requirements. For this reason, we derive an improved LM algorithm for adaptively updating weights of the neural network. It is worth noting that the improved LM algorithm can not only achieve very high accuracy, but also does not need to optimize the weight parameters layer by layer as traditional BP neural network.

In order to optimize the objective function defined in Eq. (6), we can define expression as follows,

$$F(\hat{\varpi}) = \hat{v}e^{\hat{\omega}t} + \sum_{k=1}^{n} \hat{v}_k \sin(\hat{w}_k t) + \sum_{k=1}^{n} \hat{v}'_k \cos(\hat{w}_k t) - i(t), \tag{7}$$

where, $\hat{\varpi} := [\; \hat{\omega} \quad \hat{v} \quad \hat{w}_1 \quad \cdots \quad \hat{w}_n \quad \hat{v}_1 \quad \cdots \quad \hat{v}_n \quad \hat{v}'_1 \quad \cdots \quad \hat{v}'_n \;]$.

By substituting the m samples of Eq. (5) into Eq. (7), we can obtain m equations about the weight vector $\hat{\varpi}$, as follows,

$$\begin{cases} F_1(\hat{\varpi}) = \hat{v}e^{\hat{\omega}t_1} + \sum_{k=1}^{n} \hat{v}_k \sin(\hat{w}_k t_1) + \sum_{k=1}^{n} \hat{v}'_k \cos(\hat{w}_k t_1) - i(t_1) \\ F_2(\hat{\varpi}) = \hat{v}e^{\hat{\omega}t_2} + \sum_{k=1}^{n} \hat{v}_k \sin(\hat{w}_k t_2) + \sum_{k=1}^{n} \hat{v}'_k \cos(\hat{w}_k t_2) - i(t_2) \\ \quad\quad\quad\quad\quad\quad\quad\quad\quad \vdots \\ F_m(\hat{\varpi}) = \hat{v}e^{\hat{\omega}t_m} + \sum_{k=1}^{n} \hat{v}_k \sin(\hat{w}_k t_m) + \sum_{k=1}^{n} \hat{v}'_k \cos(\hat{w}_k t_m) - i(t_m) \end{cases}, \tag{8}$$

The definition of the Jacobi matrix of Eq. (8) is shown in Eq. (9),

$$
J(\hat{\varpi}) := \begin{bmatrix} a_1 & b_1 & c_1^1 & \cdots & c_1^n & d_1^1 & \cdots & d_1^n & e_1^1 & \cdots & e_1^n \\ a_1 & b_2 & c_2^1 & \cdots & c_2^n & d_2^1 & \cdots & d_2^n & e_2^1 & \cdots & e_2^n \\ \vdots & \vdots & \vdots & \cdots & \vdots & \vdots & \cdots & \vdots & \vdots & \cdots & \vdots \\ a_m & b_m & c_m^1 & \cdots & c_m^n & d_m^1 & \cdots & d_m^n & e_m^1 & \cdots & e_m^n \end{bmatrix} \in R^{m \times (3n+2)}, \quad (9)
$$

where, $a_j = \frac{\partial F_j(\hat{\varpi})}{\partial \hat{\varpi}} = \hat{v} t_j e^{\hat{\varpi} t_j}$, $b_j = \frac{\partial F_j(\hat{\varpi})}{\partial \hat{v}} = e^{\hat{\varpi} t_j}$, $c_j^k = \frac{\partial F_j(\hat{\varpi})}{\partial \hat{w}_k} = \hat{v}_k t_j \cos(\hat{w}_k t_j)$

$-\hat{v}'_k t_j \sin(\hat{w}_k t_j)$, $d_j^k = \frac{\partial F_j(\hat{\varpi})}{\partial \hat{v}_k} = \sin(\hat{w}_k t_j)$, $e_j^k = \frac{\partial F_j(\hat{\varpi})}{\partial \hat{v}'_1} = \cos(\hat{w}_k t_m)$, $j = 1, 2, \ldots, m$,

$k = 1, 2, \ldots, n$.

By using the improved LM learning algorithm, the updating procedure of parameters $\hat{\varpi}$ can be denoted as Eq. (10),

$$
\hat{\varpi}_{s+1} = \hat{\varpi}_s + \Delta\hat{\varpi}_s = \hat{\varpi}_s - (J^T(\hat{\varpi}_s)J(\hat{\varpi}_s) + \mu_s I)^- J^T(\hat{\varpi}_s)F(\hat{\varpi}_s), \quad (10)
$$

where, $J(\hat{\varpi}_s)$ is Jacobi matrix, defined as Eq. (9), μ_s is the learning rate.

Unlike conventional LM learning algorithm, the learning rate μ_s of improved LM learning algorithm should be updated in every iteration [21–23]. Its updating scheme can be defined as Eq. (11),

$$
\mu_s := \alpha_s(\theta \|F(\hat{\varpi}_s)\| + (1-\theta)\|J^T(\hat{\varpi}_s)F(\hat{\varpi}_s)\|), \theta \in (0, 1), \quad (11)
$$

where, α_s is updated by trust region techniques. It should be updated via the following strategy,

$$
\alpha_{s+1} = \begin{cases} 4\alpha_s & \text{if } r_s < p_1 \\ \alpha_s & \text{if } r_s \in [p_1, p_2] , \\ \max(\alpha_s/4, u) & \text{else} \end{cases} \quad (12)
$$

where, $0 \le p_0 \le p_1 \le p_2 < 1$, $u > 0$,

where, r_s is the ratio of the actual decrease $Ared_s$ to the estimating decrease $Pred_s$,

$$
r_s := Ared_s / Pred_s,
$$

where, $Ared_s$ and $Pred_s$ should still be updated,

$$
Ared_s := \|F(\hat{\varpi}_s)\|_2^2 - \|F(\hat{\varpi}_s + \Delta\hat{\varpi}_s)\|,
$$
$$
Pred_s := \|F(\hat{\varpi}_s)\|_2^2 - \|F(\hat{\varpi}_s + J(\hat{\varpi}_s)\Delta\hat{\varpi}_s)\|.
$$

It is worth pointing out that the improved LM algorithm is a globally convergent method for solving nonlinear systems of equations. Global and local convergence of this new method is proved without the non-singularity assumption of the Jacobian matrix. Therefore, the improved LM learning algorithm has better convergence performance than the general gradient descent method and the conventional LM algorithm [20]. Numerical results will further show that this new method can obtain high precision.

3   Simulation Experiments

For the DC component parameter estimation of fault current in power system expressed in Eq. (1), Ref. [5] has achieved good results. In order to verify the proposed method and its learning algorithm, we will use the example of Ref. [5] for simulation analysis and performance comparison.

It is worth pointing out that in all the simulation experiments in this section, the parameters of neural network learning algorithm are as follows,

$$u = 10^{-8}, \quad \theta = 0.5, \quad \alpha = 0.1 + u, \quad p_0 = 10^{-4}, \quad p_1 = p_0 + 0.25, \quad p_2 = p_0 + 0.75,$$
$$\varepsilon = 10^{-12}.$$

For the sake of fairness, the simulation current signal we selected is the same as Ref. [5]. We illustrate the fault current signal as Fig. 2 and the corresponding mathematical expression is shown in Eq. (13),

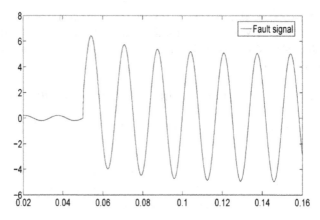

Fig. 2. Time domain waveform of fault current expressed in Eq. (13).

$$i(t) = \begin{cases} 0.4\sin(2\pi \times 60t + 1.5) & t \in [0.03 \quad 0.047) \\ (I_f/\lambda)e^{-t/\tau} + I_f \sin(2\pi \times 60t + 1.5) & t \in [0.047 \quad 0.16] \end{cases}, \quad (13)$$

where, the period $t \in [0.03 \quad 0.047)$ is normal current, the period $t \in [0.047 \quad 0.16]$ is fault current, τ is the time constant, λ is the amplitude ratio between the fundamental component and the decaying DC, i.e., $\lambda = I_1/I_0$. In our simulation experiment, τ, λ and the sampling rate f_s are exactly the same as those in the Ref. [5], i.e., $\tau = 5, 25, 50, 100, 150, 200$ ms, $\lambda = 0.2, 0.4, 0.6, 0.8, 1.0$, and sampling rate is set to 64 per cycle.

Actually, fault current signal of actual power systems usually contain a lot of noise. In order to better simulate the current signal in actual situation of power system, it is necessary for us to simulate some kinds of noise (such as Gauss white noise) in fault current signal. Therefore, the proposed algorithm will consider the existence of Gauss white noise, although Cho's and most of the other schemes [5] seldom take noise into account.

Table 1 shows the comparison results between Cho's [5] and the proposed algorithm when we take six different situations of actual time constants τ into consideration, and change the amplitude ratios λ between fundamental component and decaying DC with five different situations.

Table 1. Comparisons on estimation results of time constants between Cho's and the proposed scheme.

$\tau(ms)$		0.2	0.4	0.6	0.8	1.0
5	Cho's	**5.157**	5.143	5.138	**5.136**	5.135
	Proposed	5.000	5.000	5.000	5.000	5.000
	Proposed (GWN)	5.165	**5.009**	**5.105**	5.173	**5.120**
25	Cho's	25.173	25.148	25.139	25.135	**25.132**
	Proposed	25.000	25.000	25.000	25.000	25.000
	Proposed (GWN)	**25.001**	**24.925**	**24.948**	**24.952**	25.179
50	Cho's	50.195	50.150	50.141	50.134	**50.130**
	Proposed	50.000	50.000	50.000	50.000	50.000
	Proposed (GWN)	**49.935**	**49.877**	**50.126**	**49.997**	49.849
100	Cho's	100.225	100.162	100.140	100.130	100.123
	Proposed	100.000	100.000	100.000	100.000	100.000
	Proposed (GWN)	**100.034**	**100.084**	**99.905**	**100.029**	**100.037**
150	Cho's	150.235	150.158	**150.133**	150.120	150.112
	Proposed	150.000	150.000	150.000	150.000	150.000
	Proposed (GWN)	**149.904**	**150.031**	149.835	**149.978**	**150.032**
200	Cho's	200.233	200.144	200.118	**200.105**	**200.097**
	Proposed	200.000	200.000	200.000	200.000	200.000
	Proposed (GWN)	**200.084**	**200.072**	**200.112**	200.125	199.884

In Table 1, data of the rows labeled with "Cho's" and "Proposed" are estimation results of time constants of Cho's and our schemes in which Gauss white noise will not be took into consideration, and data of the rows labeled with "Proposed (GWN)" are estimation results of time constants of our scheme in the case of Gauss white noise (60 dB) is considered.

From Table 1, we can easily see that, when Gauss white noise will not be took into consideration, all estimation results of time constants of the proposed scheme exhibit complete agreement with the actual values, and Cho's scheme are not accurate enough. Take the case of $\tau = 5$ ms and ratio $\lambda = 0.2$ as an example, the relative error between the actual and estimated time constant of Cho's method is 3.14%. On the other hand, if the comparisons are made between Cho's (Gauss white noise is not taken into consideration) and our schemes (Gauss white noise is taken into consideration), we can see that the proposed scheme still has competitive gain than Cho's scheme in most cases.

Table 2 shows the comparison results between Cho's and the proposed schemes when the fundamental frequency changes in a small range. We take two different situations of actual time constants $\tau = 25$ and $\tau = 50$ into consideration.

Table 2. Comparisons on estimation results of time constant under the case that fundamental frequency is abnormal.

$\tau(ms)$	25			50		
	Cho's	Proposed	Proposed (GWN)	Cho's	Proposed	Proposed (GWN)
59.8	24.844	25.000	**24.970**	49.454	50.000	**49.890**
59.9	25.024	25.000	**24.986**	49.908	50.000	**49.960**
60.0	25.139	25.000	**24.948**	50.141	50.000	**50.126**
60.1	25.171	25.000	**25.110**	50.148	50.000	**50.015**
60.2	25.188	25.000	**24.909**	49.302	50.000	**50.080**

Similarly, in Table 2, data of the columns labeled with "Cho's" and "Proposed" are estimation results of time constants of Cho's and our schemes in which Gauss white noise will not be took into consideration, and data of the rows labeled with "Proposed (GWN)" are estimation results of time constants of the proposed scheme in the case of Gauss white noise (60 dB) is considered.

From the data of time constants estimated by the two methods in Table 2, we can see that, in despite of whether Gauss white noise is considered or not, the estimation accuracy of the proposed method don't tend to decrease when the fundamental frequency is changed from normal to abnormal. But if we carefully check the results of Cho' scheme, we can find that the estimation accuracy tends to decrease when the fundamental frequency is abnormal. This shows that the proposed scheme can better resist the adverse effects of the abnormal fundamental frequency even in the noisy case.

Table 3 gives the time consumption of the two schemes. Observe the data in the table, we can find the longest computation time required by the algorithm is 48.9 ms at the case $\lambda = 1.0$, $\tau = 5$, which is sufficient for the response time of the conventional relay protection system. It is worth to mention that the simulation algorithm is all in software environment: Windows XP, matlab 2012a; hardware environment: CPU: Celeron (R) Dual-Core T3500 2.10 GHz, 2.09 GHz, memory: 0.99 GB.

Table 3. Time consumption between Cho's and the proposed scheme.

$\tau(ms)$	Time consumption (s)					
	5	25	50	100	150	200
0.2	0.0190	0.0046	0.0027	0.0033	0.0035	0.0097
0.4	0.0288	0.0050	0.0038	0.0022	0.0019	0.0049
0.6	0.0212	0.0056	0.0033	0.0025	0.0022	0.0072
0.8	0.0294	0.0036	0.0034	0.0026	0.0020	0.0082
1.0	0.0489	0.0041	0.0027	0.0024	0.0020	0.0091

4 Discuss and Conclusion

Fault current signal with decaying DC component can be denoted as the sum of exponential and trigonometric functions. In general, parameter estimation of the fault current signal cannot be directly solved by traditional neural network. Based on the mathematics model of fault current signal, a specific neural network is constructed and then its corresponding objection function is pre-defined. To solve optimization problem of the pre-defined objection function, we derive an adaptive learning algorithm based on improved LM algorithm.

The proposed specific neural network can be well applied to estimate the parameters of fault current signal with decaying DC component and achieve a very high accuracy. Profiting from good nature in fault tolerance of neural network, it can be applied to the case of existence of Gauss white noise, which is closer to the actual situation. Moreover, the proposed algorithm can also achieve higher estimation accuracy for the abnormal change of fundamental frequency. The only disadvantage of our algorithm is that the time consumption is relatively a little large. Nevertheless, this response time is not a problem because it is enough for conventional relay protection system and our further work is ongoing to cut down the time consumption with a hardware realization.

Acknowledgement. This work was supported by the Key Lab of Digital Signal and Image Processing of Guangdong Province (2016GDDSIPL-02) and Research on Advanced Signal Processing Technology and Application of Department of Education of Guangdong Province (2017KCXTD015). The authors would like to thank all the reviewers for their comments.

References

1. Qian, H., Zhao, R., Chen, T.: Inter-harmonics analysis based on interpolating windowed FFT algorithm. IEEE Trans. Power Delivery **22**(2), 1064–1069 (2007)
2. Lim, Y., Kim, H.M., Kang, S.: A reliable data delivery mechanism for grid power quality using neural networks in wireless sensor networks. Sensors **10**, 9349–9358 (2010)
3. Cheng, P., Liu, W.: Design of storage system of running platform for electric SCADA System. J. Comput. Res. Dev. **48**(suppl.), 132–136 (2011)
4. Liu, Y., Wang, X., Liu, Y., et al.: Resolution-enhanced harmonic and inter-harmonic measurement for power quality analysis in cyber-physical energy system. Sensors **16**(7), 946 (2016)
5. Cho, Y., Lee, C., Jang, G., Lee, H.: An innovative decaying DC component estimation algorithm for digital relaying. IEEE Trans. Power Delivery **24**(1), 73–78 (2009)
6. Lim, Y., Kim, H.M., Kang, S.: A design of wireless sensor networks for a power quality monitoring system. Sensors **10**, 9712–9725 (2010)
7. Jin, G., Li, L., Gao, L., et al.: Real-time fundamental current extraction under inter-harmonics in power system based on high resolution harmonics tracking and fast sequential least square. Int. J. Electr. Power Energy Syst. **61**, 137–144 (2014)
8. Wen, H., Zhang, J., Meng, Z., et al.: Harmonic estimation using symmetrical interpolation FFT based on triangular self-convolution window. IEEE Trans. Industr. Inf. **11**(1), 16–26 (2015)

9. Yu, S.L., Gu, J.C.: Removal of decaying DC in current and voltage signals using a modified fourier filter algorithm. IEEE Trans. Power Delivery 16(3), 372–379 (2001)

10. Guo, Y., Kezunovic, M., Chen, D.: Simplified algorithms for removal of the effect of exponentially decaying DC-offset on the fourier algorithm. IEEE Trans. Power Delivery 18(3), 711–717 (2003)

11. Kang, S.H., Lee, D.G., Nam, S.R., et al.: Fourier transform-based modified phasor estimation method immune to the effect of the DC offsets. IEEE Trans. Power Delivery 24(3), 1104–1111 (2009)

12. Hooshyar, A., Sanaye-Pasand, M.: Accurate measurement of fault currents contaminated with decaying DC offset and CT saturation. IEEE Trans. Power Delivery 27(2), 773–783 (2012)

13. Benmouyal, G.: Removal of DC-offset in current waveforms using digital mimic filtering. IEEE Trans. Power Delivery 10(2), 621–630 (1995)

14. Granados-Lieberman, D., Romero-Troncoso, R.J., Cabal-Yepez, E., Osornio-Rios, R.A., Franco-Gasca, L.A.: A real-time smart sensor for high-resolution frequency estimation in power systems. Sensors 9, 7412–7429 (2009)

15. Granados-Lieberman, D., Valtierra-Rodriguez, M., Morales-Hernandez, L., Romero-Troncoso, R., Osornio-Rios, R.: A hilbert transform-based smart sensor for detection, classification, and quantification of power quality disturbances. Sensors 13, 5507–5527 (2013)

16. Sidhu, T., Zhang, X., Albasri, F., Sachdev, M.: Discrete-fourier-transform-based technique for removal of decaying DC offset from phasor estimates. IEE Proc. Gener. Transm. Distrib. 150(6), 745–752 (2003)

17. Rosolowski, E., Izykowski, J., Kasztenny, B.: Adaptive measuring algorithm suppressing a decaying DC component for digital protective relays. Electr. Power Syst. Res. 60(2), 99–105 (2001)

18. Xiao, X., Jiang, X., Xie, S., Lu, X., Zhang, Y.: A neural network model for power system inter-harmonics estimation. In: The 7th International Conference on Bio-Inspired Computing: Theories and Applications, vol. 9, pp. 756–760 (2010)

19. Marei, M.I., El-Saadany, E.F., Salama, M.M.A.: A processing unit for symmetrical components and harmonics estimation based on a new adaptive linear combiner structure. IEEE Trans. Power Delivery 19(3), 1245–1252 (2004)

20. Yang, L., Chen, Y.: A new globally convergent Levenberg-Marquardt method for solving nonlinear system of equations. Math. Numerica Sinica 30(4), 388–396 (2008)

21. Xiao, X., Lai, J.-H., Wang, C.-D.: A neural network for parameter estimation of the exponentially damped sinusoids. In: Sun, C., Fang, F., Zhou, Z.-H., Yang, W., Liu, Z.-Y. (eds.) IScIDE 2013. LNCS, vol. 8261, pp. 86–93. Springer, Heidelberg (2013). https://doi.org/10.1007/978-3-642-42057-3_12

22. Xiao, X., Lai, J., Wang, C.: Parameter estimation of the exponentially damped sinusoids signal using a specific neural network. Neurocomputing 143, 331–338 (2014)

23. Xiao, X., Chen, B., Yan, J.: A specific neural network for estimating decaying DC component. J. Yangzhou Univ. 21(3), 50–54 (2018). (Natural Science Edition)

Cybersecurity

Typing Technology of Virtual Character of Animation Based on Enneagram Personality

Jiang-lin Luo[1], Mei-li Zhu[1], and Qing-qing Wang[2](✉)

[1] Jilin Animation Institute, Changchun 130000, China
[2] College of Optical and Electronical Information,
ChangChun University of Science and Technology, Changchun 130000, China
286769533@qq.com

Abstract. Facial expression inevitably leads to facial deformation. In this paper, the advantages and disadvantages of feature extraction and recognition method are considered. A facial expression recognition method based on mixed feature fusion of nine types of personality is proposed. The texture features are extracted by discrete wavelet transform and standard orthogonal non negative matrix decomposition for a person's facial expression image sequence, and AAM square is used. The method calculates the coordinate difference between the expression key points of the expression frame and the neutral frame in the image sequence, and extracts the geometric deformation characteristics. Then use the canonical correlation analysis (CCA) to fuse the two features, and finally use discrete HMM to classify faces.

Keywords: Enneagram · Canonical correlation analysis · Facial expression recognition

1 Introduction

Nowadays, the vitality and expanding market value of animation in the creative culture industry has been highly valued by many European and American developed countries in the global economic integration, and has gained a vigorous development. As an important role in the animation, expression animation has also made a very important position in the game, film and television animation, human-computer interaction, and has a very important prospect application.

Expression refers to the emotional indicators of human and other animals from the appearance of the body. Most of them refer to the facial muscles and the state of the five senses, such as the smile, the anger, and the body language expressed by the body as a whole. Facial expression refers to the expression of a variety of emotional states through changes in the eye muscles, facial muscles, and the muscles of the mouth. It is the result of one or more movements or states of the facial muscles. Expression contains a wealth of human behavior information, is the most important carrier of emotion, is the embodiment of intelligence, and the study of it can further understand the corresponding psychological state of human.

Z. Pan et al. (Eds.): Transactions on Edutainment XV, LNCS 11345, pp. 61–70, 2019.
https://doi.org/10.1007/978-3-662-59351-6_6

In computer field, the research on facial expression recognition has been developing gradually in recent years. In document [1], the idea of face recognition is applied to facial expression recognition, which is identified by a static single frame expression image, and the expression is projected to "expression space". This does not reflect the change of facial expression, and does not contain time information and motion information. It is not good enough to expand and is difficult to identify mixed expressions. The expression recognition system implemented in document [2] is based on the rule based method to identify a more exaggerated single expression. Yang [3] propose a 3D facial expression recognition (FER) algorithm using convolutional neural networks (CNNs) and landmark features/masks, which is invariant to pose and illumination variations due to the solely use of 3D geometric facial models without any texture information. Li, Roivainen [4] et al. described a model based approach to use feedback control between computer graphics and computer vision processing for facial image coding systems. A robust thermal face recognition method has been discussed in this work. A new feature extraction technique named as Histogram of Bunched Intensity Values (HBIVs) is proposed by Seal [5]. Zhang [6] proposed a skin–muscle–skull structure. The construction of facial muscles is achieved by using an efficient muscle mapping approach.

It can be seen that there are many studies on facial features at present, mainly in the approach to the analysis of facial features, such as the extraction of facial features, image features, and model based classification, depending on whether the facial features are based on local operations or based on global operation or the two characteristics. In addition, there are still fewer techniques for the recognition of role expression through the role character, based on the static image or the dynamic image sequence or the three-dimensional data based on the input data. Therefore, this paper puts forward the expression recognition technology based on the nine types of personality, that is, to classify the characters according to the nine types, and the different types of personalities are different in the corresponding facial expressions. Then the role character will be integrated into the animation role making, so that the role can convey more emotions and emotions.

2 Establishment of a Nine Type Personality Expression Model

Psychology refers to the relatively stable psychological characteristics of people's attitudes and behaviors. Character is an organic unity made up of various characteristics. Character runs through all mental activities of a person and regulates the whole way of behavior. Psychologists define a number of character models. There are three dimensions of Eysenck's structure (extroversion, psychoticism, neuroticism); Yang Guoshu and other four dimensional structures (shrewd and skillful, simple and simple, impulsive and elegant); the four dimensional structure of jilforth (social activity, paranoid tendencies, introverted thinking, emotional stability); cartel's five dimensional structure (extroversion, Friendliness, strength of superego, anxiety, intelligence. The nine personality model is a widely used personality model, which mainly includes perfect, all love, achievement, artistic, intelligent, loyal, active, leader and peaceful.

People of different personalities have great differences in their expression changes. By establishing a nine type personality expression model, we can solve the problem of lack of character in the change of the character's face.

This paper uses the nine personality model as a character model. The model depicts a person's character from nine sides, which can be represented as a nine dimensional space, in which one's character corresponds to a point in the nine dimensional space. It can be expressed as, in order to further refine the role character, we can divide each dimension in detail into three intervals according to the size of the value. For example, the active type is divided into three intervals, and if the active type is taken for, it shows that the character is introverted and values in, which shows that the role is moderate in activity, and the value in, which shows the role is very active. In the process of facial expression recognition, the characteristics of different regions of different characters can be extracted to get the character of the character.

3 Expression Recognition Technology Based on Nine Personality

Facial deformation is manifested in two aspects: facial texture changes and facial shape changes. Texture features focus on extracting local subtle changes. Geometric deformation features can be used to express the macroscopic structural transformation of the face. It is a new trend to combine the two features of face texture and face shape to combine the two changes. The existing methods of extracting mixed features mostly use three-dimensional models, or use animation parameters, the algorithm is complex, which increases the cost of the system. In this paper, the advantages and disadvantages of feature extraction and recognition method are considered. A method of facial expression recognition with mixed feature fusion is proposed. The texture features are extracted by discrete wavelet transform and standard orthogonal non negative matrix decomposition for a person's face image sequence, and the method is used to calculate the image sequence. The coordinates of the key points of expression frame and neutral frame are extracted to extract the geometric deformation characteristics. Then, the two features are fused by using canonical correlation analysis. Finally, discrete HMM is used to classify faces.

3.1 Texture Feature Extraction Based on DWT-ONMF

For a sequence of images to be measured, the Daubechies series wavelet bases are selected for wavelet decomposition. Then the low frequency coefficient matrix is chosen as the research object. The low frequency coefficient matrix of each image is quantized and the whole image sequence is composed of matrices. According to formula (1), get the corresponding eigenvector moments, which are quantized into 300 dimensional column vectors.

$$f = OW^+X \tag{1}$$

Among, $OW^{+} = (OW^{T}OW)^{-1}OW^{T}$, which is the generalized inverse matrix of the standard orthogonalization matrix OW. X is the low frequency coefficient matrix of the image sequence after a DB1 wavelet transform. Then the entire image sequence matrix is vectored by each low frequency coefficient matrix.

Canonical correlation analysis is a statistical method to deal with the interdependence between two random vectors. Like principal component analysis and discriminant analysis, it occupies a very important position in multivariate statistical analysis. It is a valuable data processing method. The algorithm studies the correlation between two groups of random variables into a few pairs of variables, and the few are unrelated to the variables. Not only can the original feature dimension be compressed, but the typical correlation features of the extracted combination have good classification performance, which reflects the essential features of the image. Canonical correlation analysis has been applied in face recognition. This paper applies it to facial expression recognition based on nine character personality recognition.

Specifically, for the two random vectors x, y, which are to be considered, we find out the linear combination of its components, $a_i = \alpha_i^T x$, $b_i = \beta_i^T y$ and have the greatest correlation between the same variables, and each of them is not related to the typical variables, which is called the canonical correlation. In this way, the correlation analysis between x, y can only be achieved by analyzing the relationship between a few pairs of typical variables. Generally, the projection direction α and β can be obtained by maximizing the following criterion functions:

$$
\begin{aligned}
\rho &= \frac{E[\alpha^T x y^T \beta]}{\sqrt{E[\alpha^T x x^T \alpha] \cdot E[\beta^T x x^T \beta]}} \\
&= \frac{\alpha^T E[x y^T] \beta}{\sqrt{\alpha^T E[x x^T] \alpha \cdot \beta^T E[x x^T] \beta}} \\
&= \frac{\alpha^T S_{xy} \beta}{\sqrt{\alpha^T S_{xx} \alpha \cdot \beta^T E S_{yy} \beta}}
\end{aligned}
\tag{2}
$$

Among, S_{xx} and S_{yy} represent the covariance matrix of x and y respectively, and S_{xx} represents the cross covariance matrix between them.

Let A and B represent two characteristic vector training samples space respectively. According to the idea of canonical correlation theory, we need to find out the linear combination of the components of random vectors x and y respectively. Extract the first pair of typical variables $a_1 = \alpha_1^T x$, $b_1 = \beta_1^T y$, and make the maximum correlation between a_2, b_2 and not related to the first pair of canonical variables. Continue to do so that the relevant features of x and y are extracted. The typical features of n are obtained from a_1 and b_1, a_2 and b_2, ... a_n and b_n. Then, a_1, a_2, ..., a_n and b_1, b_2, ..., b_n are regarded as transformed feature components respectively. It is $X^* = (a_1, a_2, ..., a_n) = (\alpha_1, \alpha_2, ..., \alpha_n)^T x = W_x^T x$, $Y^* = (b_1, b_2, ..., b_n) = (\beta_1, \beta_2, ..., \beta_n)^T y = W_y^T y$. Then:

$$Z = \begin{bmatrix} X^* \\ Y^* \end{bmatrix} = \begin{bmatrix} W_x^T x \\ W_y^T y \end{bmatrix} = \begin{bmatrix} W_x & 0 \\ 0 & W_y \end{bmatrix}^T \begin{bmatrix} x \\ y \end{bmatrix} \tag{3}$$

Which is a combined feature after projection. It can be seen that in order to get the correlation characteristics between the two features, the key is to obtain transformation matrix W_x and W_y.

Because of the components of two groups of eigenvectors x and y that participate in the same pattern sample, there may be a large difference in the different or component changes of the dimension selection, which is not conducive to the extraction of typical features. In order to eliminate the adverse effects of the two features of the participation combination on the numerical or the dimensionality, this paper first standardized the two sets of features, x and y, respectively, before the feature fusion.

$$x* = \frac{x - \mu_x}{\sigma_x}, y* = \frac{y - \mu_y}{\sigma_y} \tag{4}$$

In the formula, $\mu_y = E(y)$ and $\mu_x = E(x)$ are the mean vectors of training samples respectively. $\sigma_x = \frac{1}{m}\sum_{j=1}^{m}\sigma_{xj}, \sigma_y = \frac{1}{n}\sum_{j=1}^{m}\sigma_{yj}$, Here σ_{xj} and σ_{yj} are the standard deviations of the j characteristic components of the training samples, namely the mean of the standard difference vectors of the training samples for the σ_x and σ_y respectively in each component.

In the field of pattern recognition, especially in face image recognition, it is often necessary to deal with the problem of high dimension small sample. In this kind of problem, the overall scatter matrix or covariance matrix of the sample is generally singular, so the covariance matrix is irreversible, so the problem of canonical correlation analysis under the case of high dimension and small sample is solved. The concrete solution process is summarized as follows:

Step 1: the eigenvector matrices extracted from the two methods are X and Y respectively, and the covariance matrix S_{xx}, S_{yy} and cross covariance matrix S_{xy} are calculated after preprocessing.

Step 2: find the standard orthogonal eigenvectors corresponding to the non-zero eigenvalues of S_{xx} and S_{yy}. So $P = (\xi_1, \xi_2, \ldots, \xi_r)$, $Q = (\eta_1, \eta_2, \ldots, \eta_l)$.

Step 3: then calculate the covariance matrix $\tilde{S}_{xx} = P^T S_{xx} P$, $\tilde{S}_{yy} = Q^T S_{yy} Q$ in the r dimension and l dimension space respectively. And the mutual covariance matrix $\tilde{S}_{xy} = P^T S_{xy} Q$ between them.

Step 4: let $H = \tilde{S}_{xx}^{-1/2} \tilde{S}_{xy} \tilde{S}_{yy}^{-1/2}$ calculate the non zero eigenvalue $\lambda_1^2 \geq \lambda_2^2 \geq \ldots \geq \lambda_r^2$ of $G_1 = HH^T$ and $G_2 = H^T H$, and the corresponding orthogonal orthogonal eigenvectors u_i and $v_i (i = 1, 2, \ldots, r)$.

Step 5: let $\tilde{\alpha}_i = \tilde{S}_{xx}^{-1/2} u_i, \tilde{\beta}_i = \tilde{S}_{yy}^{-1/2} v_i$, $i = 1, 2, \ldots, r$. $\overline{W}_x = (\tilde{\alpha}_1, \tilde{\alpha}_2, \ldots, \tilde{\alpha}_d)$, $\overline{W}_y = (\tilde{\beta}_1, \tilde{\beta}_2, \ldots, \tilde{\beta}_d)$, $\overline{W}_x$ and $\overline{W}_y$ are transformation matrixes for canonical correlation analysis.

For the two feature vectors extracted from an image sequence to be processed before feature fusion, the two feature vectors are first standardized. Then the normalized x and y are transformed as follows: $\tilde{x} = P^T x$, $\tilde{y} = Q^T y$, so $Z = (\overline{W}_x^T \, \overline{W}_y^T) \begin{pmatrix} \tilde{x} \\ \tilde{y} \end{pmatrix}$. That is, the new feature vectors obtained after the fusion of the two features, Among $\overline{W}_x = \tilde{\alpha}$, $\overline{W}_y = \tilde{\beta}$. According to the algorithm step 1–5 proposed in this paper, the feature fusion is carried out. The dimension of the $\overline{W}_x$ to the transformation matrix is 65 * 65, the dimension of the $\overline{W}_y$ is 89 * 65, and the dimension of the feature vector Z after the feature fusion is 65 dimension. The normalized value is used as the observed value vector of discrete HMM.

3.2 Classification Recognition Based on HMM

Expression is a dynamic process. The dynamic information of expression contains many information that is beneficial to expression recognition, so the dynamic information of the expression can be modeled by the hidden Markov model, and the category of the sample is judged by detecting the maximum posterior probability of the sample sequence. Since all events in the computer need to be discretized, the Discrete Hidden Markov model is actually used.

When applying hidden Markov models in facial expression recognition, we first choose the topological structure of the model. This is related to specific problems. Different problems require different topologies, and the effects of different topologies on different problems are different. Another problem is the training problem of multiple observation sequences. In order to get a satisfactory model, a lot of training data are often needed. In practical applications, in order to overcome the shortage of training data, multiple observation sequence training algorithms are often used. Then, when training HMM for L observation value sequence, the revaluation formula of Baum-Welch algorithm should be modified, and the observation value is $O^{(l)}, l = 1, \ldots, L$, in which, $O^{(l)} = O_1^{(l)}, O_2^{(l)}, \ldots, O_{T_l}^{(l)}$, assuming that each observation value sequence is independent, at this time,

$$P(O|\lambda) = \prod_{l=1}^{L} P\left(O^{(l)}|\lambda\right) \tag{5}$$

Since the revaluation formula is based on the frequency of different events, the recomputation formula for L training sequences is revised to:

$$\bar{\pi}_i = \sum_{l=1}^{L} \alpha_1^{(l)}(i)\beta_1^{(l)} / P\left(O^{(l)}|\lambda\right), 1 \le i \le N \tag{6}$$

$$\overline{a_{ij}} = \frac{\sum_{l=1}^{L}\sum_{t=1}^{T_l-1} \alpha_t^{(l)}(i)a_{ij}b_j\left(O_{t+1}^{(t)}\right)\beta_{t+1}^{(l)}(j)/P(O^{(l)}|\lambda)}{\sum_{l=1}^{L}\sum_{t=1}^{T_l-1} \alpha_t^{(l)}(i)\beta_{t+1}^{(l)}(j)/P(O^{(l)}|\lambda)} \qquad 1 \leq i \leq N \qquad (7)$$

$$\overline{b_{jk}} = \frac{\sum_{l=1}^{L}\sum_{t=1\,and\,O_t=V_k}^{T_l-1} \alpha_t^{(l)}(i)\beta_t^{(l)}(j)/P(O^{(l)}|\lambda)}{\sum_{l=1}^{L}\sum_{t=1}^{T_l-1} \alpha_t^{(l)}(i)\beta_{t+1}^{(l)}(j)/P(O^{(l)}|\lambda)} \qquad 1 \leq i \leq N,\ 1 \leq k \leq N \qquad (8)$$

According to the specific problem of expression recognition, we will introduce the topology of the hidden Markov model used in this paper, select the state number N, the initial state probability distribution vector, the state transition probability matrix and the observation value probability matrix. Typical facial expressions include anger, disgust, fear, joy, sadness, surprise, these six basic expressions. In this paper, we use the model to distinguish six basic expressions. We must establish a HMM model for each expression, that is, determine the parameters of each model $\lambda_i(i = 1, 2, \ldots, 6)$. The Baum-Welch algorithm of multiple observation sequences is used to train HMM. Through experiments, the left and right model of the state is selected. The left and right model, that is, can only be transferred to its own and its right state, and can not be transferred to the left. The topology structure of the model is shown as the following figure. a_{ij} is the element in the state transition matrix A, and $b_j(o)$ is the column vector of the B of the observation matrix. The initial condition probability vector $\pi_i = 1(i = 1)$ $\pi_i = 0(2 \leq i \leq N)$, A and B matrices of the model usually satisfy the definition of the model. Mixed features may be negative as observed values, and will be normalized to [0, M-1].

Therefore, the system flow of facial expression recognition can be summarized as follows: for a sample sequence, the texture features and geometric deformation characteristics are extracted first, then the two features extracted are fused by canonical correlation analysis, and the eigenvectors of the obtained dimension are classified as the observation value vector. Algorithm, a probability value is obtained, and the expression class corresponding to the maximum probability value is the expression category of the image sequence (Fig. 1).

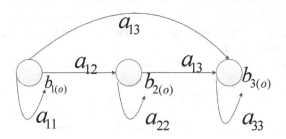

Fig. 1. HMM's state transition diagram

4 Experimental Results and Analysis

The database used in the experiment is the Cohn-Kanade activity unit encoding expression database, which is a standard expression database established by the Robotics Research Laboratory of Carnegie Mellon University in 2000. The library contains nearly 2000 image sequences of 6 facial expressions of more than 200 people, and the expression library does not control light conditions. Each sequence starts from neutral expression to the maximum state of expression.

In this paper, we choose the facial expression image of 40 people to do the experiment. Each expression of each person's expression from neutral to facial expression contains 10 images, 6 expressions and 240 images in a total of 2400 images. 10 of them used to train the model, then randomly selected the image sequences from the 40 person's image sequences to conduct recognition tests respectively. Table 1 shows the recognition results of six basic expression image sequences, and the last two are recognition rate and judgement rate respectively.

Table 1. Recognition results of six expressions

	Angry	Disgust	Fear	Happy	Sad	Surprise	Rejection	Recognition rate	Rejection rate
Angry	35	1	0	0	2	0	2	87.5%	5%
Disgust	1	34	0	0	1	0	4	85%	10%
Fear	0	0	35	1	1	0	3	87.5%	7.5%
Happy	0	0	0	39	0	0	1	97.5%	2.5%
Sad	1	0	0	1	34	0	4	85%	10%
Surprise	0	0	0	0	0	38	2	95%	2%

From the above table, we can see that the recognition rate of surprise and pleasure is high, while the recognition rate of disgust and sadness is low. The average recognition rate of this paper is 89.58%.

In this paper, a comparison graph of recognition rate, misjudgement rate and rejection rate is given. According to the six probability values calculated by HMM, the first two maximum probability values are taken. If the difference is greater than the given threshold, it is considered that the degree of the area is enough to distinguish the waiting expression, then the expression is judged to be the expression of the expression represented by the HMM model with large probability value. Category, otherwise, it is considered indistinguishable. Here, the size of the threshold is determined by repeated experiments, as shown in Fig. 2.

It can be seen that the average recognition rate of this paper is 89.58%. The average misjudgement rate is 3.75% and the average rejection rate is 6.67%. In other words, the probability of misjudging is smaller when it is not correctly identified, which is of great practical value in practical application. In addition, the method is based on the two dimensional image model and is relatively simple to implement.

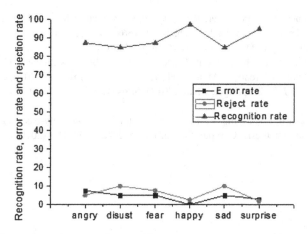

Fig. 2. Comparison diagram of recognition rate, miscarriage rate and rejection rate

5 Conclusion

Facial expression extraction is a key step in facial expression recognition. The quality of feature extraction directly determines the effect of facial expression recognition. In this paper, a hybrid feature phase fusion method based on texture and geometric deformation features is proposed in view of the defect that most facial expression recognition algorithms use only one single feature as the basis of facial expression classification. This paper uses canonical correlation analysis for feature fusion, which takes the correlation feature between two groups of feature vectors as effective discriminant information, which not only achieves the purpose of information fusion, but also eliminates the information redundancy between features. In this paper, the expression recognition hidden Markov model is used in this paper. Finally, the experimental results of facial expression recognition using the fusion feature and hidden Markov model are given, and the experimental results are analyzed and compared. The experimental results show that the recognition rate of this method achieves good results and the average misjudgement rate is low.

Acknowledgments. This work was supported by The Education Department of Jilin Province. I would like to thank those who took care of me, encouraged me and helped me when I am finishing this paper.

References   ,

1. Jia, X., Wen, C.C., Bao, X.Y.: Expression recognition based on dynamic image sequence. J. Beijing Univ. Technol. **9**, 1360–1365 (2013)
2. Wang, L., Liu, J., Fu, X.: Facial expression recognition integrating local features and depth belief network. Laser Optoelectron. Prog. **1**, 198–206 (2018)
3. Zhao, J., Mao, X., Zhang, J.: Learning deep facial expression features from image and optical flow sequences using 3D CNN. Visual Comput. **34**, 1–15 (2018)

4. Li, H., Roivainen, P., Forcheimer, R.: 3-D motion estimation in model-based facial image coding. IEEE Trans. Pattern Anal. Mach. Intell. **15**(6), 545–555 (1993)
5. Seal, A., Bhattacharjee, D., Nasipuri, M., Gonzalo-Martin, C., Menasalvas, E.: Histogram of bunched intensity values based thermal face recognition. In: Kryszkiewicz, M., Cornelis, C., Ciucci, D., Medina-Moreno, J., Motoda, H., Raś, Z.W. (eds.) RSEISP 2014. LNCS (LNAI), vol. 8537, pp. 367–374. Springer, Cham (2014). https://doi.org/10.1007/978-3-319-08729-0_38
6. Zhang, Y., Prakash, E.C., Sung, E.: Efficient modeling of an anatomy-based face and fast 3D facial expression synthesis. Comput. Graph. Forum **22**(2), 159–169 (2010)

E-learning

The Style-Based Automatic Generation System for Xinjiang Carpet Patterns

Xiao Gang Hou and Hai Ying Zhao[✉]

Institute of Network Technology,
Beijing University of Posts and Telecommunications, Beijing 100876, China
zhaohaiying@bupt.edu.cn

Abstract. Xinjiang carpet patterns have flowery color, strong contrast, and the overall harmony, how to design a carpet patterns with Xinjiang style feature is a challenging problem. This paper puts forward a method based on interactive choice mechanism and establishment color constraint rules in order to create Xinjiang carpet patterns. First, we can establish pattern design model through the medallion pattern, corner pattern and brink pattern; then according to the user's choice, we can get sample pattern, and establish respectively dominant color matrix of samples and generated patterns; finally, through the color similarity to generate design constraints, the simulation experiment shows that method of the paper can innovatively design more inherited color style of Xinjiang carpet designs, and enrich the research methods of Xinjiang carpet style design.

Keywords: Xinjiang carpet pattern ·
Three kinds of motif (medallion, corner, brink) · Interactive choice ·
Dominant color matrices · ISDS (Interactive style design system)

1 Introduction

Xinjiang carpet patterns as a part of the intangible cultural heritages, has a very high aesthetic value and application value, which is known as the 'soft gold' in the international world. However, more than ten years, especially the past five years, Xinjiang carpet pattern design is deficiency, shrinking rapidly and extinction. There are only several kinds of Xinjiang carpet pattern in 1950, and it increased to 77 in 1953. In 1966, they reached to 100 various designs. In 1972 years later, the breeds of design and color of Xinjiang carpet had a leap development. Their transplantation and innovation pattern were more than 300. The contents are extremely rich. By the 90 s, they had reached more than 700. However, in recent years the industry with carpet has been shrinking rapidly, design patterns did not increase, but disappeared with the loss designers. We need to increase the Xinjiang carpet pattern by the method of transplantation and innovative design, in order to make Xinjiang carpet industry really

This work was supported by the Project of Science and Technology Committee of Beijing (D171100003717003).

Z. Pan et al. (Eds.): Transactions on Edutainment XV, LNCS 11345, pp. 73–83, 2019.
https://doi.org/10.1007/978-3-662-59351-6_7

brilliant. However, one of the most elusive goals in computer aided design is artistic design and pattern generation [1]. Element, configuration and color also constitute a complex ornament and decorative symbol. In many applications, from architectural design to industrial design and decorative design, an effective algorithm for generating a pattern is more important. This paper presents a novel method for generation carpet patterns, with color as constraint under the interactive choice mechanism. The proposed design algorithm generates various carpet patterns only by changing choice of user. Therefore designer can find their favor pattern. The rest of the paper is organized as follows. Section 2 reviews some of previous works in ornamental design. Section 3 presents a new method for carpet design and prototype system. Section 4 explains the function and implementation results. Finally, conclusion and future work are discussed in Sect. 5.

2 Background

A large number of researches have been devoted to the visualizing ornamental designs, including islamic star patterns, Kolam patterns, plant decoration pattern and the Chinese paper-cut design in the published literature. (1) symmetrical patterns, Alexander [2] developed a FORTRAN program for generating the 17 types of design in the Euclidean plane. Khajeh [3] seeks to design a fashion system utilizing a set of fabric patterns through the interactive genetic algorithm to produce artistic creativity and a set of clothes designs. Zhang [4] propose a computer-aided generation approach of mandala thangka patterns, which can construct parameterized models of three stylistic patterns used in the interior mandalas of Nyingma school in Tibetan Buddhism according to their geometric features, namely the star, crescent and lotus flower patterns. Glassner [5] studied frieze patterns, which can be used for generating band ornaments. Izadi propose a novel computerized and heuristic algorithm to produce various complicated symmetric patterns [6]. Darani [7] present study develops a method to tackle the user fatigue problem in the interactive genetic algorithm using the candidate elimination algorithm. (2) Islamic Geometrical Pattern (IGP), most work related to IGP analysis is to use symmetry groups [8]. Albert propose a new method for analysing mosaics based on the mathematical principles of Symmetry Groups [9]. Rasouli [10] proposed two new algorithms for computer generated Islamic Geometrical Patterns. Zarghili and Bouatouch [11] propose a method for the indexing of an Arabo-Moresque decor database which is not based on symmetry. They use a supervised mosaicing technique to capture the whole principal geometric information (spine) of a pattern. (3) kolam patterns, these traditional designs also seem to imbibe mathematical properties have been done extensively by Gerdes [12]. Recently Nagata [13] has used arrangement of diamond shaped tiles by placing them corner to corner to form kolam patterns. Lalitha [14] proposed a novel method of generating kolam patterns using Petri Nets. (4) Ornamental pattern based on mathematical function: Based on mathematical model of quasi-regular patterns generation [15], Pattern Design of Textile Printing Based on The Transform of The Julia Set [16], The Application to Fractal of Complex Dynamics System on Innovative Design of Textile Pattern [17], Auto Generation of Textile Patterns Based on IFS [18]. Niu proposed a new algorithms to improve the IFS algorithm based on fractal theory thought described by irregular geometry, and then apply the algorithms to packaging design especially in packaging and decoration design [19]. (5) Cut paper patterns [20–22] have got a great attention and acquired good effect in many art fields [23]. During the creation process, the user first composes the outline of the paper-cut image, and then picks up some patterns from the bank to fill the space inside the paper-cut image. Although paper-cut patterns have got a great progress, the computer aided technology is involved very little as a traditional art.

Compared to all of the previous work in the field of pattern generation, our approach presents a new method for carpet pattern design, which is efficient in generating new carpet patterns and algorithm simplicity. On the other hand, in our approach, a color feature has been used to solve the problem of based style design.

3 Carpet Design Method and Prototype System

Aimed at the research questions, Xinjiang carpet pattern is analyzed by computer technology and the feature model established of generation object; and put forward some interactive choice mechanism and the design method of color constraint generating design. According to experts Xinjiang carpet are divided into the following categories: Keliken, Qiaqiman, Ameanguli, Bexiqiqiekeguli, Ediyale, Bogu, Ximunusika, Yilannusika, Worship pad, etc. This paper by analyzing the features of patterns extract structure style features; establish pattern combination structure; introduce dominant color matrix description pattern color style; with users interactive choice mechanism, combine and design the user's preference pattern.

3.1 Representation Model Based on the Features of Carpet Pattern

There are some characteristics in analysis the Xinjiang carpet design and shown in the following aspects: Xinjiang carpet pattern takes these independent geometry or plant elements as a basic motif. They aren't obvious periodical and direction, but contain abundant connotation and meaning. Located in the central region of the pattern is medallion elements (uygur, called AYiGuLi namely the moon flowers) which are comprise of one to three round motif. Surrounding space to add size different flowers, branches and leaves as brink, and in the carpet corners decorated with corner elements, a pattern configuration is obtained (Fig. 1).

So a representation model of pattern can be formed. Each pattern consists of three part, they are medallion elements, corner elements and brink elements.

$$\text{Pattern representation model}: \quad \text{Pattern} = p(m, c, b) \tag{1}$$

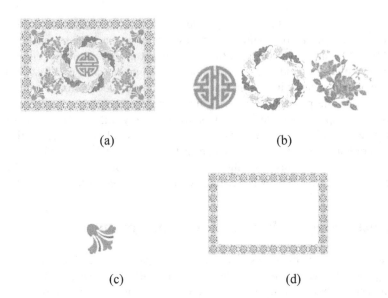

(a)   (b)

(c)   (d)

Fig. 1. (a) original pattern (b) medallion element (c) corner elements (d) brink element

3.2   Pattern Color Representation – Dominant Color Matrices

Xinjiang carpet makes use of plant fluids to dye carpet with color, its dyestuff include pomegranate skin, walnut, red, and blue grass leather, etc. Plus regional characteristics also often be rosy, amaranthine, sapphire blue, bright yellow gorgeous color such as used in the carpet. Thus formed a red and scarlet, yellow, green, red, hector and soil red, Ultramarine blue, Beige Latte, brown, black, yellow, turquoise, ultramarine, light tan as the main body of the 12 colors, and make carpet color comparative and intense, harmonious and unified.

Humans are particularly sensitive to large patches of color, and most of the images are dominated by a small number of colors, these dominant colors contribute more to the discrimination of the image with other images. The method proposed by Knakanhalli, Mehtre and Wu [24] and Celenk [25, 26] can be used to obtain these dominant colors. Denoting the dominant color set of the pattern by $\bar{f}$, which is expressed as:

$$\bar{f} = \{C_k | k = 1, 2, \ldots \mu\} \tag{2}$$

Where C_k is a dominant color, m is number of carpet dominant color.

We propose dominant color matrices for representing the distribution of dominant color in pattern. As first step, the pattern is divided into $m \times n$ number of blocks, we denote by $B_{i,j}$ a block, where $i = 1, 2, \ldots m$ and $j = 1, 2, \ldots n$. Let size of the pattern be $f_{xsize} \times f_{xsize}$, then the size of each block is $s_x \times s_y$.

$$\begin{cases} S_x = \frac{f_{xsize}}{m} \\ S_y = \frac{f_{ysize}}{n} \end{cases} \tag{3}$$

Each block $B_{i,j}$ is examined to determine the fraction $\lambda_{C_k}(i,j)$ of the pixels having dominant color C_k. C_k. $\lambda_{C_k}(i,j)$ is expressed as:

$$\lambda_{C_k}(i,j) = \frac{1}{s_x \times s_y} \sum_{x,y \in B_{x,y}} \begin{cases} 1 & f(x,y) \in C_k \\ 0 & otherwise \end{cases} \tag{4}$$

After computing the fraction of each block in the pattern, we can produce μ number of dominant color matrices $\pounds = \{\pounds_{C_k} | k = 1, 2, \ldots \mu\}$. $\pounds_{C_k}$ denote a dominant color matrix with dominant color C_k. If fraction of block $B_{i,j}$, $\lambda_{C_k}(i,j)$ is greater than a pre-defined threshold value T_{pre}, element $\pounds_{C_k}(i,j)$ of dominant color matrix $\pounds_{C_k}$ be assigned by $\lambda_{C_k}(i,j)$, otherwise, be assigned by 0. The dominant color matrix $\pounds_{C_k}(i,j)$ is defined as Eq. (5)

$$\pounds_{C_k}(i,j) = \begin{cases} \lambda_{C_k}(i,j) & for \ \lambda_{C_k}(i,j) > T_{pre} \\ 0 & otherwise \end{cases} \tag{5}$$

μ number of dominant color matrices can be obtained to represent the feature information of the pattern. According to carpet dominant color, μ number is assigned 12.

3.3 Interactive Choice Mechanism

The system produces randomly a carpet design. Users choose the kept design part according their preference (medallion, corner and brink). The system provides 8 kinds of combination design ways: 1, 2, 3, 12, 13, 23, 0, 123. One means to keep the medallion pattern; 2 means corner pattern; 3 means brink pattern; 12 means the medallion and corner pattern; 13 as the medallion and brink to keep; and 123 means generation designs for the users needed design, retain and exit the system. If users input 0, means that the medallion, corner and brink pattern are not retain pattern. That's to say generation design style is not in conformity with the requirements, and we need to generate randomly combination patterns.

3.4   Color Constraint Rules

In order to generate the carpet pattern which is similar with the selected sample pattern, we need to have a method to determine whether two patterns between selected sample pattern and generated pattern are similar based on their dominant color-contents as constraint generation.

Let S be the sample pattern and I be a generated pattern. The factor is considered in defining similarity between S and I. That is color and spatial location similarity: how well does the color of one pattern match another. We introduce the method for computing the color-spatial similarity regarding dominant color matrices. Let S_{C_k} denote the dominant color matrices of the selected sample pattern S, and I_{C_k} denote dominant color matrices of generated pattern I, where k = 1, 2, ... μ.

We introduce the color-spatial similarity between S and I based on dominant color matrices, since these matrices give both chromatic and position information of color. Assuming $g(S_{C_k}, I_{C_k})$ be matching distance between S_{C_k} and I_{C_k} whose size are $m \times n$, then the color-spatial similarity can be defined as Eq. (6).

$$ss(S, I) = \sum_{k=1}^{\mu} W_k \times g(S_{C_k}, I_{C_k}) \tag{6}$$

Where W_k is weight, which controls the relative importance of dominant color C_k, and $\sum_{k=1}^{\mu} W_k = 1$.

Due to the matching distance in our paper would be the color constraint generation, so between the selected pattern and generated patter is evaluated by their similarity. To obtain matrix matching distance $g(S_{C_k}, I_{C_k})$ between S_{C_k} and I_{C_k}, we use histogram intersection operator to compute the similarity between pattern.

3.5   System Framework of ISDS

This illustration shows the system framework of ISDS. The system mainly consisted of two modules: designs library, interactive choice mechanism and color constraint rule generation pattern. Designs library consists of three kinds of library. They are the foundation of the pattern generation. Interactive choice mechanism provides users 8 ways to choose, as a pilot of generation pattern, and color constraint rule is filled with samples of screening randomly generated pattern design, and obtained the most similar generation pattern.

The main purpose of ISDS is generating carpet pattern of user preferences. Therefore, the paper realizes a method to generate the most similar style carpet pattern, according to the dominant color matrices as constrains conditions to match generation pattern (Fig. 2).

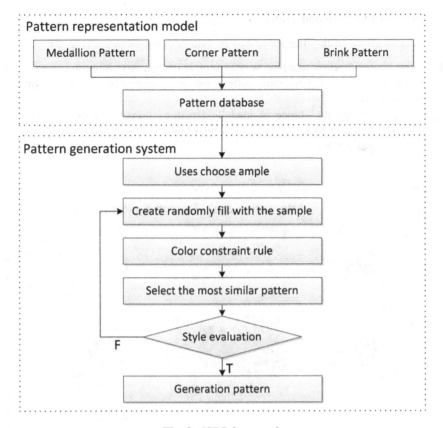

Fig. 2. ISDS framework

4   System Function and Implementation Results

4.1   Algorithm Describe

STEP 1. Generate randomly a pattern, according to the pattern combination model.

STEP 2. Users select a generation model for retaining, and compute dominant color matrix of sample.

STEP 3. Select randomly motif to fill incomplete pattern from the pattern database, according to user's choice way, in order to get generated pattern and to computer its dominant color matrix.

STEP 4. The most similar generation pattern will be selected, according to the color constraint rule to compute the similarity of dominant color matrix between sample pattern and generation pattern.

STEP 5. Users choose and evaluate the generation pattern. If users think the design complies with the design requirements, then he can input 123 for keeping the generated pattern, or continue to step 3.

4.2   System Interface and Functions

The main functions of the interactive carpet style design system are (Fig. 3):

(1) Users choose freely a retaining way as sample design. According to color similar constraints rules, a generation pattern can be gotten whose color is overall coordinating.

(2) If users give up the choice of medallion pattern, corner pattern or brink, the system can repeat to select randomly three kinds of pattern in order to combination carpet pattern.

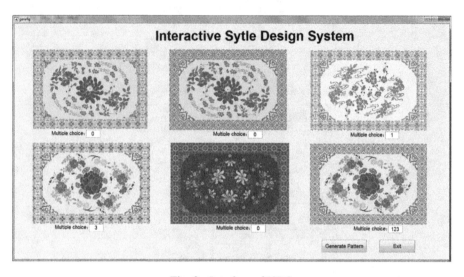

Fig. 3. Interface of ISDS

4.3   Pattern Generation Example and Style Evaluation

(1) According to the user's selection, generating different carpet pattern based on color constrains (Fig. 4)

(2) Style evaluation of generating carpet pattern

According to user's subjective evaluation, establish the style assessment form of the generated patterns. We select randomly 50 minorities as a test of 10 patterns (serial number 1 to 6 from generation patterns, serial number 7 to 10 from the primitive carpet patterns). The evaluation options have the following 3 choices: similar, not similar, and neutral. The results are as follows (Table 1):

Analysis: the evaluation of six generation patterns were an average of 72%, and rest four were 84%. The result explains that that ethnic minority fabric design has a unanimous approval degree, and the generated in the pattern design using gene, which inherits the certain national style. So it also gets the high style identity, and could be used in national pattern design by genuine.

(a)

(b)

(c)

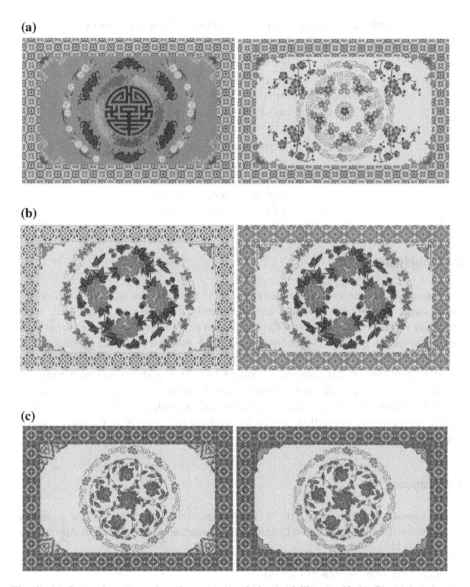

Fig. 4. (a) Generating pattern based on users to choice medallion motif, (b) Generating pattern based on users to choice brink motif, (c) Generating pattern based on users to choice corner motif

Table 1. Assessing form of style similarity of generating pattern

Number	Similar	Dissimilar	Neutral
1	86.54%	5.00%	8.46%
2	56.67%	14.50%	28.83%
3	91.00%	4.65%	4.35%
4	46.64%	15.50%	37.86%
5	67.32%	21.00%	11.68%
6	81.69%	13.31%	5.00%
7	90.00%	3.67%	6.33%
8	77.61%	3.33%	19.06%
9	84.67%	14.00%	1.33%
10	83.37%	12.00%	4.63%

5   Conclusion

This design generation system has many characteristics, displays in: Firstly, this system using image representation model can completely describe the design part, more important is that it could represent the connection of different pattern's features; build more innovation patterns. Secondly, through the interactive choice mechanism to extend effectively the space design, and help the users' preference design style; better solve the problems of Xinjiang carpet pattern lacking of stylized design. Finally, the system can generate optimization design for others; through the interactive choice and iterative generation users preference pattern; and according to the dominant color matrix, constrain the generation pattern and converge effectively in the users' preference design space.

References

1. Bastanfard, A., Mansourifar, H.: A novel decorative Islamic star pattern generation algorithm. In: 2010 International Conference of Computational Science and Its Applications, pp. 111–117 (2010)
2. Alexander, H.: The computer/plotter and the 17 ornamental design types. In Proceedings of IGGRAPH 1975, pp. 160–167 (1975)
3. Khajeh, M., Payvandy, P., Derakhshan, S.J.: Fashion set design with an emphasis on fabric composition using the interactive genetic algorithm. Fashion Text. 3(1), 8–24 (2016)
4. Zhang, J., Zhang, K., Peng, R., et al.: Computer-aided generation of mandala thangka patterns. In: International Symposium on Visual Information Communication & Interaction. ACM (2017)
5. Glassner, A.: Frieze groups. IEEE Comput. Graph. Appl. 16(3), 78–83 (1996)
6. Izadi, A., Rezaei (Ghahroudi), M., Bastanfard, A.: A computerized method to generate complex symmetric and geometric tiling patterns. In: Plemenos, D., Miaoulis, G. (eds.) Intelligent Computer Graphics 2010 Studies in Computational Intelligence, vol. 321, pp. 185–210. Springer, Heidelberg (2010). https://doi.org/10.1007/978-3-642-15690-8_10

7. Darani, Z.S., Kaedi, M.: Improving the interactive genetic algorithm for customer-centric product design by automatically scoring the unfavorable designs. Human-centric Comput. Inf. Sci. **7**(1), 38–45 (2017)
8. Kaplan, C.S., Salesin, D.H.: Islamic star patterns in absolute geometry. ACM Trans. Graph. **23**(2), 97–119 (2004)
9. Albert, F., et al.: A new method to analyse mosaics based on symmetry group theory applied to Islamic Geometric Patterns. Comput. Vis. Image Understand. **130**, 54–70 (2014). https://doi.org/10.1016/j.cviu.2014.09.002
10. Rasouli, P., Bastanfard, A., Rezvanian, A., Jalilian, O.: Fast algorithms for computer generated islamic patterns of 8-ZOHREH and 8-SILI. In: Huang, Y.-M.R., et al. (eds.) PCM 2008. LNCS, vol. 5353, pp. 825–829. Springer, Heidelberg (2008). https://doi.org/10.1007/978-3-540-89796-5_91
11. Zarghili, A., Gadi, N., Benslimane, R., Bouatouch, K.: Arabo-moresque decor image retrieval system based on mosaic representations. J. Cult. Herit. **2**(2), 149–154 (2001)
12. Gerdes, P.: Reconstruction and extension of lost symmetries: examples from tamil of South India. Comput. Math Appl. **17**(4–6), 791–813 (1989)
13. Nagata, S., Robinson, T.: Digitalization of kolam patterns and tactile kolam tools. In: Formal Models, Languages and Applications. Series in Machine Perception and Artificial Intelligence, vol. 66, pp. 353–362 (2006)
14. Lalitha, D., Rangarajan, K.: Petrinets generating kolam patterns. Indian J. Comput. Sci. Eng. **3**(1), 68–74 (2012)
15. Suyi, L., Leduo, Z.: Textile pattern generation technique based on quasi-regular pattern theory and their transform. In: 2008 IEEE Pacific-Asia Workshop on Computational Intelligence and Industrial Application, pp. 264–266 (2008)
16. Zhang, Z., Suyi, L.: Pattern design of textile printing based on the transform of the julia set. In: VECIMS 2009 International Conference on Virtual Environments, Human-Computer Interfaces and Measurements Systems Hong Kong, China, 11–13 May 2009
17. Zhang, Z., Wang, M.: The application to fractal of complex dynamics system on innovative design of textile pattern. In: 2011 Workshop on Digital Media and Digital Content Management, pp. 330–335 (2011)
18. Zhao, X., Yang, X.: Auto generation of textile patterns based on IFS. In: 2009 Fifth International Conference on Natural Computation, pp. 451–454 (2009)
19. Niu, X., Yuan, X.: Packaging design of IFS algorithm based on fractal theory. Revista de la Facultad de Ingeniería U.C.V. **32**(14), 502–507 (2017)
20. Xu, J., Kaplan, C.S., Mi, X.: Computer-generated paper cutting. In: 15th Pacific Conference on PG 2007, pp. 343–350, 29 Oct–2 Nov 2007
21. Lei, H.: A survey of digital paper-cutting. Comput. Aided Drafting Des. Manufact. **22**(3), 12–17 (2012)
22. Chi, M.T., Liu, W.C., Hsu, S.H.: Image stylization using anisotropic reaction diffusion (2016)
23. Peng, D., Liu, X., Sun, S.: An information view: digitalizing theory and methods in nonmaterial cultural heritage protection. J. Comput.-Aided Des. Comput. Graph. **20**(1), 117–123
24. Kankanhalli, M.S., Mehtre, B.M., Wu, J.K.: Cluster-based color matching for image retrieval. Pattern Recognit. **29**(4), 701–708 (1996)
25. Celenk, M.: A color clustering technique for image segmentation. Comput. Vis. Graph. Image Process. **52**, 145–170 (1990)
26. Senthilkani, A.S., Ananth, C., et al.: Overlap wavelet transform for image segmentation. Int. J. Electron. Commun. Comput. Technol. (2017)

Research on Teaching Experiment of Color and Digital Color

JianWen Song[1(✉)], ZheFeng Ma[1], Peng Song[1], and ZhiGeng Pan[1,2]

[1] Creating Design Manufacturing Collaborative Innovation Center,
China Academy of Art, Hangzhou 310024, China
songjw888@126.com
[2] DMI Research Center, Hangzhou Normal University,
Hangzhou 310013, China

Abstract. Color is one of the most familiar physical phenomena and common sense in daily life. However, to understand color is a very complicated learning processing, which takes a long period of time with great effort in professional color application and design practice to mastering the basic laws of color application. Therefore, how to develop a visual teaching system for learning basic law of color and how to make this system more acceptable by students becomes an urgently issue among all art colleges. In this paper, we start with the color digitization issue, establishing the basic relations and orders of color by using color cube and virtual reality technology. Moreover, within this system, it offers an easy way to extract The Color Family System from any image and build a harmonious color relationship. This paper provides a new and high level of color teaching standard, also, solves the key problems between teaching and learning effectively.

Keywords: Color cube · Digital color · Teaching experiment ·
Image analysis · Color family · Virtual reality

1 Introduction

It is a complex process for people to understand the basic laws of color, which needs a long-term training and a large experience accumulated. In process of art design, both teachers and students have strong subjectivity in color cognition. Because they gain color experience from their daily life. However, the existing color standards and digital color design system makes it more difficult to learn the laws of how to use color in a short period of time, especially for ordinary people and students, who do not have a lot of previous experience in manipulating color. Therefore, in the paper, the color digitization system aims at establishing a set of suitable tools, which is a technical system provides an easy method in teaching and learning the laws of color application and benefits for both teachers and students. Our research started with color digitization issue, establishing the basic relations and orders of color by using color cube and virtual reality technology. By using the system, students can easily learn the basic rules of color in a simple method to cognize Color Family from any given image. It greatly enhances the teaching results.

Z. Pan et al. (Eds.): Transactions on Edutainment XV, LNCS 11345, pp. 84–92, 2019.
https://doi.org/10.1007/978-3-662-59351-6_8

2   The Issues Occur During the Process of Teaching and Learning

In most cases, universities hire teachers who practice background close to color design instead of the real professional color experts, which lead to many common problems in color teaching domain. In teachers' perspective, teaching knowledge of color is often influenced by the subjective experience of the himself/herself, also, the traditional teaching approaches to interpret the laws of color application. Usually, it is hard to explain the basic structure of color cube and how to use the color without a visual tool.

Moreover, from the student's perspective, learning color classification and other color knowledge from a class or a traditional color study tutorial becomes a main obstacle for students who study color. Because, in this way, students cannot be able to establish a highly efficient connection between knowledge and application.

In practical level, especially in the color design process, the more important fact is that the results of color palette are usually not only based on the basic laws of color but also influenced by some other elements such as politics, economy, religion, folk custom and so on.

3   The Relationship Between Color Digitization and Color Order

3.1   Color Study Commonly Used Color Cube

In Colorimetry, it combines lightness, hue, colorful degree as a coordinate axis describes the relationship between colors in 3D space, called "Color Cube". Color digitization is the process that use color measurement tools to test nature light in order to obtain tristimulus values as x, y, z, and chromaticity coordinates x, y to match the three-dimensional space, point to point until every color represents by digital formula. The color cube is based on the three-dimensional digital models, and its color are formed by the long-term practice of human who continually exploring and summarizing the nature. At present, the world's most famous color cube space as follow:

(1) RGB [1] color cube space; (2) CIE XYZ [2] color cube space; (3) Munsell [3] color cube space; (4) HSI color space; (5) Lab [4] color cube space; shown as Fig. 1.

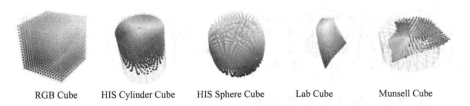

RGB Cube   HIS Cylinder Cube   HIS Sphere Cube   Lab Cube   Munsell Cube

Fig. 1. Commonly used color stereo space digital map

3.2 Research and Application of Color Digitization in the World

In early 1990s, a project worked on The Chinese Color System [5] conducted by Daheng Wang et al. from Institute of psychology, China Academy of Sciences was focusing on color visual experience of Chinese people, in the project, they established the theoretical models of Chinese Color System and the Chinese Color System Sample Volumes. Based on these studies, China Textile Information Center and China Fashion Color Association established "CNCSCOLOR (China National Color System Color) System for FASHION" in 2008 [6–8]. This system is designed as standard platform and system tools in fashion color application, so that it helps enterprises to improve service and management quality. Meanwhile, their progresses have already achieved in the research field of color digitalizing and visualization. Shigenobu's color image scale was devised by the use of an original color-projection technique, analysis of variance, cluster analysis, factor analysis, and the semantic differential method. It can be used for representing and evaluating color images considering perceptual factors. Yamazaki and Kondo introduced a method of editing color schemes in Kansei scales, which adopted human perception, e.g. "warm to cool," "soft to hard," and "natural to artificial", to represent emotional feeling [9]. Meier et al. developed a set of interactive color palette tools that provide eight visualized methods for color mixing: palette browser, image and composition tools, gradient mixer, dial-a-color tool, frequency visualizer, palette breeder, name IPT, and grouper. Hu et al. presented an interactive method for generating harmonious color schemes in the visualized HSV/HSL color space, in which user can obtain harmonious color schemes by simply sitting a few personal parameters [10].

4 Building Color System

4.1 Building Color Cube

In general, color model is the color theory system, which named by the order according to their own characteristics and some certain distribution laws.

From the meaning of mathematical analysis, in Euclidean three-dimensional space, we use x, y, z axis to represent tristimulus long wave L, medium wave M, and shortwave S. Also, set origin point (l, m, s) to (0, 0, 0) in black. As result, these color systems are established and classified based on three attributes of colors.

In this study, we will control the color value of the current [11, 12], and its main functions are realized:

(1) The digital transformation model of the general color standard and color cube model in the world; (2) RGB color cube digitization; (3) HIS column face color cube digitization; (4) HIS spherical color cube digitization [13]; (5) Lab color cube digitization and (6) Munsell color cube digitization.

4.2 Building Color Analysis System

The system design is made up by three parts: (1) Color Cube Analysis System; (2) Color Order Analysis System; (3) Color Analysis Database System. Data is transferred from system to system through the multi process client/server structure (C/S) technical solutions to achieve data synchronization updates and seamless links (in Fig. 2).

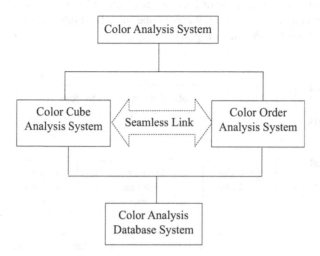

Fig. 2. Color analysis system logic structure

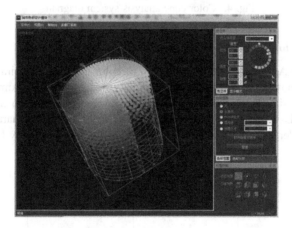

Fig. 3. HSV color cube Space slice experiment

1. Color cube analysis system

According to the way artists using color, researchers commonly use color cube model (shown in Fig. 1) as a whole, which create an OpenGL based color space, and each color cube can be met the needs of teaching, by cutting the profile freely (as shown in Fig. 3). By using the system, it helps student make more intuitive and objective color analysis and application, even more, students are allow to convert different type of cube to fit the specific needs. it made the teaching/learning processing easy and convenient. Color Cube Analysis System is mainly a system that most of normal international color cubes are integrated in this system, based on the client's user experience design, with an up to date interface. It is convenient for students to operate and understand and arbitrary cutting color cube internal structure, achieve arbitrary switching between three-dimensional color cube models. It offers a standard reference system for students (as shown in Fig. 4).

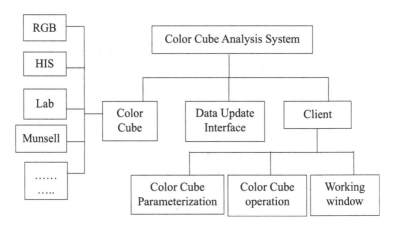

Fig. 4. Color cube analysis system diagram

2. **Design of color spatial analysis system**

Color Order Analysis System is the core of color teaching experiment, Users can equally divide any given image to calculate average of the approximate color and extract them as single color based on weighted average in order to make a mosaic analysis chart. Extracted the limited Key master color to form a harmonious color system and render them within a color cube. Allows users Intuitively Understand the

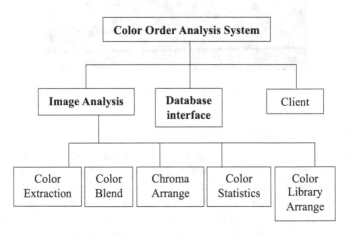

Fig. 5. Color order analysis system diagram

logical relationship between the colors in the image and when they present in color space. That is the process of how the system help user to realize the color order of any image (as shown in Fig. 5).

3. Color analysis database system design

Color Analysis Database System uses JPG as the general format of image processing, and this paper design a standardized document format for color teaching: **(1) ccp (color cube plate) file:** Color cube plat is the color order that forms in the process of image processing, which the color order (shown in Fig. 9) based on the statistical color scale. **(2) cpl (color cube lib) file:** color cube palette I/O interface is mainly interface that user can adjust and change color order after the image is processed, when the color cube set up. **(3) ccd (color cube database) file:** The data storage format of the color order system, which mainly complete the data transfer between client/server (C/S) and the main data storage format of the system resource database about this paper (as shown in Fig. 6).

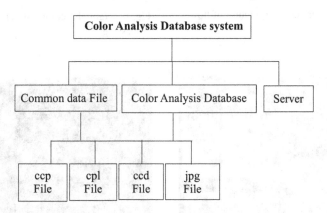

Fig. 6. Color analysis database system diagram

The three systems as above is an important part of the experimental teaching system of color, data transmission through the communication between processes achieve seamless link synchronous real-time transmission, for teaching process provides a good user experience (as shown in Figs. 7, 8, 9 and 10).

5 The Order of Color and the Color of the Family

5.1 Natural Order of Color

Order is the logical relationship formed by a certain law among the objective world. The natural order of color refers to the color relation formed in nature, such as the seasonal color in the spring, summer, autumn, winter, or the colors of flowers as shown in Fig. 7. The image analysis (in Fig. 8) shows that the natural order of colors generated by the system. It is notable that the order relations remain the same when user enlarge the size of the mosaic (as shown Fig. 9). In the color cube space, the system extracts approximation of color automatically according to the principle of weighted average, which means that the system automatic eliminating similar color and only keeping different colors to generate the color map of the natural order, as shown in Fig. 10.

Fig. 7. Nature color in picture of flower

Fig. 8. Natural color order of image processing

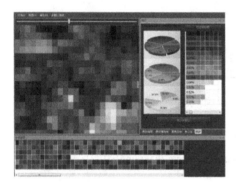

Fig. 9. Increasing the range of mosaic

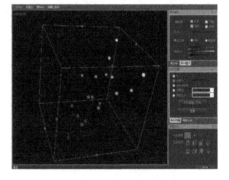

Fig. 10. The natural color order in system

5.2 The Relationship of Family Color

In the system of Color Order Analysis in Fig. 7 for example, we established the natural order of the colors (Fig. 9) and built the main tone as the core of color order. Each color order has a main color tone and the rest colors are serve as auxiliary tones, We named it as main color tone oriented family relationship (as shown in Fig. 11). There are five color families: blue, green, yellow, red and mixed color. The pictures below are examples of these five color families used in design practice (Fig. 12).

Fig. 11. Color family's relationship   **Fig. 12.** Effect of color family in cylindrical vessel (Color figure online)

6 Color Teaching Practice

6.1 Establishing the Logical Relationship Between Teaching and Learning

It is significance for both teacher and students who engage digital color teaching. In the class, students would learn how to establish thinking logic between teaching and learning. Student can select any picture (in Fig. 7) to complete the following steps:

(1) Analysis of natural color in the photo, and analysis the natural order of color from the picture; (2) establishes a certain number of color families; (3) Sorts the color families they established; (4) Apply the color families to the actual objects; (5) find out the optimum color schemes works for actually product design.

6.2 Practical Cases of Students Hands-on Operation

According to the steps described in Sect. 6.1, students start to analyze the comprehensive color families relationship from Fig. 7, and practice for real product design which is similar to the shape of the objects, in order to have more detailed observation between color and object (as shown in Fig. 13). To compare the different color schemes

Fig. 13. Color family with relationship of the cubs   **Fig. 14.** Real product the with color family

above [14, 16], it is clear to figure out that the green and yellow scheme have very soft visual effect. They fit the needs of food products, Fig. 14 shows the final products in selected schemes (as shown in Fig. 14).

7 Conclusion

In the paper, we present a method, which can automatically do the equally divide calculation for any given image and extracted a single color by doing weighted average of the approximate colors from the image. Then regenerate a new mosaic analysis image with the extracted colors in order to have a certain number of key colors to form a harmonious color family system, which can be rendered and present in the color cube. This paper revealed the basic laws of the family color system, and it would benefit for students by introducing them a new method and theory to visualize the convert process from the natural color system to the subjective color system. It shows the significant value both in theory and practice and also be seem as a remarkable achievement in color teaching in China.

References

1. ICC. Why Color Management? The two PCS's in the ICC system are CIE-XYZ and CIELAB. Accessed 16 Apr 2008
2. http://dba.med.sc.edu/price/irf/Adobe_tg/models/munsell.html
3. http://www.adobe.com/digitalimag/adobergb.html
4. http://www.iso.org/iso/home.html
5. Shenzhen HaiChuan color technology, Ltd,Chinese color system standard sample volumes, GSB16-2062-2007
6. The People's Republic of China, Chinese color system (GB\T15608-2006). China Standard Press (2006). ISBN 0661285545
7. Shigenobu, K.: Color Image Scale. Kodansha Ltd, Tokyo (2001)
8. Yamazaki, H., Kondo, K.: A method of changing a color scheme with kansei scales. J. Geom. Graph **3**, 77–84 (1999)
9. Meier, B.J., Spalter, A.M., Karelitz, D.B.: Interactive color palette tools. IEEE Comput. Graph Appl. **24**, 64–72 (2004)
10. Hu, G.S., Pan, Z.G., Zhang, M.M., Chen, D., Yang, W.Z., Chen, J.: An interactive method for generating harmonious color schemes. Color Res. Appl. **39**(1), 70–78 (2012)
11. Song, J.: Color design in France—Sutdy on French color scientist Jean Philippe LENCLOS, Teaching and social practice. Shanghai people's Fine Arts Publishing House (1999). ISBN:9787532221899
12. http://en.wikipedia.org/wiki/Category:Color_space
13. Hunter Lab Versus CIE 1976 L*a*b*, HunterLab Applications Note, vol. 13, no. 2
14. Song, J.: The golden giant building creating elegant—Nanjing South Railway Station architectural color design notes, architectural creation, vol. 154, pp. 72–76
15. Song, J.: Reading The Colors of Macao New Geographies 3 Urbanisms of Color, pp. 125–141. Harvard University press. ISBN 978-934510-26-2
16. Song, J.: Hangzhou color expression—Hangzhou city color planning practice experience, Public Art, vol. 5, pp. 28–34

Cybersecurity Curriculum Design: A Survey

Djedjiga Mouheb, Sohail Abbas(✉), and Madjid Merabti

Department of Computer Science, University of Sharjah,
Sharjah, United Arab Emirates
{dmouheb,sabbas,mmerabti}@sharjah.ac.ae

Abstract. The threat of cyber attacks continue to grow with the increasing number of sophisticated and successful targeted cyber attacks throughout the globe. To address this issue, there is a dire need for cybersecurity professionals with adequate motivation and skills to prevent, detect, respond, or even mitigate the effect of such threats. To this end, several cybersecurity educational programs and concentrations have been established over the past years both at the graduate and undergraduate levels. Moreover, a number of initiatives taken by the government standard bodies in the cybersecurity domain have emerged to help in framing cybersecurity education. Due to the interdisciplinary (and sometimes multidisciplinary) nature of cybersecurity, educational institutions face many issues when designing a cybersecurity curriculum. In this context, we believe that there is a desideratum to provide a big picture of the overall efforts done so far in the direction of cybersecurity curriculum design. In this paper, we present an overview and comparison of existing curriculum design approaches for cybersecurity education. This survey will help the researchers and educators to have an overview of the existing approaches for the purpose of developing a suitable and more effective cybersecurity curriculum in their future endeavour.

Keywords: Cybersecurity · Teaching · Learning · Curriculum · Education

1 Introduction

In recent years, a dramatic increase in the number and sophistication of cyber attacks targeting governments, organizations, and end-users has been observed. In fact, the continuous emergence of new mobile devices and the wide adoption of Internet of Things (IoT), and the so-called Bring Your Own Device (BYOD) trends, have brought many cybersecurity challenges and opened new doors to cyber criminals to exploit vulnerabilities of these systems. In its 2015 Cyber Threat Report, Symantec Corporation [1] reports that, as a conservative estimate over half a billion personal records were lost or destroyed in 2015, there were over one million cyber attacks against people each day, 75% of all legitimate

© Springer-Verlag GmbH Germany, part of Springer Nature 2019
Z. Pan et al. (Eds.): Transactions on Edutainment XV, LNCS 11345, pp. 93–107, 2019.
https://doi.org/10.1007/978-3-662-59351-6_9

web sites were vulnerable to attacks in such a way as to potentially infect users, a new form of attack was appearing roughly once every week. The recent Cyber Security Breaches Survey from the UK government [12] reports that two thirds of large UK businesses were hit by a cyber breach or cyber attack in the past year, with one in four being hit by a breach at least once per month. The cost of these attacks often runs into millions of pounds/euros/dollars. In short, cyber issues pose a serious threat to everyone and to all organisations.

This situation is exacerbated by the lack of appropriate cybersecurity skills to cope with the emerging cyber threats. Companies and organizations are constantly facing severe shortages in valued and highly-skilled cybersecurity professionals. The lack of such expertise leaves them vulnerable to cyber threats, resulting in theft of sensitive information, financial loss, and reputation damage. The scale of the problem, rapid growth and technical nature of cyber attacks widen the gap between the fast growing need for cybersecurity professionals and the lack of appropriate security skills. As reported in [6], experts from the International Information Systems Audit and Control Association (ISACA) [5], a non-profit IT governance group, predict a global shortage of two million cybersecurity professionals by 2019. On the other hand, cyber training environments don't currently reflect real-world cyber scenarios, contributing to the widening skills gap. In this context, there is a strong demand for skilled professionals in the cybersecurity profession now and for the future.

To address this issue, a number of initiatives and government standard bodies in the cybersecurity domain have emerged to help in framing cybersecurity education. Among these initiatives, we can cite: The National Cybersecurity Workforce Framework (NCWF) by NICE (National Initiative for Cybersecurity Education) [4], which proposes the categories and skill sets that should be considered in the cybersecurity field; An educational reference framework proposed by the Committee on National Security Systems, which proposes a reference standard of the content of an Information Security Curriculum [10]; The National Information Assurance (IA) Education and Training Programs (NIETP) Center of Academic Excellence (CAE), etc.

On the other hand, several cybersecurity educational programs have emerged over the past years. Indeed, cybersecurity education is no longer confined to a number of courses introduced in a computer science discipline. Instead, a number of specialized cybersecurity programs and concentrations have been established at the graduate and undergraduate levels, or even at the high-school level. These programs usually offer a wide range of courses, from general and fundamental cybersecurity courses to more specific ones, including malware analysis, digital forensics, ethical hacking, penetration testing, cryptography and network security, secure software development, information systems management, etc.

Because of the wide range of cybersecurity subjects and applications, when developing a cybersecurity course or educational program, a number of issues need to be addressed, such as: (i) What are the cybersecurity topics and subjects that should be covered in the curriculum? (ii) What are the skills and competencies expected from the graduates at the end of the course or educational program? At which educational level should a cybersecurity program be offered? What is the methodology that should be followed for teaching cybersecurity subjects? What are the evaluation components needed to assess students' knowledge related to cybersecurity? How to ensure that graduates are equipped with enough skills and expertise to work as cybersecurity professionals?

In this context, several attempts have been made in the existing literature offering different kinds of proposals for security curriculums. However, in most cases, these proposed curriculums guidelines focus only on one aspect from the aforementioned issues. We believe that there is a dire need to provide an overview of the overall efforts done so far in the direction of the cybersecurity curriculum design. This will help the researchers to have a big picture of the overall efforts. To the best of our knowledge, no previous efforts have been done on comparing and analyzing curriculum design approaches for the cybersecurity domain. In this paper, we present a review and comparison of the state-of-the-art curriculum design approaches for cybersecurity education. Our goal is to come up with some conclusions and answers that would help in developing a suitable and more effective cybersecurity curriculum.

The rest of the paper is organized as follows. In Sect. 2, we discuss the general categorization of cybersecurity curriculum design approaches in three different facets, i.e., education, industry, and government/defense. Section 3 encompasses the comparison of existing proposals. In Sect. 4, we present a discussion of the proposed approaches. Section 5 provides an overview of non-traditional approaches to cyber security teaching. The paper is concluded in Sect. 6.

2 Cybersecurity Curriculum Approaches

Cybersecurity education is becoming imperative more than ever, especially with the widespread of cyber attacks worldwide. In this context, several approaches have been proposed offering different kinds of cybersecurity curriculums. In this section, we review and survey the existing literature on cybersecurity curriculum design approaches. We categorize these approaches according to their main focus as educational, industry, and defense/Home Land Security based approaches.

2.1 Educational Approaches

In this category, we present cybersecurity curriculums which focus on improving cybersecurity education from different perspectives.

Reflections about the contents that should be included in a graduate-level cybersecurity curriculum are discussed in [31]. The authors reviewed the content and skill sets that should be considered in a cybersecurity curriculum. In particular, the authors referenced two well-known educational frameworks, namely, the National Cybersecurity Workforce Framework (NCWF) by NICE (National Initiative for Cybersecurity Education) [3] and an educational reference framework proposed by the Committee on National Security Systems [2]. In order to master the multidisciplinary nature of cybersecurity, it was suggested that students should also learn the STEM (Sciences, Technology, Engineering and Mathematics) principles. The authors also emphasized the importance of developing critical thinking and problem solving skills in addition to technical skills since these competencies are important to assess risk, detect emergent threat, respond to attacks and identify potential adversaries. Moreover, the authors addressed the need to develop security skills that are related to the professional environment, understand cybersecurity ethical and moral issues, as well as develop cross-disciplinary collaboration to be able to communicate cybersecurity knowledge to technical and non-technical audience.

Furthermore, the authors also discussed the topics that should be considered in a cybersecurity curriculum. The authors reviewed three main activities that have been suggested by researchers, namely, Prepare, Defend and Act [30]. It was proposed that these activities be grouped into three distinct phases, namely, Prevention, Detection and Response [23]. In the Prevention activity, the authors suggested to include topics, such as penetration testing, ethical hacking and advanced persistent/evasive threats, implementation of secure software and awareness. In the Detection activity, the authors proposed to cover intrusion detection systems and penetration testing. As for the Response activity, topics such as digital forensics and incident response, and auditing, as well as other areas related to cultural and global standardization, legal issues, and awareness. Due to the dynamic nature of cybersecurity threats and vulnerabilities, it was also suggested to timely adjust the activities and strategies in each phase.

The importance of teaching behavioral security was addressed in [27]. Behavioral security is a field that deals with the behavioral human aspects needed in the study and analysis of cybersecurity events. The importance of the problem lies in the fact that the greatest security challenge is in the human weaknesses rather than in technical solutions. To address this issue, an undergraduate course on Behavioral Cybersecurity has been developed at Howard University as a complement to the cybersecurity course. The course also allows the participation of students from Psychology or behavioral science majors, to whom special tutorials were provided with behavioral security background. The course followed the flipped classroom approach that required a lot of reading and lively discussion. The course included topics related to password meters, biometrics, steganography, hacker profiling, game theory, risk assessment, gender differences, etc. The evaluation of the course was based on five components: class participation, tests, written assignments and labs, oral presentations, and a final paper. It was noted that the course increased the students' participation and interest, as well as opened promising further developments in the field of cybersecurity.

A cybersecurity curriculum that teaches children the basic concepts of cybersecurity and information assurance was proposed in [21]. After presenting a set of requirements to analyze the effectiveness of computer-security curricula, the authors came up with recommendations for a cybersecurity curriculum targeting children with basic computer skills. The authors concluded that cybersecurity education should be flexible enough to cover a wide group of users, teaching cybersecurity in an interactive and motivational way, and teach computer-security skills in a simple way that children can understand.

Ethical and legal issues related to teaching ethical hacking skills in an information security curriculum are discussed in [34]. This is due to the fact that some students would use the acquired offensive skills in an inappropriate and illegal ways, which might put their careers, education, and even their entire information security program at risk. As such, the authors raised the importance of teaching students ethical hacking rules and techniques, which are fundamental in an Information Security curriculum. To this end, the authors presented a case study that consists of implementing a comprehensive ethical hacking hands-on lab exercises for teaching common Denial of Service (DoS) attacks, namely, the Land, the TCP SYN (synchronization) flood, and the Teardrop attacks, in an isolated network laboratory environment. The paper discussed also common defense techniques for detecting DoS attacks, including Intrusion Detection Systems (IDS) and Software tools, such as Snort tool, during the hands-on lab exercises. Through this case study, the authors presented the necessary steps that should be taken by schools and educators to make students aware of the consequences of any misconduct and ensure that they are responsible for their actions. The authors also discussed the effectiveness of adding hands-on exercises in information security education, which greatly enhances students' performance in terms of achieving program's outcomes.

The role of students' assessment in cybersecurity education was discussed in [18]. It was noted that there is a lack of focus on assessment task design in most ethical hacking courses. The other issue is related to the fact that many students delay their engagement with cybersecurity teaching material until faced with assessment tasks [2]. In this context, the authors used a case study on the re-design and critical assessment of an undergraduate ethical hacking and countermeasures course at Bournemouth University. First, the authors reviewed the design of existing course work. The assessment consists of asking students to plan, conduct, and document four exploits of their choice, which gave them flexibility by working with technology they were comfortable with. The main issues related to this assessment approach are mainly: engaging students in the technical skills but failing to engage them with the underlying practices; difficulty of providing feedback on the underlying problems related to theory, and difficulty of minimising plagiarism. To address these weaknesses, the authors re-designed the coursework assignment for the course by requiring students to demonstrate various cybersecurity practices through realistic scenarios. In contrast to the first assessment approach, students worked on a real-world case study, and involved social, physical, as well as logical security elements. The revised assignment was critically evaluated based on its alignment with the course outcomes, students' engagement, and opportunities for plagiarism. It was suggested that constructive alignment of the redesigned assignment could be further improved by adding guidelines about the adequate form that assignments might take. This could also require revision of the expected learning outcomes to fit the level of students.

The inclusion of cybersecurity modules in the undergraduate computing degree programs was discussed in [19]. This inclusion of modules is the direct consequence of the societal change, i.e. the current advancement of mobile computing (smart phones and tablets) and cloud computing technology. The aim of the work was to ensure that all computing students, irrespective of their degree programs, received instructions regarding security concepts. The basic idea was to include self-contained instructional modules in the relevant classes of various computing disciplines, i.e. Information Technology, Computer Science, Computer Engineering, Network Security, etc. Each module was defined to be a distinct unit of course work materials, for instance, teaching or lab component which may be included into the existing courses of the curriculum without requiring any changes in the courses, degree programs, or curricular approval. The scope of modules included, technical, ethical, and legal aspects of cybersecurity covering range of details, i.e. from introductory material to more technical concepts. These could be incorporated into a standalone course or series of courses. It was suggested that both module and instructional designers may work together in order to create modules that are self-contained, steady and may be linked together to construct larger blocks of instruction. The authors devised three modules, focussing on secure coding, piloted to students as short non-credit seminars. The author claimed from the initial students' feedback that the method increased students' interest in the field of cybersecurity.

The authors in [14] described a fourteen years transitional period of their cybersecurity undergraduate curriculum. In 2002, the authors' institution (Towson University) launched a security track named as the Cyber Operations. The difference between the curriculum of general computer science program and the security track was that the upper-level CS elective courses were converted to deeper and security focussed. For example, Operating System was converted to Operating System Security, Data Communication and Networking was converted to Network Security, etc. Initially, the security track included courses, such Computer Ethics, Introduction to Computer Security, Network Security, and Introduction to Cryptography; however, later on these courses had also been added to general CS program, for example, Computer Ethics and Introduction to Computer Security are required courses for about all computing majors. As a result, the security track students found these courses as redundant. The solution proposed for this was to convert the existing (redundant) courses as security focussed and to include two more courses as alternate, i.e. Advanced Programming Concepts and Reverse Engineering and Malware Analysis. The former is the pre-requisite for the latter. The Reverse Engineering and Malware Analysis course was added to the curriculum because students needed more than just learning the basics; their final projects usually involved the reverse engineering of live malwares.

The challenges of integrating security into the Computer Science curriculum were addressed in [32]. The discussed challenges were mainly included the lack of faculty for teaching security, scarcity of effective teaching resources, and insufficient room in CS curriculum to accommodate security. Among the challenges, the authors also targeted the development of the faculty expertise in cybersecurity field and provided and elaborated various projects. The author aimed at improving the cybersecurity educators' expertise in order to build a community of CS educators that would prepare and produce computing graduates meeting the current and future challenges of cybersecurity.

A multidisciplinary paradigm for undergraduate cybersecurity education was proposed in [25]. The approach focused on algorithm choice and implementation as well as trade-offs between hardware and software. Three departments of the Rochester Institute of Technology namely, Computer Science, Computer Engineering and Software Engineering, put efforts in designing a multidisciplinary course integrating algorithmic, engineering, and practical aspects of security. They took applied cryptography as their case study and presented the course structure, topics to be covered, lab tools and also the final results of the two offerings of this course. This multidisciplinary approach differed than the traditional approach which mainly focused on the theoretical and mathematical aspects of cryptography without focussing on the practical implementation issues. The author also emphasized the active learning pedagogy that immediately engages students with hands-on exercises during the class after covering the theoretical aspects of a topic. The student groups need to compose of individuals belonging to each category of hardware or software. The computer engineering students belong to the hardware discipline whereas software engineering or computer science belongs to software discipline. The authors' proposed approach may suffer from the following issues. First, since the method depended on mixture of students from different departments, a good balance sometimes may not be possible. Second, the author demonstrated only the applied cryptography course; however, the proposed work needs to provide guidelines or a framework for transforming the existing courses or designing new courses to their proposed multidisciplinary approach.

The authors in [24] emphasized on the importance and hence the inclusion of hardware components in the curriculum of undergraduate and graduate level cybersecurity programs, in both CS and IT disciplines. The author proposed a new pedagogical model to improve cybersecurity students' skill thereby introducing hardware concepts and design skills in the network intrusion detection course. After focussing on the fundamental concepts, the curriculum of the course should highlight the main topics of the course, such as network traffic analysis, system configuration, rule-based detection and basic hardware design and experiments. During the course, hands-on projects were also designed to hone the students' technical skills.

2.2 Industrial Approaches

Due to the rise of cybersecurity threats, opportunities of employment in the cybersecurity field have dramatically increased over the past years. Unfortunately, having a degree in cybersecurity is not always enough to meet the needs of the cybersecurity profession. A cybersecurity professional is not only required to have broad and fundamental knowledge of cybersecurity concepts, but also should be equipped with adequate expertise and hands-on experience. Indeed, employers are constantly looking for cybersecurity professionals who can hit the ground running in very specialized areas. To ensure that graduates meet the needs of the workplace and stay current with the latest cybersecurity technologies, there has been several efforts focusing on cybersecurity professional training and certification. In this context, some approaches focused on cybersecurity curriculum requirements in terms of industry needs.

The issue of cybersecurity professional certification, i.e., the lack of a standard ways to assess cybersecurity skills and competencies of Information Security professionals was discussed in [33]. The authors highlighted the issue that university IT programs only incorporate security components into the curriculum, but do not prepare graduates for certification. In this context, the authors study the effectiveness of university IT programs in providing the necessary knowledge and skills to graduates to work as computer security professionals. The authors reviewed certification requirements for the most accepted certifications in the cybersecurity field. To address this issue, the authors presented a model for designing and evaluating a cybersecurity program based on quality standards that are established by accreditation bodies such as ABET. The program's development relied on three parts that formulate the program's mission, educational objectives and career goals, and desired outcomes and competencies. The authors also paid attention to the necessity of continuously updating and changing the program in place for constant improvement.

The current efforts to promote cybersecurity education and to adapt it to the current education and industry needs in the United States were discussed in [17]. The efforts were analyzed in order to establish how these efforts can be exploited to create programs to benefit industry, education, and the graduates. The author considered student success element as one of the important factors for a successful program. Because, the technical elements alone may not deliver the desired workforce outcomes required for the current cyber-enabled environment. The author also analysed the gaps in aligning industry and education in cybersecurity domain as follows. The industry complains that graduates do not have ample hands-on skills to carryout routine jobs. It is important that the difference between education and training be understood. In education, graduates focus on "why", i.e. the theory and mechanism behind the material; whereas, the industry expects training, in which students focus on "how", i.e. working of current technology and methods. The academia mostly focuses on education; however, the industry usually demands for educated as well as trained graduates. So, the universities should also focus on both in order to meet the industry demands and to broaden the scope of job market for their security graduates.

The authors in [15] considered cybersecurity to be a broad field and mostly the industry wants graduates in specific fields, not in the broad field of cybersecurity. The authors advocated specialities in graduate programs in the cybersecurity domain thereby proposing curriculum for three specialities: cyber intelligence, cybersecurity data analysis, and health care information security and privacy.

2.3   Homeland Security Approaches

Following the establishment of the Department of Homeland Security (DHS) in 2003, the need for educational programs for DHS employees has increased. In this context, several efforts have been made to address the issue of what should be included in DHS educational programs in terms of security courses and subjects. Examples of such efforts include a workshop of the Committee on Educational Paradigms for HS in 2004, a Master's degree curriculum proposed by the Naval Postgraduate School, etc. At the same time, the number of educational programs targeting Homeland Security has greatly increased. In the following, we review existing work related to cybersecurity education targeting Homeland Security.

A study of the educational needs for the Department of Homeland Security employees was conducted in [29]. The authors addressed the questions of where the field of Homeland Security should fit in academia, the type of degrees that should be provided, and the relevant courses that should be included in the curricula. To this end, the authors conducted a survey, namely, The HS Education Needs Assessment [29], to gather information from DHS employees working in fields related to law enforcement and security. The employees were asked about the subjects they believed should be part of Homeland Security undergraduate curriculum. The participants were given a list of fifty-two courses and subjects and asked to rank them in the order of importance in a HS undergraduate education program. The results of the survey suggested that Terrorism and Fundamentals of HS were the two most important courses for HS education curricula. The next most important subjects were general education courses, including Critical Thinking/Analytical Skills, Ethics, Technical Writing, English Composition, and Informational and Oral Communication.

A course of study specifically for Homeland Security (HS) students in the cybersecurity domain was proposed in [22]. The authors pointed out that currently information security and HS programs are largely disjoint. Which is due to the fact that most of the information security degrees are technical in nature, their aim is to produce tool developers; however, the HS on the other side is based on a non-technical paradigm of applied social science curricula. The former approach does not meet the needs of HS students, who need "computer security for the social sciences". The author suggested a multidisciplinary approach, that is, the HS programs should not only provide the opportunity for the students to study subjects like risk management, emergency management, terrorism studies, and infrastructure protection; but also to motivate students study information security course in-depth.

3   Comparison of Curriculum Approaches

Table 1 summarises and compares the reviewed cybersecurity curriculum programs according to the following defined criteria:

- Target audience (i.e., undergraduate students, graduate students, or general public)

- Focus (i.e., the focused domain of the paper)
- Assessment (i.e., whether the approach includes an evaluation component)
- Practicality (i.e., whether the proposed curriculum is practical or theoretical)

4   Discussion

In the above discussed literature, the main question posed to the authors was that what should a cybersecurity professional be acquainted with and what sort of skills they must possess? The question is one but the answers were more than one and differing in nature. One of the main reasons of the difference of opinion is due to the interdisciplinary (and sometimes multidisciplinary) nature of cybersecurity which is used in numerous roles covering many disciplines. Some of the issues related to this question are given below.

- Mostly the proposed changes in the curriculum are in nascent state which needs proper assessment and evaluation before and after the implementation phase. It is evident from Table 1 that most of them are just proposals that have not been applied yet.
- The cybersecurity programs should be designed according to their resulting careers' objectives, i.e. academia, industry, or government. Several authors proposed changes that would make the degree as a mixture of courses belonging to different domains and skill sets. For example, if the students are intended to be trained for the industry, they should be taught more technical and hands-on skill based courses whereas if the objective of the degree is to educate the students for higher education and research, they should be taught with courses having more depth and understanding. To our belief such mixing will detract students who have already set their future goals and targets, i.e. to go for higher education or industry but not both.
- One of the issues that is posed by many authors and also noted by DHS CyberSkills Report [4] is that the industry usually criticizes higher education programs and complains about the graduates being deficient in hands-on skills in cybersecurity field. In simple words, universities educate students while industry demands for trained graduates rather than educated ones. Some authors addressed this issue, such as [17] by suggesting that universities should educate as well as train students in order to fill the gap between academia and industry. We believe that mixing training with education in a single program will not be an interesting idea. Because, if some students already set their future targets as to extend their careers in a single direction, i.e. industry or academia not both; then they might lose interest in such programs. A viable solution would be either to offer degrees in these two flavours separately or to designate some of the semesters as the specialized ones, i.e. flavouring education and training.

It is suggested that the cybersecurity education programs should be based on the core knowledge and skills having a computing based foundation. The courses of the program should encompass concepts and techniques that hone

Table 1. Cybersecurity curriculum approaches - summary and comparison

Proposal	Audience	Focus	Assessment	Practicality
[31]	Graduate	Cybersecurity content and skills	N.A	Proposal
[27]	Undergraduate	Behavioral security	Given	Flipped classroom
[21]	Children	Improving cybersecurity education	N.A	Proposal
[33]	Undergraduate	Cybersecurity certification	N.A	Proposal
[34]	Undergraduate	Ethical/Legal issues	N.A	Practical
[18]	Undergraduate	Students evaluation	Given	Applied
[29]	Undergraduate	Government and defense	N.A.	Proposal
[17]	General	Industry and education	N.A.	Proposal
[15]	Graduate	Industry	N.A.	Proposal
[19]	Undergraduate	Improving cybersecurity education	N.A.	Applied
[14]	Undergraduate	Improving cybersecurity education	N.A.	Applied
[32]	Cybersecurity educators	Improving cybersecurity education	N.A.	Projects and workshops
[25]	Undergraduate	Multidisciplinary	Given	Applied
[24]	Undergraduate and graduate	Improving cybersecurity education	Given	Applied
[22]	Undergraduate	Government and defense	N.A	Proposal

the skills of the cybersecurity graduate and that should be applicable to a broad range of cybersecurity domain. In addition to emphasizing the ethical obligations and responsibilities, the program should be flexible enough in order to adapt its curriculum to any specialized needs.

5   Non-Traditional Approaches

5.1   Gamification

The use of computer games in education have recently gained attention; especially in Cyber security. One of the benefits of this approach is to reduce the stress prevailed during Cyber security exercises and to produce a fun environment to the students. In the long run this approach may change the students' habit from tense to fun mode during carrying out real time Cyber security tasks. Some of work done in this arena is as follows. Nagarajan et al. [26] propose a Cyber security training game, called CyberNEXS. The game enables the users learn topics including social engineering and phishing techniques, password management, shielding from spamwares and malwares, etc. Another effort in this direction is the work proposed by [20], called CyberCiege which is a game developed for educating students regarding information assurance and network security concepts. The game has different scenarios ranging from basic training and awareness to advanced network security concepts. I-SEE is game based Cyber security training that uses web-based and 3D technologies in order to promote less technical and abstract level Cyber security concepts. After learning the high level concepts, the students may then put these concepts to carryout tasks in competitive group activities. Video games are considered as good and interesting tools for Cyber security teaching and learning. However, they are not used for technical topics. They are used only for teaching general and less technical concepts in order to promote awareness of high level issues. Mostly, video games are preferred to be used for teaching basic education and raising Cyber security awareness in the public.

5.2   Virtualization

Virtualization allows the creation and use of virtual environments for a physical machine, network or operating system. Virtual environments are useful as they allow the use of different operating systems/networks on the same physical machine. Virtualization is also particularly useful for cybersecurity teaching and learning as it can be used to simulate different kinds of attacks without causing damage to the host physical machine/network. Moreover, some attacks such as man-in-the-middle, requires at least three machines for the attacker and the two victims. This could be simulated using three VMs on a single physical machine.

SEED Labs project [9] provides a pre-built virtual machine image, which is preconfigured to run over 30 practical cyber security labs. VLabNet [28] is a virtual platform developed for cyber security education based on the open-source Xen software. Tele-Lab [10] is a cloud-based platform for practical cyber security education. This platform was enforced with security through VPN tunnel. The Xen Worlds platform was adopted to teach information assurance classes. This platform is based on Xen hypervisor, which supports many VMs, and where each students uses his own VM [13]. ReSeLa [16] is a virtual platform based on multiple VMs. The platform was introduced to give students remote access in order to experiment with malware and ethical hacking in a secure environment.

Virtualization can be setup on a desktop machine or cloud-based infrastructure. Desktop-based virtual environments allow the use of virtual machines with different Oss, all sharing the resources of the host machine. This allows students to run applications that require different platforms. The main challenge with desktop-based virtualization is the size of the VMs, which is often quite large. Additionally, students need to have high-performance machines in order to run multiple VMs. Also, the VMs may require special configuration such as installing and configuring cybersecurity software/libraries, which requires additional skills from students who need to do the configuration by themselves. To overcome these issues, an alternative solution is to set a cloud-based virtualization environment, which can also be accessed by the students outside the campus.

5.3 Competitions

Cyber security competitions are widely adopted with the aim of raising security awareness among students and identifying the top cyber security talents. Some of these competitions are sponsored and run by governments and companies to help identifying candidates with best cybersecurity skills for recruitment. These competitions are usually run through virtual environments or online. They could be also offered in a two modes, either single-user or multiple-user.

The international Capture the Flag (iCTF) [11] is one of the most popular ethical hacking competitions, which has reached more than thousands of students. Several academic institutions, governments and organizations organize such hackathons worldwide to challenge contestants with cyber security problems. The Cyber Security Challenge UK [7] is a competition supported by the UK Government and several partnering industries to support cyber security training. The competitions consists of several single-user exercises provided through online video games. Top-ranked contestants are selected to further compete in multi-user challenges set by sponsors who are looking to recruit the best cyber security talents. The UAE CyberQuest competition [8] is designed by the Signals Intelligence Agency and targets school and University students to raise awareness and identify cyber security talents. The competition is developed in two forms: capture the flag competition for school students and cyber security exercise for University students. Training is offered by the organizing agency to help participants prepare for the final competition.

Although these competitions are a good way for identifying cyber security talent, however, they are limited in terms of training new talent. Most of the time, competitions do not offer training to the contestants, but instead students are expected to already have enough cyber security knowledge. We believe that training is necessary to allow students to be at the competitive level required by these competitions.

6   Conclusion

The cybersecurity landscape is extremely fast moving and rapidly changing. The need for adept professionals in this field continues to grow; hence, education systems are responding to it in a variety of ways. Advanced countries, at governmental and organizational levels initiated efforts to help educational institutions in framing appropriate cybersecurity curriculum in order to fulfill this rising demand of cybersecurity professionals. Also, various researchers have proposed cybersecurity curriculum design proposals and suggestions. In this paper, we categorized and surveyed those efforts into three main categories focusing on education, industry, and government/defense. We also cross compared them highlighting our own suggestions. This work, we believe, will help the educationists to have an overview of the overall efforts undertook in the cybersecurity landscape and will also help them develop more effective cybersecurity curriculums in their future efforts.

References

1. Symantec Corporation. http://www.symantec.com
2. National Training Standard for Information Systems Security (INFOSEC) Professionals (1994). http://www.sis.pitt.edu/jjoshi/courses/IS2150/Fall11/nstissi_4011. pdf
3. National Initiative for Cybersecurity Education Strategic Plan. Building a Digital Nation (2011). http://www.cssia.org/pdf/20000168-NationalInitiativeforCybersecurityEducationStrategicPlan.pdf
4. DHS Task Force on CyberSkills: CyberSkills Taks Force Report. D.o.H, Security, Washington, DC (2012)
5. International Information Systems Audit and Control Association (ISACA) (2017). https://www.isaca.org/
6. The Fast-Growing Job With A Huge Skills Gap: Cyber Security (Forbes article) (2017). https://www.forbes.com/sites/jeffkauflin/2017/03/16/the-fast-growing-job-with-a-huge-skills-gap-cyber-security/#465297be5163
7. Cyber Security Challenge UK (2018). https://www.cybersecuritychallenge.org.uk/
8. CyberQuest Competition (2018). https://cyberquest.ae/en
9. SEED Labs (2018). http://www.cis.syr.edu/~wedu/seed/lab_env.html
10. Tele-Lab (2018). https://hpi.de/meinel/security-tech/security-awareness/tele-lab-it-security.html
11. The International Capture The Flag ("iCTF") Competition (2018). https://ictf. cs.ucsb.edu/
12. Cyber Security Breaches Survey 2017, April 2017. https://www.gov.uk/ government/statistics/cyber-security-breaches-survey-2017
13. Anderson, B.R., Joines, A.K., Daniels, T.E.: Xen worlds: leveraging virtualization in distance education. SIGCSE Bull. **41**(3), 293–297 (2009). http://doi.acm.org/10.1145/1595496.1562967
14. Azadegan, S., O'Leary, M.: An undergraduate cyber operations curriculum in the making: a 10+ year report. In: 2016 IEEE Conference on Intelligence and Security Informatics (ISI), pp. 251–254. IEEE (2016)
15. Bicak, A., Liu, X.M., Murphy, D.: Cybersecurity curriculum development: introducing specialties in a graduate program. Inf. Syst. Educ. J. **13**(3), 99 (2015)
16. Carlsson, A., Gustavsson, R., Truksans, L., Balodis, M.: Remote security labs in the cloud ReSeLa. In: 2015 IEEE Global Engineering Education Conference (EDUCON), pp. 199–206, March 2015
17. Conklin, W.A., Cline, R.E., Roosa, T.: Re-engineering cybersecurity education in the US: an analysis of the critical factors. In: 2014 47th Hawaii International Conference on System Sciences (HICSS), pp. 2006–2014. IEEE (2014)
18. Faily, S.: Ethical hacking assessment as a vehicle for undergraduate cyber-security education. In: BCS 19th Annual INSPIRE Conference (2014)
19. Howles, T., Romanowski, C., Mishra, S., Raj, R.K.: A holistic, modular approach to infuse cybersecurity into undergraduate computing degree programs. In: Annual Symposium On Information Assurance (ASIA), Albany, NY, pp. 7–8 (2011)

20. Irvine, C.E., Thompson, M.F., Allen, K.: Cyberciege: gaming for information assurance. IEEE Secur. Priv. **3**(3), 61–64 (2005)
21. Iv, A.L.Z.: Cyber-Security Curricula for Basic Users. Thesis at Naval Postgraduate School, Monterey, California (2013)
22. Kessler, G.C., Ramsay, J.D.: A proposed curriculum in cybersecurity education targeting homeland security students. In: 2014 47th Hawaii International Conference on System Sciences (HICSS), pp. 4932–4937. IEEE (2014)
23. LaPiedra, J.: The Information Security Process Prevention, Detection and Response (2002). https://www.giac.org/paper/gsec/501/information-security-process-prevention-detection-response/101197
24. Lo, D.C.T., North, M., North, S.: Hardware Components in Cybersecurity Education. DigitalCommons@ Kennesaw State University (2014)
25. Lukowiak, M., Radziszowski, S., Vallino, J., Wood, C.: Cybersecurity education: bridging the gap between hardware and software domains. ACM Trans. Comput. Educ. (TOCE) **14**(1), 2 (2014)
26. Nagarajan, A., Allbeck, J.M., Sood, A., Janssen, T.L.: Exploring game design for cybersecurity training. In: 2012 IEEE International Conference on Cyber Technology in Automation, Control, and Intelligent Systems (CYBER), pp. 256–262, May 2012
27. Patterson, W., Winston, C.E., Fleming, L.: Behavioral cybersecurity: a needed aspect of the security curriculum. In: SoutheastCon 2016, pp. 1–7 (2016)
28. Powell, V.J.H., Davis, C.T., Johnson, R.S., Wu, P.Y., Turchek, J.C., Parker, I.W.: VLabNet: the integrated design of hands-on learning in information security and networking. In: Proceedings of the 4th Annual Conference on Information Security Curriculum Development, InfoSecCD 2007, pp. 9:1–9:7. ACM, New York (2007). http://doi.acm.org/10.1145/1409908.1409918
29. Ramirez, C.D., Rioux, G.A.: Advancing curricula development for homeland security education through a survey of DHS personnel. J. Homeland Secur. Educ. **1**, 6–25 (2012)
30. Rowe, D.C., Lunt, B.M., Ekstrom, J.J.: The role of cyber-security in information technology education. In: Proceedings of the 2011 Conference on Information Technology Education, SIGITE 2011, pp. 113–122. ACM, New York (2011). http://doi.acm.org/10.1145/2047594.2047628
31. Santos, H., Pereira, T., Mendes, I.: Challenges and reflections in designing cyber security curriculum. In: 2017 IEEE World Engineering Education Conference (EDUNINE), pp. 47–51, March 2017
32. Siraj, A., Taylor, B., Kaza, S., Ghafoor, S.: Integrating security in the computer science curriculum. ACM Inroads **6**(2), 77–81 (2015)
33. Smith, T., Alex Koohang, R.B.: Formulating an effective cybersecurity curriculum. Issues Inf. Syst. **XI**(1), 410–416 (2010)
34. Trabelsi, Z., Ibrahim, W.: A hands-on approach for teaching denial of service attacks: a case study. J. Inf. Technol. Educ. Innovations Pract. **12**, 299–319 (2013)

Teaching as a Collaborative Practice: Reframing Security Practitioners as Navigators

Patricia A. H. Williams[1,3](✉) and Lizzie Coles-Kemp[2]

[1] Flinders University, Adelaide, SA, Australia
patricia.williams@flinders.edu.au
[2] Royal Holloway University of London, Egham, UK
Lizzie.Coles-Kemp@rhul.ac.uk
[3] Edith Cowan University, Joondalup, WA, Australia

Abstract. The need is growing for a workforce with both technical skills and the ability to navigate existing and emerging information security challenges. Practitioners can no longer depend upon process-driven approaches to people, processes and IT systems to manage information security. They need to be navigators of the entire environment to effectively integrate controls to protect information and technology. The research presented in this paper trialed an innovative tactile learning activity developed through the European Technology-supported Risk Estimation by Predictive Assessment of Socio-technical Security (TREsPASS) project with tertiary education students, designed to provide students with experience in real-world modelling of complex information security scenarios. The outcomes demonstrate that constructing such models in an educational setting are a means of encouraging exploration of the multiple dimensions of security. Such teaching may be a means of teaching social, organization and technical navigation skills necessary to integrate security controls in complex settings.

Keywords: Information security · Security practitioner · Collaborative learning

1 Introduction

Information security uses processes, tools and techniques to protect the confidentiality, integrity, and availability of information and information systems. Current information security practice in organizations is carried out through the assessing of risk and performing of risk treatments, the creation of policy and the demonstration of compliance, planning, incident management, and business continuity. Through these actions, the practice of information security management is presented as a systematic approach to the protection of information, and includes people, processes and IT systems.

In government policy [1, 2], information security is promoted as an important means with which to protect an organization's activities and information (assets) upon which an organization relies to undertake day-to-day business. Protection from disrupted business operations, theft of sensitive or valuable information, and reputational

Z. Pan et al. (Eds.): Transactions on Edutainment XV, LNCS 11345, pp. 108–128, 2019.
https://doi.org/10.1007/978-3-662-59351-6_10

damage are important. In the security management discourse there are many examples of the impacts of information breaches [3]. For example, the loss of availability of an IT system for a bank may impact the organization financially; the exposure of personal health information may breach confidentiality and impact an individual's privacy; and intentional manipulation of student grades challenges the integrity of results.

At the forefront of bringing security know-how into organizations and helping organizations defend against information breaches is the information security professional, often termed "security practitioner". There are many types of security practitioner but broadly speaking a security practitioner helps an organization to identify and manage its risk from data breaches and attacks on technological systems [4]. Such security professional roles include: IT Security Officer, Information Security System Manager, Information Security System Officer, and Security & Information Risk Advisor [5]. As such, an information security practitioner sits at the intersection between business, technology and regulation. An information security practitioner must also be able to communicate across an organization with individuals and groups from different educational, professional and social backgrounds.

This paper explores the changing role of information security professionals, security practitioner skills, and conceptualization of security roles, and discusses what is needed in education to respond to these changes. Increasingly, security practitioners are required not only to ensure the protection of technology and information but also to integrate this protection into the wider organizational setting. Such integration requires skills that enable security practitioners to engage with, travel through and bring together the social, economic, political, cultural as well as technical aspects of an organization. This requires building a skill set that sees the security practitioner become both an individual that not only designs and deploys information security controls and protection but can also navigate an organization by making sense of the different aspects of an organizational setting, understand the connections between those aspects and communicate the importance of those connections.

In this paper, a re-positioning of the security practitioner as such a navigator of the organization is explored and a navigation visual modelling tool activity trialed. In particular, the work of November et al. [6] influences this perspective. In this paper, we reflect on the outputs of a mapping exercise to consider how information security practitioners can construct and use a map of the organizational landscape in order to navigate an organization through risky territory. Whilst the security practitioner is often characterized as a facilitator (e.g. [7]) and technology tools are available that describe the processes of identification and management of risk as navigation (e.g. [8]) the navigation role of the security practitioner is less well considered in the information security practice literature.

The structure of this paper is as follows: in Sect. 2 information security practice as a profession is discussed, outlining the current skills matrix from the professional bodies, the role of tertiary education and the contribution of November et al. [6] to the discussion of navigation as practice and how this conceptualization might prompt a new way of looking at the skills matrix. Section 3 presents the design of a case study that examines how a mapping exercise might contribute to the teaching of the role of navigator. In Sect. 4 the study results are presented. The discussion in Sect. 5 includes reflections from the students and facilitators as to the strengths and weaknesses of the navigation approach. This is followed in Sect. 6 with the conclusion.

2   The Profession of an Information Security Practitioner

Information security has a long and varied history and its evolution shows how information security is an umbrella term for many types of information protection [9]. With the advent of computing, information security became a field of study [10] and as the uptake of computing spread, the field of study has become more diverse. As organizations have become increasingly dependent on computerized production, circulation, protection and curation of information, information security as a recognized professional practice has also emerged and diversified [11].

2.1   Security Practitioner Skills

Whilst there exist international standards, for instance the ISO/IEC 27000 - *Information Security Management* family of standards [12], and other information security frameworks and guidelines to assess and treat the risks [13], security practitioners must have a range of skills in the processes, tools and techniques of information security. The standards for the management of security [12] emphasize that security practitioners must also have the skills to understand the social, organizational and political context in which these are applied. The traditional methods for managing information security rely on controls of distinct types including those at the administrative or bureaucratic layer of an organization, logical and physical controls within computer systems and architectures, classification of information and information protection techniques such as encryption. These controls are implemented and managed through organizational processes such as governance and assurance, incident response, and business continuity. Within information security practice, there is increased recognition of sociotechnical challenges brought about through ubiquitous computing, big data analytics [14] and the persistent collection of data from the Internet of everything [15]. These sociotechnical challenges can, in one sense, be described as the interactions between the social, organizational and the technical facets.

This awareness of the sociotechnical challenge requires new perspectives on understanding the attack methods, attack phases, continuous monitoring, rapid attack detection as well as the mitigations that are required [14]. The new perspectives that integrate the social and the organizational into what has historically been primarily technical and mathematical thinking require us to rethink our approach to managing information security. In this paper we suggest that one way to reconceptualize security practitioners is to frame practitioners as navigators who chart the organizational landscape anticipating information security harms and plotting a safe and secure course in light of these harms rather than people who simply 'do' information security. As a navigator, security practitioners may oversee the development of policies, the performance of risk assessments and treatments and the design and implementation of security controls. However, their primary role is to help the organization to find a way through the complex and knotty challenges by helping the organization to understand the risk signposts, identify and understand the security relationships between different aspects of the organization, reflect on the potential for information security hazards as the organization undertakes its activities, and both communicate and collaborate with other members of the organization to respond to the anticipated risks along the way.

In this reframing, the role of information security education therefore becomes as much about teaching and nurturing navigation skills as it does teaching information security engineering skills. Navigational skills also require an understanding of the broader theoretical concepts of security and the connections between individual, organizational, societal, economic, political and technical securities to understand the complexity of the landscape security practitioners are charting. For example, as the study by Shedden et al. [16] illustrates there are significant limitations with current risk assessment methodologies resulting from a lack of recognition of the social and knowledge aspects of organizational processes which are integral to the environment to be protected. It is therefore imperative that we move beyond the teaching of the traditional risk and asset-protection approach to security practice and, instead, teach security concepts, techniques and theories that can be assembled in limitless ways in real-world environments. Such an education will then enable security practitioners who use their knowledge to read and interpret risk cues and signposts as they navigate an organization through the complex cyber security environment to meet their business goals and organizational governance requirements.

2.2 Navigating the Risk Landscape

November et al. [6] discuss the role of the map in exploring risk landscapes, and eloquently describe using digital technologies both to map terrains and to interact with digital maps in a way that was not possible in the pre-digital age. This interaction enables a community to use the map as a means of navigation and to bring into a single picture both the physical, social, political and human geographical dimensions. The authors argue that such digital mapping techniques liberate the mapping process from being tied to transcribing the physical space as the base of the map and enable the navigator to foreground different perspectives of a space. Digital techniques and technologies, examples of which can be found in [47], enable an individual to map routes through the socio-physical space using a series of risk signposts and building an understanding of the relationship between those signposts. Navigating in this way requires skills to reflect, identify and resolve conflict and to both wrestle with and form a position on ambiguous risk cues that emerge in organizational settings. In this paper, we argue that information security practitioners too have taken on this role of navigator and in so doing must also foreground skills for reflection, conflict management and the resolution of ambiguity. This paper examines one of the techniques that tertiary education in information security might adopt to achieve this.

2.3 Tertiary Education and Cyber Security

In recent years, tertiary education has embraced the teaching of information security. Indeed, governments around the world have encouraged the establishment of new information security courses with a view to increasing national capabilities in information security. The perceived value of information security has been heightened by the shift in framing from information security to cyber security – where the technological aspects of information security are complemented with a political dimension [17]. As part of this shift, a cyber security skills shortage narrative emerges and tertiary education globally has responded to this narrative with a rise in information security courses, often branded as cyber security courses. Cyber security skills shortage has been defined [18] as difficulty to identify and retain appropriately skilled staff for cyber security related roles. Much of the content of such courses therefore focuses on what are regarded as the appropriate skills, namely the technical skills needed to implement secure computers and secure networks. Students enroll on such courses with the promise of future employment. For example, the UK's National Audit Office published a report [19] on the cyber skills shortage in which it estimated that it would take 20 years for the UK to close the cyber security skills gap. This position is reinforced by the ISC2 report [20] that suggests that the difference between the demand driven projection for cyber security workers and the supply constrained projection will be about 1.5 million people globally by 2019. However, the skills gap is largely perceived as an engineering one and whilst there is some focus on governance and assurance skills, these skills are understood through the prism of technology.

In an attempt to refine and differentiate the skills needed for Information and Communications Technology (ICT) and security, the cyber security industry is directing its attention to developing a skills matrix. For instance, the Skills Framework for the Information Age (SFIA) [21] is an ICT skills and capabilities matrix, designed to align skills with job roles and responsibilities. The framework is careful to distinguish between technical knowledge and professional skills, and maps these skills to seven specific levels of attainment for specific job roles. These levels reflect the amount of autonomy and responsibility expected in each role and consist of: 1-Follow, 2-Assist, 3-Apply, 4-Enable, 5-Ensure and advise, 6-Initiate and influence, and 7-Set strategy, inspire and mobilize. The upper levels, similar to the construction of Blooms Taxonomy for education [22], reflect skills that require industry application such as 'influence'. An essential element of the framework is the experience and qualification, where experience gives practical demonstration of application and consequently capability [21]. Higher education is attempting to embed the practical interpretation of higher-level skills into the curriculum and produce graduates who are job-ready [23, 24]. This is at the behest of both the cyber security industry and the students themselves [25] and poses a significant challenge for higher education in how to achieve this [26].

At the same time, the SFIA framework is used by accreditation and professional bodies worldwide to ensure a shared understanding and commonality of language across industry for defining for IT based and associated jobs, the roles and responsibility skills, including those applicable to security. Interestingly, all security related skills are listed at SFIA level 3 and above. Information security skills are levels 3 to 6, information assurance skills at levels 5 to 7, and security administration at levels 3 to 6. This indicates that mere rote learning and understanding of skills is not sufficient. University degrees help students develop generic higher-level skills yet "many struggle in the labour market", "University IT graduates are not well matched with workplace needs", and "In IT, universities are not supplying the graduates needed by a fast-moving industry" [25].

Frameworks such as SFIA have been used internationally to map specific skills to job roles. For example, the Australian Computer Society [27] identified the skills required for twenty-five common ICT roles. This included an ICT Security Specialist for which 61 different skills are needed with skill levels predominantly at SFIA level 5 and above. Other roles across the ICT spectrum were also identified as requiring security skills, such as the role of Network Administrator. When broadening the skill base to include IT governance, of which security is a component, the number of higher level roles with associated high-level skills (SFIA 7) demanding these skills expands rapidly.

Similarly, in the UK, CESG/National Cyber Security Centre (NCSC) [5] has mapped SFIA and the Institute of Information Security Professionals (IISP). For roles, such as Security and Information Risk Advisor, IT Security Officer, and Communications Security Officer, CESG/NCSC defines three levels of role aligned to SFIA level 2, 4 and 6. This acknowledges that in some roles entry level abilities can be catered for in roles that assist in application and monitoring of policy [5]. Such a skills matrix highlights the need for practical application and understanding of the environment holistically, to enable risk management, policy development and conformance, as well as technical skills. Indeed, technical skills themselves are rarely mentioned.

Despite the mapping attempts and skills frameworks, there is still a shortage of appropriately skilled graduates particularly in cyber security. This is due, in part, to the demand for experience (usually five years) in advertised cyber security positions, and a lack of clarity about the skills needed for roles in cyber security [48]. This creates a disconnect between the labour market and the job market, particularly where graduates are concerned. This problem is exacerbated by a lack of recognition of the need for cyber security capability in many organizations, and it is argued that this situation will become critical in the future as organizations realize the need for specialized cyber security capacity [48].

When looking at the governance and information assurance tracks of tertiary education programs in cyber security, it quickly becomes apparent that risk thinking, risk assessment and risk modelling are regarded as significant tracks of the education program [4]. Education in this area focuses on the 'doing' of risk assessment and risk modelling and there is a distinct focus on the protection of information and technological assets and how to achieve this. Within such education programs there is less focus on organizational knowledge, understanding and how information and technological protection interacts with and is shaped by the organizational landscape through which the information flows and in which it is produced. Consequently, our current methods of teaching information security rarely capture this broader perspective, yet it is necessary to be able to understand and apply tools and techniques to the way organizations are experienced and understood [16].

Over the last decade, several voices have articulated the need for change in the education program of information security. For example, there is a view that "academic programs exposing the students to theoretical concepts and problem-solving experience are critical for preparing graduates for jobs in information security" [28]. Equally there is also the view that meeting the requirements for today's information security practitioner, means certifications that focus on vocational training based on core competencies that potentially limit the ability of the student to expand their knowledge base.

The difference in tertiary education is that it seeks to elicit broad educational objectives with discipline specific knowledge and academic abstraction [29]. However, whilst voices have acknowledged the need for change in direction in information security education since the turn of the century, the skills gap is still perceived as a largely engineering and technical one and does not include the skills traditionally found in tertiary education that would support the development of a security practitioner as navigator.

A contributing factor to this stalemate in curriculum development is that of the traditional training and certification methods used by the cyber security industry to date. Professional and vendor specific certifications have been popular over the past 10 years. However, in a rapidly expanding and increasingly complex cyber security environment such certifications do not prepare graduates to be sufficiently adaptable. This issue is not new but yet persists. Further, to be at the leading edge of information security protection, education in the field requires innovation and research. Whilst certifications can provide knowledge in the short term, by definition, their content needs renewal periodically and in the cyber security environment this renders knowledge out of date quickly.

2.4 Security Practitioners as Navigators

The University of Queensland and the Australian Information Security Association (AISA) collaborated with the UK's Research Institute in the Science of Cyber Security to conduct parallel studies in the UK and Australia [4, 30] to ascertain the type of work security practitioners undertook and the skills that are needed to undertake that work. From both studies, it was discovered that engagement, and specifically, relationship building and communication, formed the core of a security practitioner's everyday work. It was also discovered that security practitioners wanted new ways of engaging with communities together with clear, evidence-based advice on which engagement methods should be used and when. When the term "community" is used in this context the focus is on groups of people bound together by common characteristics and goals within an organization. The studies showed that successful engagement is key for a security practitioner because the quality of the working relationship between security and the organization is an important factor in ensuring the effectiveness of cyber security processes.

From both studies it was concluded that information security practitioners often come from an IT background that ill-prepares them for the relationship building, management and communication skills that are needed in real-world security management. In the video summary of the research that forms part of [30], the need to acquire communication skills and capabilities for understanding the cultural implications of technological security is clearly identified. The complexity and highly situated nature of what constitutes information security is highlighted by the diffuse definitions of information security highlighted in the Australian study [4]. The research in [30] articulates the complexity of the organizational setting and the need to navigate and make connections between different aspects of the organization in order to understand the relationships between cyber security technology and the organizational environment. The responses of participants articulated in [4, 30] highlight the centrality of the risk concept in security practice and, yet, how this concept has to hold multiple interpretations of what constitutes the protection of information and technology and how to achieve it.

As both studies show, security practitioners have to develop and maintain specific skills and knowledge beyond the technical, including:

- Skills
  - Communication
  - Conflict identification and management
  - Relationship building and management
- Knowledge
  - Understanding of social, organizational and political as well as technical risk signposts
  - Understanding of the relationship between information security and organizational well-being.

This list indicates that to develop good navigators, we need to educate and train security practitioners with good communication skills in order to convince organizations to take and remain on a particular path, strong conflict identification and management skills to keep the organization on course when different communities want to take different risk directions and effective relationship building and management skills keep the organization on the same path, moving in the same direction towards a common risk outcome. These skills, however, are not enough on their own and a wider understanding and appreciation of the world in which an organization operates is necessary. This requires security practitioners to be educated with a theoretical understanding of the security relationships between social, organizational, political and technical aspects of an organization so that security practitioners are not only able to read the risk signposts but to understand the relationships between those signposts. Education of students of information security, therefore, needs to take a broader perspective and a more constructive approach. Whilst it is essential for students to obtain core technical knowledge that enables them to identify, prevent and respond to technical attacks, they must also develop the skills and the confidence to navigate an organization through that complexity when anticipating and responding to attacks on their digital infrastructure.

2.5   TREsPASS and the Navigation Metaphor

To address the difficulty in assessing and identifying the risks associated with the interaction between people and technology, known as socio-technical security, the European Union funded Technology-supported Risk Estimation by Predictive Assessment of Socio-technical Security (TREsPASS) [31] was established. The project aimed to improve the resilience of businesses and create a standardized framework analyzing the socio-technical aspects of security. The project [31, 32] developed methods and tools to analyze and visualize information security risks in dynamic organizations, as well as possible countermeasures in response to so-called social engineering attacks where human behaviour as well as technical weaknesses are targeted by attackers. As the project description [31] identifies, examples include StuxNet, in which infected USB sticks were used to sabotage nuclear plants, and the DigiNotar attack, in which fake digital certificates were used to spy on website traffic. New attacks cleverly exploit multiple organizational vulnerabilities, involving physical security and human behaviour.

The navigation metaphor was central to the TREsPASS project [31]. The tools and technologies developed through TREsPASS research [31, 32, 47] were built on the philosophy that security practitioners need to make rapid decisions regarding which attacks to block, as both infrastructure and attacker knowledge change rapidly. Being able to visualize the risk trajectory [32, 47] was regarded as central to these capabilities as the researchers believed that attack opportunities will be identified and prevented only if people can envisage them. In today's dynamic attack landscape, this process is too slow and exceeds the limits of human imaginative capability. The project objectified its navigation metaphor with the development of an Attack Navigator tool to help security practitioners model which attack opportunities are possible and most pressing, and which countermeasures are most effective.

The project also produced an Attack Navigator Map [47] to help the security practitioner navigate the intended risk trajectory calculation by the Attack Navigator. The Attack Navigator Map presented visualizations that combine information visualizations with techniques from critical cartography and digital humanities to articulate different socio-technical dimensions of risk and provide tools through which to explore these dimensions.

The TREsPASS visualization strategy drew on three types of visualization [32, 46]:

- Artistic visualizations, which foreground the social, cultural, economic and political dimensions to security risks and critique security and risk logics;
- Journalistic visualizations, which situate risks and the data flows within an organization and examine the relationships between those risk pictures and the workings of a risk model; and
- Scientific visualizations, which contribute to the quantification of the qualitative risk data, articulate the attack and defence interaction (for which attack-defence trees are our start point) and enable the user to calculate risk from different perspectives and perform root cause analysis on risks to complex information flows.

Using the TREsPASS tools and techniques, a paper prototype kit was used within two tertiary education programs. The activity provided a hands-on example exploring the physical, digital and social aspects of risk. It promoted the application of risk analysis concepts to a use case. It was not made clear to the students, intentionally, that the basis for the activity was mapping risk analysis approach to the construction of a real-world space. This was only explained to the student after they have undertaken the activity and was part of the post activity whole-class discussion.

2.6   Educational Theory and Methods

Paper prototyping, an output of the TREsPASS [31] research (work package 4 – visualization and tools), was used to inform and enhance education of tertiary students on the construction of security and assessment of risk. This provides an example of the practical application of security visualization. It further contributes to meeting the outcomes of the undergraduate and postgraduate topics (CSI2102 and CSI5133) Information Security, parts of the Bachelor of Science (Cyber Security), Bachelor of Science (Security), and Master of Cyber Security, at Edith Cowan University, Western Australia. The academic outcomes that this activity in assessing and managing risk contributes to include:

1. Describe and apply concepts, principles and techniques relating to the security of information;
2. Describe the role of risk analysis and contingency planning in information security; and
3. Describe and apply classification systems for information.

Education at the tertiary level in information security has not diverged from the traditional university education model. Whilst there have been attempts at innovative initiatives such as involving students in cyber defense competitions and workflow technology [33, 34] these are not part of the main stream university teaching. There is little doubt that active learning techniques increase student engagement and the use of case studies has been a common method to enact this in information security [35]. However, as articulated in the industry reports, and demonstrated by the increasing emphasis on job readiness using Work Integrated Learning, what is still lacking is the ability of graduates to demonstrate real-world application, in place of experience. The need for students to study and experience complicated information security scenarios, and practice analytical skills is clear.

Paper prototyping has been used successfully as a design methodology for assisting software designers to simulate realistic experience with multiple dimensions [36, 37]. These methods allow identification of real-world issues and provide insights into the environment under study. The application of this method to security education is a novel and innovative approach to learning. It provides a user-centred approach to physical and information architectures and provides the ability to visualize and manoeuvre artefacts representing real situations. Further, if the paper prototyping method include colour coding and physical construction, a multi-method approach, then greater immersion in the task and improved engagement can be achieved [38]. This can provide the learner with experience of situational construction and subsequent analysis, which is vitally important in learning about information security and risk.

It is recognized that the use of visualization methods to assess students in both recognizing security risk and relating this to a specific organizational environment is important in developing an understanding of how being technical and social aspects of risk assessment integrate and impact one another [39]. Based upon General Principle 1. Awareness, skills and empowerments which states that "all stakeholders should understand digital security risk and how to manage it" [39, p. 9], it is pivotal for students to gain multiple perspectives on how this can be achieved, starting with how they can construct this for themselves. The development of a solid understanding of digital security risk resulting from the interplay of technology, social factors, physical environment, and organizational process, is vital to the effective management of security in dynamic real-world environments. Further, that effective security requires risk assessment that acknowledges the highly complex and interconnected nature of organization and information systems [40].

The practice of analytical skills to solve complex problems uses cognitive load theory [41] where the short-term memory is not overloaded in favour of developing longer-term learning skills. Paper prototyping purposefully provides a visual stimulus rather than relying on memory to manipulate an environment and formulate a solution to a complex problem. This approach uses constructivism learning theory with an instructional design to construct knowledge and meaning from the experience of the prototyping activity. It achieves this using a real-world team simulation thus promoting learning through communication in a safe and supported learning environment. This joint and shared learning experience promotes discussion and negotiation of the task.

Consequently, this approach aligns with cognitive load theory [42] in which the learner is encouraged to optimize intellectual performance. The security concepts used in the prototyping activity are not new to the student in the courses in which the activity was undertaken, and therefore short-term memory overload is minimized. This allows the student to think critically about the task. However, it is acknowledged that there may be some students for whom this method presents limitations where they have not acquired the necessary knowledge prior to the activity. The activity uses a generalized schematic knowledge structure to apply to situational analysis and problem solving, making the skills learned transferable to other problems [43].

3   Method

Three different cohorts of students undertook the paper prototyping activity. In each case the students were given a modelling objective: namely to model the security risks to a sensitive data (in this example exam papers) stored on a server.

This scenario was developed and used because it was a scenario that would be familiar to all students. As a project, TREsPASS worked with several scenarios including the security of ATMs, security of micropayments through IPTV and the installation of malware on memory sticks [32]. Preparation for activity incorporated:

1. Pre-preparing packs of resources for each student group
2. Direction to students regarding readings, lecture, and activity.

3.1   Structure of the Modelling Session

The students were presented with an activity pack containing: a paper prototyping kit and written instructions that replicated the information presented to them by the activity's facilitator. To assess whether the activity can be run independently of the creators of the activity, a different facilitator was used each time the modelling activity was run. Following a lecture on risk assessment, the activity was undertaken in class, with an allocated time of 1.5 h. The facilitator presented the scenario, presented the content of the packs and presented the activity guidance shown in Table 1.

Table 1. Activity guidance

	Consideration/activity construction objective
1	Considering the security disposition of the physical and digital space
2	Identifying the assets and actors
3	Analyzing the security strengths and weaknesses of the assets and actors
4	Producing measures of risk for the threat of unauthorized access mark

The students split into groups of between 4–6 participants. Each group was asked to assign the following roles to group members:

- Scribe – notes down the actions of the group.
- Observer – observes the group and checks at the end of the session with the scribe's notes to see if more needs to be added.
- Map constructor – assembles the completed elements as they are made by the group members
- Asset constructor – assembles the asset elements identifying the security strengths and weaknesses of the asset
- Actor constructor – assembles the actor elements identifying the security strengths and weaknesses of the actor (don't forget that attackers are actors)
- Risk constructor – assembles a summary of the risks resulting from the analysis
- All – contribute to the discussion about the values at work.

The following scenario was presented to the groups:

A physical server is used to store sensitive student material, in particular the exam papers for each module. The server is located in the university, in a server room that is protected physically and digitally (via a firewall and host-based security features). The sysadmin employed by the university has full access to the server, two operational administrators have access to the server but not to the exam papers and the module leader has access to the exam papers but not to the underlying operating system. Both the sysadmin and the module leader can edit the exam papers using remote access protocols as well as by locally logging on to the server. The server is logically separated from the rest of the university network (protected by routers and an internal firewall).

The following areas of analysis were outlined:

Please explore the threat of unauthorized access to the exam papers by:

- Considering the security disposition of the physical and digital space;
- Identifying the assets and actors;
- Analyzing the security strengths and weaknesses of the assets and actors; and
- Producing measures of risk for the threat of unauthorized access to the exam papers.

Students were given 1 h to complete the activities. Whole-class discussion took place for 30 min following the completion of the hour. During the hour taken to complete the tasks, groups could ask questions of the facilitator and lecturing staff.

The paper prototyping kit contained lengths of assorted colours that were used to represent physical, digital, organizational and social boundaries. The thickness of the line represented the strength of the boundary from attack. The pack also contained hexagons that were used to represent assets and actors (Fig. 1). These assets could be decorated in different ways to represent asset qualities (Fig. 2). In addition, assets were also represented using circles to reflect assets that were protected by other assets (Fig. 1).

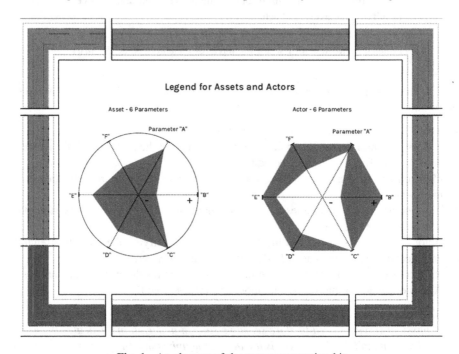

Fig. 1. An element of the paper prototyping kit.

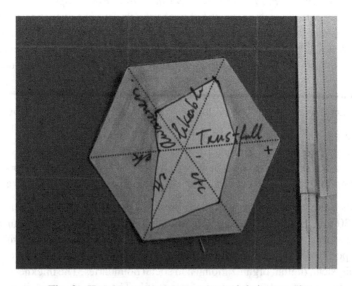

Fig. 2. Hexagon to represent assets and their strength

The activity was completed three times over 18 months with information security students on equivalent programs. In each session, data was gathered through photographs taken during the sessions and through annotation of group and whole-class discussions. In addition, reflection feedback was gathered from students at the end of the course and feedback was gathered from lecturers. For this type of activity, there is no model answer as the study is focused on the nature of the process of navigating rather than the results arrived at. Similarly, the analysis focuses on the process rather than the results produced by each student group, although examples of student solutions are provided in Sect. 4.

4 Results

The student model constructions were analyzed and the results presented in this section. The reflections from students of their learning and from the facilitators is integrated into the discussion section as this relates directly to the synthesis and interpretation of the results. Analysis of the photographs of the group results, together with discussion with the groups during the activity revealed the following general observations:

- Of the four activities the groups were guided to consider (Table 1), analysis of the strength and weakness of assets and actors (item 3) using the specified activity method was overlooked or not considered as important as identification of the factors and how they interacted. The mapping of the strengths and weaknesses using the kite diagram (using up to six parameters) was not undertaken by most of the groups.
- The modelling of the assets and actors was well understood (item 2).
- The concept of using height of the colouring to reflect the magnitude of the vulnerability was not embraced or explored by any group.
- The delineation between the physical and digital space was well understood by the end of the activity, although some students has difficulty conceptualizing and representing the difference between the physical and digital assets (item 1). For instance, where a server holds the data to be protected.

These observations highlight the limitations of the students in discerning the strength of association between threats. Much of this type of knowledge is learned from experience. As the lecturer feedback demonstrates (given in the discussion), activities such as the mapping exercise are an important means to enable students to consider information security as a multidimensional problem within the class room environment.

4.1 Describing the Physical Space

Students were asked to build a frame to represent the server room in the scenario, to consider the security features of the physical space and to use colour and line thickness to reflect the strength of the space.

As Figs. 3 and 4 show, the activity was successful in enabling students to consider the interplay between digital (denoted by pink) and physical space (denoted by blue).

Fig. 3. Example of student model construction - sample 1 (Color figure online)

4.2 Differentiating Between Physical, Social, Organizational and Digital Characteristics

The activity guidance encouraged students to differentiate between the physical strengths, social strengths, organizational strengths and digital strengths of the server room and indicate these differentiations using colour. By examining the relative strengths of the different dimensions, the students were encouraged to think about how the different strengths complemented each other and how you might combine these strengths. As Figs. 3 and 4 show, students were able to differentiate between the physical and digital strengths of a space but found it hard to bring in the third and fourth dimensions, social and organizational strengths, indicating that this is an area that would benefit from future focus during lectures and seminars.

Fig. 4. Example of student model construction - sample 2 (Color figure online)

5 Discussion

5.1 Reflection from Students

Students were highly engaged both in the task – particularly in understanding the parameters of the activity and construction of the use case, and in group discussion negotiating what risks were present, the strength of these risks, and how to calculate the magnitude of any risks present (Table 1, item 4). Further, the activity promoted the interpersonal communication required and team work to build consensus within the group. The prototyping activity presents multifaceted learning through personal understanding enhanced by team communication and demonstration through modeling. This method aligns to good cognitive load theory and indeed, Kirschner et al. [44] affirm that groups working on complex problems can spread 'working-memory' across the group thus allowing for enhanced critical constructions.

There were differences, as may be expected, between the function of the post-graduate and undergraduate groups. The postgraduate students took longer to start the construction of the environment using the materials provided – initial discussion was heavily focused on understanding the use case and getting the solution 'right'. In some ways these students were less adventurous in exploring the activity, with an expectation of providing an ideal answer. This group was more focused on engineering a solution rather than exploring the environment and adapting their responses as they learned more about the environment.

By contrast, many of the undergraduate groups were less concerned with a correct answer, rather focusing on the construction and integration of the elements of the task. In this undergraduate cohort, participants were more willing to combine dimensions of the space they were modelling to develop ways of both understanding and mitigating the risks they were asked to investigate. They reacted to the model in a more intuitive way and examined how the risks were shaped by the environment.

There was therefore a notable difference between the groups who actively started with construction and were comfortable to adapt and change as their understanding of the task changed, and those groups who 'needed' to fully understand all elements before beginning any construction, resulting in them taking longer to understand what they were to achieve and how to go about this. In the former group, there was more evidence of navigation skills, a different type of communication and a more holistic understanding of the system security. It is also noteworthy that the postgraduate groups had a more engineering, solution-oriented approach, an approach potentially learned in undergraduate classes and security practitioner experiences.

The activity provided an alternative method for learning and apply the concepts using visualization. Research demonstrates that "student perceptions of visualization" result in the usefulness of it as a method to address complex issues [45], and in this experience students appreciated the method to enhance their learning. Student comments from the Edith Cowan University – Unit Teaching and Evaluation Instrument indicate that the class activities, including this activity, helped their learning:

- "I found the lecture activities to be the best aspect- I was skeptical at first, but really enjoyed them"
- "Each and every lecture followed by a real-life situation"
- "Being able to utilize real-world scenarios"
- "Out of the box activities".

5.2   Reflection from Facilitators

"The approach of using a visual representation really "turned the lights on" of the students. The interaction and cooperation of the group was very helpful to the topic, but also for me. I have been trying to get more openness and interaction happening between the students and this was a great way of doing this".

"The staged breakdown into "chewable" chunks also allowed for the students to complete a relatively complex task in a logical and methodical manner which takes away the perceived enormity of the task. That said.... For those that went through the process the feedback to me in the tutorial was that when you really drill down its can be quite a complex and thorough exercise, which is what separated a "tick and flick" from "proper" risk assessments".

The students started to think about how the elements connect in the one environment, and this demonstrates a type of wayfinding or navigation. It exposes a method of cognitive reasoning using colouring and different icons that reflects wayfinding and reveals a progression of conceptual understanding about the space on the paper that can be observed as navigating the space under construction.

5.3 Future Activity Refinements

Development of the activity into a 3D space, for instance using Lego, might enhance the activity for those students who need a more tactile experience and who can better identify and make sense of the different aspects of an organization through construction and making. The addition of string to indicate links and weak points might increase the ability of students to define a richer picture and consider an organization in terms of connections and relationships. Whilst consideration of inclusion of the threat sources would be beneficial it is also a limitation given the timeframe allocated to learning sessions. However, including a mechanism for showing physical threats that influence the confidentiality, availability and integrity of information would be a useful addition, particularly for threats from an authenticated insider, as much of the student focus was from the external perspective. Another aspect of complexity that could be added for those with more security experience, or as a follow-on activity, might be highlighting how foregrounding different aspects of an organization (such as social, cultural, economic or political) re-shapes information security risk, and posing the question of how multiple perspectives of risk and information security might be responded to within an information security strategy. This would further highlight the role of the security practitioner as a navigator through increased complexities and nuances of the context under exploration.

In the exercises trialed, students observed other groups working on the problem and the resultant models. In future iterations inclusion of peer presentation of the outcomes discovered would be likely to reinforce learning and to promote discussion and learning by those outside individual groups.

From the outcomes observed, the overlay of the three essential aspects of physical security, logical security and security perception were problematic for some student groups to grasp initially but highlighted to the students the multiple layer and perspectives needed to navigate real-world security landscapes. This aspect of the exercise might be simplified by practice roles to participants, e.g. an information security manager (logical), a CEO (perception) and a physical security manager (physical). The results would illustrate the differences in perspective when all aspects were bought together.

6 Conclusion

The granularity expected to be produced from the construction and analysis appeared to be beyond the cognitive ability of some students with the preliminary level of knowledge and security experience. As part of the cutting-edge EU research on the quantification of risk, and part of the EU TREsPASS project, the students were immersed in concepts designed to prompt thinking as well as make sense of a specific real-world example. The skills and knowledge that such scenarios demand raise the question of whether the traditional risk-based information security practitioner approach to security has reached its 'use by' date. There is no argument that the pervasive nature of computing has created complex and technologically interwoven work and home environments, which, in turn, create increasingly challenging problems for effective information security. The role of the security practitioner is evolving, and the expectations of the skills required shifting from purely risk analysis and implementation to that of a person who can see across perspectives and steer a path through the complexities of organizations- in other words a navigator.

Acknowledgments. The researchers would like to thank the participants for their efforts, energy and contributions. Coles-Kemp's contribution was by supported by the European Commission through the FP7 project TREsPASS (grant agreement n. 318003). The materials for the workshop were developed as part of Work Package 4 outputs for the TREsPASS project by art studio LUST.

References

1. Australian Government: Protective Security Policy Framework. Australian Government, Attorney-General's Department (2016). https://www.protectivesecurity.gov.au/information security/Pages/default.aspx. Accessed 30 Nov 2017
2. GOV.UK: Security Policy Framework. Cabinet Office, Government Security Profession and National Security Intelligence (2014). https://www.gov.uk/government/publications/security-policy-framework. Accessed 30 Nov 2017
3. TechWorld: 28 of the most infamous data breaches (2017). https://www.techworld.com/security/uks-most-infamous-data-breaches-3604586/. Accessed 30 Nov 2017
4. Burdon, M., Siganto, J., Coles-Kemp, L.: The regulatory challenges of Australian information security practice. Comput. Law Secur. Rev. **32**(4), 623–633 (2016)
5. NCSC: CESG Certification for IA Professionals and Guidance to Certification for IA Professionals documents. National Technical Authority for Information Assurance, UK. (2015). https://www.ncsc.gov.uk/articles/cesg-certification-ia-professionals-and-guidance-certification-ia-professionals-documents. Accessed 30 Nov 2017
6. November, V., Camacho-Hübner, E., Latour, B.: Entering a risky territory: space in the age of digital navigation. Environ. Plan. D Soc. Space **28**(4), 581–599 (2010)
7. Coles-Kemp, L., Overill, R.E.: On the role of the facilitator in information security risk assessment. J. Comput. Virol. **3**(2), 143–148 (2007)
8. Vasenev, A., Montoya, L., Ceccarelli, A., Le, A., Ionita, D.: Threat navigator: grouping and ranking malicious external threats to current and future urban smart grids. In: Hu, J., Leung, Victor C.M., Yang, K., Zhang, Y., Gao, J., Yang, S. (eds.) Smart Grid Inspired Future Technologies. LNICST, vol. 175, pp. 184–192. Springer, Cham (2017). https://doi.org/10.1007/978-3-319-47729-9_19
9. de Leeuw, K.M.M., Bergstra, J.: The History of Information Security: A Comprehensive Handbook. Elsevier, Amsterdam (2007)
10. Saltzer, J., Schroeder, M.: The protection of information in computer systems. Proc. IEEE **63** (9), 1278–1308 (1975)
11. Reece, R., Stahl, B.: The professionalisation of information security: perspectives of UK practitioners. Comput. Secur. **48**, 182–195 (2015)
12. ISO: ISO/IEC 27000:2016 Information technology – Security techniques – Information security management systems – Overview and vocabulary (2016). https://www.iso.org/standard/66435.html. Accessed 30 Nov 2017
13. NIST: Cybersecurity Framework. National Institute of Standards and Technology (2014). https://www.nist.gov/cyberframework. Accessed 30 Nov 2017

14. Giranldi, B., Martin, D., Nguyen-Duy, J., Santana, M., Schwartz, E., Weber, D.: Transforming traditional security strategies into an early warning system for advanced threats: big data propels SIEM into the era of security analytics. RSA Secur. Brief **11** (2012). https://www.emc.com/collateral/software/solution-overview/h11031-transforming-traditional-security-strategies-so.pdf. Accessed 30 Nov 2017
15. CISCO: Internet of Everything (IoE) value index (2013). http://internetofeverything.cisco.com/sites/default/files/docs/en/ioe-value-index_Whitepaper.pdf. Accessed 30 Nov 2017
16. Shedden, P., Scheepers, R., Smith, W., Ahmad, A.: Incorporating a knowledge perspective into security risk assessments. VINE J. Knowl. Manag. **41**(2), 152–166 (2011)
17. Hansen, L., Nissenbaum, H.: Digital disaster, cyber security, and the copenhagen school. Int. Stud. Q. **53**(4), 1155–1175 (2009)
18. Libicki, M., Senty, D., Pollak, J.: Hackers Wanted: An Examination of the Cybersecurity Labor Market. RAND Corporation, Santa Monica (2014)
19. National Audit Office: The digital skills gap in government: survey findings (2017). https://www.nao.org.uk/report/the-digital-skills-gap-in-government-survey-findings/. Accessed 30 Nov 2017
20. Frost and Sullivan: The 2015 (ISC)2 Global Information Security Workforce Study (2015). https://www.boozallen.com/content/dam/boozallen/documents/Viewpoints/2015/04/frostsullivan-ISC2-global-information-security-workforce-2015.pdf. Accessed 30 Nov 2017
21. SFIA Foundation: SFIA 5 Framework Reference (2017). https://www.sfia-online.org/en/sfia-5. Accessed 30 Nov 2017
22. Universities Australia: Landmark strategy to make graduates more 'job ready' (2015). https://www.universitiesaustralia.edu.au/news/media-releases/Landmark-strategy-to-make-graduates-more–job-ready-#.WEMoFfl97D4. Accessed 30 Nov 2017
23. Bloom, B., Englehart, M., Furst, E., Hill, W., Krathwohl, D.: Taxonomy of Educational Objectives: The Classification of Educational Goals. Handbook I: Cognitive Domain. Longmans Green, New York (1956)
24. University Alliance: Job Ready: universities, employers and students creating success (2014). http://www.unialliance.ac.uk/wp-content/uploads/2014/07/UA06_JOB_READY_web.pdf. Accessed 30 Nov 2017
25. Norton, A., Cakitaki, B.: Mapping Australian higher education 2016, Grattan Institute (2016). http://grattan.edu.au/wp-content/uploads/2016/08/875-Mapping-Australian-Higher-Education-2016.pdf. Accessed 30 Nov 2017
26. Matthews, K.E., Mercer-Mapstone, L.D.: Toward curriculum convergence for graduate learning outcomes: academic intentions and student experiences. Stud. High. Educ., 1–16 (2016). https://doi.org/10.1080/03075079.2016.1190704
27. ACS: Common ICT job profiles & indicators of skills mobility: ICT skills white paper. Australian Computer Society (2013). http://www.acs.org.au/information-resources/ict-skills-white-paper. Accessed 30 Nov 2017
28. Hentea, M., Dhillon, H.S., Dhillon, M.: Towards changes in information security education. J. Inf. Technol. Educ. **5**, 221–233 (2006)
29. Yasinsac, A.: Information security curricula in computer science departments: theory and practice. Georg. Wash. Univ. J. Inf. Secur. **1**(2), 5 (2002)
30. Lewis, M., Coles-Kemp, L.: I've Got Something To Say: The Use of Animation to Create a Meta-Story about Professional Identity (2014). https://www.riscs.org.uk/2014/06/22/ive-got-something-to-say-the-use-of-animation-to-create-a-meta-story-about-professional-identitylewis-m-coles-kemp-l/. Accessed 25 Nov 2017
31. TREsPASS: EU TREsPASS (Technology-supported Risk Estimation by Predictive Assessment of Socio-technical Security) project (2015). http://www.trespass-project.eu/. Accessed 20 Nov 2017

32. Coles-Kemp, L.: TREsPASS Exploring Risk (2016). https://bookleteer.com/collection.html?
    id=27
33. Conklin, A.: Cyber defense competitions and information security education: an active
    learning solution for a capstone course. In: Proceedings of the 39th Annual Hawaii
    International Conference on System Sciences (HICSS 2006) (2006)
34. He, W., Kshirsagar, A., Nwala, A., Li, Y.: Teaching information security with workflow
    technology–a case study approach. J. Inf. Syst. Educ. **25**(3), 201+ (2014)
35. Zurita, H., Maynard, S., Ahmad, A.: Evaluating the utility of research articles for teaching
    information security management. In: Proceeding of Australasian Conference on Information
    Systems 2015 (2016). https://arxiv.org/abs/1606.01448
36. Bailey, B.P., Biehl, J.T., Cook, D.J., Metcalf, H.E.: Adapting paper prototyping for
    designing user interfaces for multiple display environments. Pers. Ubiquitous Comput.
    12(3), 269–277 (2008). https://doi.org/10.1007/s00779-007-0147-2
37. Tonkin, E.: Multilayered paper prototyping for user concept modeling: supporting the
    development of application profiles. In: Proceedings of the International Conference on
    Dublin Core and Metadata Applications, 2009, pp. 51–60 (2009)
38. Linek, S.B., Tochtermann, K.: Paper prototyping: the surplus merit of a multi-method
    approach. Forum Qual. Soc. Res. **16**(3) (2015)
39. OECD: Digital Security Risk Management for Economic and Social Prosperity: OECD
    Recommendation and Companion Document (2015). https://doi.org/10.1787/97892642-
    45471-en, http://www.oecd.org/sti/ieconomy/digital-security-risk-management.pdf. Acces-
    sed 02 Nov 2017
40. NIST: Managing Information Security Risk Organization, Mission, and Information System
    View, NIST Special Publication 800-39, 88 (2011). http://csrc.nist.gov/publications/
    nistpubs/800-39/SP800-39-final.pdf. Accessed 30 Nov 2017
41. Kirschner, P.A., Ayres, P., Chandler, P.: Contemporary cognitive load theory research: the
    good, the bad and the ugly. Comput. Hum. Behav. **27**(1), 99–105 (2011)
42. Sweller, J.: Cognitive load during problem solving: effects on learning. Cogn. Sci. **12**(2),
    257–285 (1988)
43. Kalyuga, S., Hanham, J.: Instructing in generalized knowledge structures to develop flexible
    problem solving skills. Comput. Hum. Behav. **27**(1), 63–68 (2011)
44. Kirschner, F., Paas, F., Kirschner, P.A.: Superiority of collaborative learning with complex
    tasks: a research note on an alternative affective explanation. Comput. Hum. Behav. **27**(1),
    53–57 (2011)
45. Swords, J., Askins, K., Jeffries, M., Butcher, C.: Geographic visualisation: lessons for
    learning and teaching. Planet **27**(2), 6–13 (2013). https://doi.org/10.11120/plan.2013.00001
46. Hall, P., Heath, C., Coles-Kemp, L., Tanner, A.: Examining the contribution of critical
    visualisation to information security. In: Proceedings of the 2015 New Security Paradigms
    Workshop 2015, pp. 59–72. ACM, September 2015
47. TReSPASS mapping tools and techniques for cyber security. https://visualisation.trespass-
    project.eu/ Accessed 24 Feb 2017
48. AISA: The Australian Cyber Security Skills Shortage Study 2016. Australian Information
    Security Association (2016). https://www.aisa.org.au/Public/Training_Pages/Research/AISA
    %20Cyber%20security%20skills%20shortage%20research.aspx. Accessed 30 Nov 2017

Pedagogical Approach to Effective Cybersecurity Teaching

Abdullahi Arabo$^{(\boxtimes)}$ and Martin Serpell

Department of Computer Science and Creative Technologies,
The University of the West of England,
Coldharbour Lane, Bristol BS16 1QY, UK
Abdullahi.Arabo@uwe.ac.uk

Abstract. Initial research ruled out many factors that were thought may correlate to student academic performance. Finally, a strong correlation was found between their academic performance and their motivation. Following on from this research teaching practice was restructured to improve student motivation, engagement, and interest in cybersecurity by contextualizing teaching material with current real-world scenarios. This restructuring led to a very significant improvement in student academic performance, engagement and interest in cybersecurity. Students were found to attend more of their lectures and practical sessions and that this had a strong positive correlation with their academic performance.

Keywords: Education · Cybersecurity

1 Introduction

Learning as a concept can mean different things to different people. Some might see it as a way of exploring a giving fact and driving a new meaning or understanding of an existing theory or fact. While others might just see it as an abstract form of knowing or memorizing an existing fact without the need to analyze or re-interpreted that fact into a body of knowledge. Learning can also be different depending on the size of the class and facilities used to convey such a message to the audience.

The need for careful and deliberate considerations in designing and implementing educational and training activities to enhance cybersecurity teaching and adaptability is of paramount importance, so as to make it more of an interactive, engaging and exciting discipline. The current skills gap in the field of cybersecurity is growing. Some employers have to wait for up to six months to the recruit suitable candidate for a role. Therefore; there is a need for a change in the pedagogical approach to teaching cybersecurity so as to provide the necessary technical skills to reduce the skills gap. The current practice makes use of some available tools and textbook oriented teaching methodologies.

In this paper, we explored the use of real-world and live scenarios with aid of available tools to contextual learning and teaching in cybersecurity so as to provide the concept of students as co-creators and higher learners rather than just presenting theoretical and textbook materials with some out of date scenarios.

© Springer-Verlag GmbH Germany, part of Springer Nature 2019
Z. Pan et al. (Eds.): Transactions on Edutainment XV, LNCS 11345, pp. 129–140, 2019.
https://doi.org/10.1007/978-3-662-59351-6_11

This paper has drawn its data from various practical approaches that have been tested with three sets of cohorts, where teaching materials are contextualized with real-world scenarios, judging the engagement of students within these cohorts in terms of their active engagement within and outside lectures with the teaching materials and teaching team. At the end of each cohort statistical data has been kept and evaluated to compare the end result both in terms of technical cybersecurity capability, obtaining placements/full-time work after graduation and final marks for taught cybersecurity and programming technical modules.

The rest of the paper is structured as follows: related background work in terms of teaching theories, pedagogy used in industrial controls systems and the use of available tools are presented. We then addressed the issues of technical programming skills and use of real-world examples to contextualize learning and its effect on enhancing teaching and learning in cybersecurity. The paper further presents our finding from a different set of cohort and compared this to available data when such methodologies have not been used. Finally, the paper then concludes with our concluding remarks and future study to enhance and provide a better road map and pedagogy for enhanced technical skills and students engagement for teaching cybersecurity.

2 Background

Ramsden classifies the concepts of learning into three main theories: teaching as a means of transmission, teaching as student activity and teaching as making learning possible [1]. The basic concept of the first theory lies in the fact that, the teacher is the main source of authoritative content/body of knowledge, while the student role is just a positive receiver of such knowledge; without the need of analyzing it. The theory utilize the input-output model without any processing in-between. It fosters a surface learning approach as explained by Biggs [2]. The theory is also of the opinion that there are good and bad students. If a student fails, it is entirely their fault but nothing to do with the teacher, programme or the institution. Biggs also discusses two concepts of constructive alignment: students get meaning from what they do to learn and teachers align such derivatives to planned learning activities with the expected learning outcomes [2]. Hence, constructive alignment is all about trying to associate assessment and outcomes. Ramsden's second theory was the principle that teaching is seen as a student activity [1]. The theory emphasis is on the need to establish procedural rules by improving teaching via the use of a set of strategies; the content not being important whereas the conditions of learning are. Ramsden's third theory focuses on the combination of the first two theories [1]. Saying that teaching is a process of making learning possible; hence, teaching, students, and subjects are inter-linked. Each takes their own responsibilities and work in harmony to enhance and provide a more positive environment. The major principle of this theory is that a teacher needs to engage with and get involved with their students by; encouraging students interest, demonstrating concern and respect for students, providing appropriate feedback, presenting students with clear goals, giving students independence and modifying ones teaching practice in response to student learning outcomes.

Development of reflective thinking and practice needs to be a cornerstone of each discipline and part of the pedagogy of teaching cybersecurity to students. This is, however, not an area of learning and teaching which is regularly discussed, despite being recognized across the literature as complex and challenging for lecturers for a variety of reasons teaching reflective practice is neither obvious or easy [3]. The range of reflective approaches available is extensive for example the work of [4–11, 16]. The challenges of introducing reflective practice are varied. For example, the literature suggests that theory is needed to underpin learning as without a guiding theory/structure, student reflections may remain shallow, not providing the anticipated depth of learning [12]. However, use of simplified and technicity prescriptions in the implementation of a theory or structure can mean that reflection becomes a checklist ticking or recipe following exercise [13]. There is potential tension between reflections as a personal, individual experience but also one that is undertaken to be assessed [14]. The risk of gamification and emotional performativity in reflective assessment writing can arise with more sophisticated students [15]. Most resonant is Wong et al. (2016) experience that despite the introduction of models and examples and provision of writing examples and templates, it never quite works for them [17] and that many students still write descriptively rather than reflectively.

Cybersecurity students need to be proficient in computer programming. Much research has already been done on how to teach computer programming. A tremendous variation in the ability to learn computer programming was reported by Bishop-Clark as long ago as 1995 [27]. Ranjeeth and Naidoo used of statistical analysis of students performances in a computer programming related assessments tasks to conclude the same [28]. However, it is believed that an aptitude for computer programming is closely related to an aptitude for mathematics [29].

Student motivation has been found to play a large part in students learning programming [20, 21]. Learning how to motivate students will improve teacher effectiveness and student learning [22]. The motivating factors individual attitude and expectation, clear direction and reward and recognition have been identified [23] as have the ability to make decisions that positively affect the quality of your work and the perception that your work is interesting and challenging [24]. However, it may not be easy measuring the motivation of new students rather it is something that must be instilled by the teacher; this aligns with the theories put forward by Ramsden [1].

Statistical analysis by Turley and Bieman (1995) found that exceptional computer programmers were more likely to be people that saw the big picture, had a bias for action, were driven by a sense of mission, exhibited and articulated strong convictions, played a proactive role with management, and helped other programmers [18]. They also found that programming ability improved with experience. Colley et al. interviewed computer programmers and found that enjoying working with machines, liking technology and enjoying solving complex problems were linked to programming ability whereas being good at maths and being good at science was not [19].

3 Teaching Methodology

3.1 Introducing Computing and Cybersecurity

In their first year, students were introduced to computer architecture and cybersecurity via lectures supported by formative self-assessment tests. There were two pieces of programming coursework which were designed to be very different. As many of the students had never programmed before, the first piece of coursework had the students doing a lot of repetitive programming under the guidance of their module tutors. They were required to write a computer program in the C programming language to emulate the instruction set of an 8-bit microprocessor. The objective was to get students familiar with both computer programming and computer architecture. This piece of coursework was designed to be grueling whereas the next was designed to be fun. The second piece of programming coursework had the students working on an open problem. They had to write software that controlled a battleship that they could see on a large screen. Their battleship bot was in competition with their fellow students' bots, marks were allocated based on how many of their fellow student's battleship bots that they had sunk. This piece of coursework was aimed at developing students networking and problem-solving skills. To stretch the better students they were encouraged to think of creative solutions to this task. Students were not punished for using underhanded techniques such as man-in-the-middle or denial-of-service attacks against their fellow students but rewarded with bonus marks instead.

Student performance in both pieces of coursework was recorded along with their responses to a questionnaire, 76 students took part. The questionnaire contained questions relating to students programming experience, technology experience, problem-solving experience, work plans and programming attitude.

- Programming experience
    - Number of years programming at school?
    - Number of years programming at work?
- Technology experience
    - Do you like Science Fiction [Y/N]?
    - Do you run Linux at home [Y/N]?
    - Do you own a Raspberry Pi or other development board [Y/N]?
    - Have you built a website before [Y/N]?
    - Have you installed an Operating System before [Y/N]?
    - Have you built a PC from component parts before [Y/N]?
- Problem-solving experience
    - Do you like solving puzzles e.g. Sudoku [Y/N]?
    - Are you good at, or have ever been good at, chess [Y/N]?
- Work plans
    - Do you intend to go on a placement year [Y/N]?
    - Do you have a specific career path in mind [Y/N]?
    - Do you have a part-time job [Y/N]?
    - Do you want to work in a technical role when you leave university [Y/N]?

- Programming attitude
  - How much do you enjoy computer programming (Please answer 0 to 10 where 0 = not at all, 10 = very much)?
  - How many hours a week did you spend doing your battleship bots assignment?

Similarly, student performance in both pieces of coursework was recorded against their aptitude test results. A number of students volunteered to take the following aptitude tests; numeric (30), verbal (28) and non-verbal (25). The lessons learned, from the student survey and aptitude tests, were then fed back into their teaching in following years.

3.2 Cybersecurity in-depth

Ramsden's (1992) third theory is applied to teaching cybersecurity in-depth. Teachers make use of a well-established framework rather than relying on an authoritative body of knowledge or an encyclopedic transmission of information to students. This theory works better if the teacher is able to be dynamic, reflective, make use of the wealth of experience form students and link the concept of teaching, student and subject by applying to real world and current examples to help students conceptualize the principles and how it can be applied in the world of work (WOW), we refer to this as a WOW factor. Being dynamic is part of the framework of teaching, using these principles helps students in understanding ideas and linking of ideas to form meaning wholes rather than just as a surface of possible facts and concepts. It also makes and identifies the big ideas that structured the course, as this might not be in any one part of the lectures or seminars or practical's. By way of linking this concept from session to session and pointing out the possible applications in life, it stimulates discussion and engagement with students in both large and small groups. Coursework marks and student attendance before and after the introduction of the new WOW teaching framework were recorded for later analysis.

Švábenský et al. [25], has pointed out adversary thinking as an essential skill that is required for cybersecurity experts. These enable them to understand possible cyber-attacks as well as to set up effective defenses. Their study is based on a set of practical classroom scenarios that enables participants to cope with numerous interdisciplinary tasks throughout the semester while at the same time exercising a broad spectrum of technical and soft skills such as system administration, penetration testing, game design, teamwork, project planning, communication, and presentation.

Byrd [26], has also conducted a study that indicates/clarifies the importance of certain math topics as a core set of skills that is essential or crucial for the developing and can be helpful for a program of study in cybersecurity which will eventually that will enable such individual with this skill set to succeed in the profession and evolving cybersecurity environment.

4 Results

4.1 Introducing Computing and Cybersecurity in the First Year

Student Prior Programming Experience. It was reasonable to believe that those students with prior programming experience, either while at school or at work, would outperform the other students in their programming coursework. However, tests using Person Correlation showed that there was no significant correlation between the experience of programming at school or work and programming performance in their coursework, see Table 1. This was unexpected and is most likely explained by the students without prior experience quickly catching up with those that had prior experience.

Table 1. Correlation between student prior programming experience and their first-year coursework performance

Question	Test result	8-bit emulator	Battleship bots
Number of years Programming at school	Pearson correlation	0.170	0.142
	Sig. (2-tailed)	0.131	0.258
Number of years Programming at work	Pearson correlation	0.216	0.060
	Sig. (2-tailed)	0.100	0.391

Student Prior Technology Experience. Certain pass-times, like running Linux at home, liking science fiction, owning a development board, building websites, installing operating systems and building PCs can be indicative of a type of person who enjoys handling technology. This type of student might be expected to do well in programming assignments, however, the Mann-Whitney test, see Table 2, showed that none of these activities correlated to better performance in either piece of coursework.

Table 2. Correlation between student prior technology experience and their first-year coursework performance

Question	Test result	8-bit emulator	Battleship bots
Do you like science fiction	Mann-Whitney U	379.500	426.000
	Wilcoxon W	484.500	2317.000
	Z	−0.648	−0.014
	Asymp. Sig. (2-tailed)	0.517	0.989
Do you run Linux at home	Mann-Whitney U	506.500	564.500
	Wilcoxon W	1682.500	942.500
	Z	−1.566	−0.922
	Asymp. Sig. (2-tailed)	0.117	0.356

(continued)

Table 2. (*continued*)

Question	Test result	8-bit emulator	Battleship bots
Do you own a Raspberry Pi or other development board	Mann-Whitney U	445.000	562.000
	Wilcoxon W	1930.000	2047.000
	Z	−1.712	−0.367
	Asymp. Sig. (2-tailed)	0.087	0.714
Have you built a website before	Mann-Whitney U	483.000	461.000
	Wilcoxon W	2136.000	2114.000
	Z	−0.704	−0.966
	Asymp. Sig. (2-tailed)	0.482	0.334
Have you installed an Operating System before	Mann-Whitney U	312.500	322.000
	Wilcoxon W	2523.500	2533.000
	Z	−0.270	−0.123
	Asymp. Sig. (2-tailed)	0.787	0.902
Have you built a PC from component parts before	Mann-Whitney U	539.500	605.000
	Wilcoxon W	890.500	956.000
	Z	−1.213	−0.493
	Asymp. Sig. (2-tailed)	0.225	0.622

Student Prior Problem Solving Experience. Solving puzzles and playing chess involve the ability to apply concentration. The results of the Mann-Whitney Tests were very interesting, see Table 3. They showed that a like for solving puzzles did not help students with their first piece of coursework ($U = 541$, $p = 0.914$) but it was very helpful with their second piece of coursework ($U = 309.5$, $p = 0.004$) and similarly being good at Chess did not help students with their first piece of coursework ($U = 595$, $p = 0.497$) but it did help with their second piece of coursework ($U = 470$, $p = 0.039$). This is most likely explained by the nature of the two pieces of coursework, the first requiring a lot of directed repetitive programming and the second undirected problem-solving. This agrees with the findings of Colley et al. (1996) were" enjoying solving complex problems" was one of the attributes linked to programming ability [19].

Student Plans for Work. Students planning their work career has little effect on their performance in their first-year coursework, see Table 4, only the wish to work in a technical role had any correlation. Wishing to work in a technical role did not help with the first piece of coursework ($U = 93.5$, $p = 0.094$) but did help with the second piece of coursework ($U = 80.5$, $p = 0.050$). This is a similar result to enjoying solving puzzles and being good at chess. It may be those students who wish to work in a technical role enjoy the challenges that come with solving technical problems, again as found by Colley et al. [19].

Student Attitude Towards Programming. It was believed if a student enjoyed programming then they would be more motivated when carrying out the programming components of their piece of coursework. The Pearson Correlation test, shown in Table 5, shows a correlation between programming enjoyment and the marks received for the programming portion of each piece of coursework. For the first piece of coursework ($r = 0.447$, $p = 0.000$) the enjoyment of programming contributed 20% to

Table 3. Correlation between student prior problem-solving experience and their first-year coursework performance

Question	Test result	8-bit emulator	Battleship bots
Do you like solving puzzles e.g. Sudoku	Mann-Whitney U	541.000	309.500
	Wilcoxon W	751.000	519.500
	Z	–0.108	–2.883
	Asymp. Sig. (2-tailed)	0.914	0.004
Are you good at, or have ever been good at, chess	Mann-Whitney U	595.000	470.500
	Wilcoxon W	1456.000	998.500
	Z	–0.680	–2.064
	Asymp. Sig. (2-tailed)	0.497	0.039

Table 4. Correlation between student plans for work and their first-year coursework performance

Question	Test result	8-bit emulator	Battleship bots
Do you intend to go on a placement year	Mann-Whitney U	163.500	227.000
	Wilcoxon W	191.500	255.000
	Z	–1.316	–0.139
	Asymp. Sig. (2-tailed)	0.188	0.890
Do you have a specific career path in mind	Mann-Whitney U	564.000	669.000
	Wilcoxon W	1384.000	1335.000
	Z	–1.628	–0.531
	Asymp. Sig. (2-tailed)	0.104	0.596
Do you have a part-time job	Mann-Whitney U	654.500	677.500
	Wilcoxon W	1395.500	1418.500
	Z	–0.516	–0.270
	Asymp. Sig. (2-tailed)	0.606	0.787
Do you want to work in a technical role when you leave university	Mann-Whitney U	93.500	80.500
	Wilcoxon W	108.500	95.500
	Z	–1.676	–1.956
	Asymp. Sig. (2-tailed)	0.094	0.050

the mark given and for the second piece of coursework ($r = 0.303$, $p = 0.008$) enjoyment contributed 9%. However we cannot say which is the dependent variable, it could be that when a student finds that they are good at programming the task becomes enjoyable. This result again agrees with the findings of Colley et al. [19]. It is also reasonable to expect that the longer a student spent working on a piece of coursework the higher the mark that they would achieve. The Pearson Correlation test, see Table 5, showed that the time spent on the Emulator positively correlated ($r = 0.292$, $p = 0.010$) to the marks achieved, emulating an Intel 8080 microprocessor involved a lot of repetitive programming and the more time spent would expectantly lead to a higher mark. This link between student motivation and programming achievement was reported by Jiau et al. and Serrano-Cmara et al. [20, 21]. The contribution time made to the mark achieved, however, was not great (<1%). There, however, was no strong correlation between the time spent working on the Battleship Bots piece of coursework and the mark achieved. This is most likely explained by the fact that the second piece of coursework required a brain, not brawn.

Table 5. Correlation between student attitude towards programming and their first-year coursework performance

Question	Test result	8-bit emulator	Battleship bots
Enjoy computer Programming	Pearson correlation	0.447	0.303
	Sig. (2-tailed)	0.000	0.008
Hours spent on Coursework	Pearson correlation	0.292	0.202
	Sig. (2-tailed)	0.010	0.080

Student Aptitude Test Results. Aptitude tests are frequently used in industry as a means of selecting suitable applicants for jobs that entail computer programming. In the literature, positive correlations have been found between the ability to score highly in numeric aptitude tests and the ability to programme computers. The Pearson Correlation test was used to determine the strength of the relationship between the student's aptitude test results and their coursework performance; the results are shown in Table 6. No significant correlations were found between the numeric, verbal or non-verbal aptitudes of the students and their coursework performance. A possible correlation (<1%) between the non-verbal aptitude of the students and the second piece of coursework may indicate that a strength in non-verbal reasoning may help with problem-solving.

Table 6. Correlation between student aptitude test results and their first-year coursework performance

Question	Test result	8-bit emulator	Battleship bots
Numeric Aptitude	Pearson correlation	0.221	0.172
	Sig. (2-tailed)	0.240	0.364
Verbal Aptitude	Pearson correlation	0.090	0.212
	Sig. (2-tailed)	0.649	0.364
Non-verbal Aptitude	Pearson correlation	–0.002	0.348
	Sig. (2-tailed)	0.993	0.088

4.2   Cybersecurity In-Depth

The coursework marks achieved by the 2015-16 cohort of year 2 students was compared to that of the 2016-17 cohort of year 2 students. The 2015-16 cohort was taught prior to the introduction of the new teaching framework, the WOW factor and the 2016-17 cohort after. The coursework marks were compared using the Wilcoxon Signed Ranks Test, it showed with 99.9% confidence that the marks were significantly different. Table 7 shows that the average coursework mark is significantly better for the 2016-17 cohort.

Table 7. Average coursework marks for the year 2015-16 and 2016-17 cohorts

Year	Mean	Std. Dev.
2015-16	36.32	20.15
2016-17	58.85	32.25

This improvement was explained by students being more motivated and their improved attendance at both lectures and practical sessions where discussion of the latest cybersecurity news, and its implications, took place. This improvement agrees with results published in [20, 21]. A Pearson's Correlation Test between attendance (the independent variable) and the 2016-17 cohort coursework mark was carried out. It showed that with >99.9% confidence that a positive correlation ($R = 0.750$) exists between student attendance and the coursework mark that they achieve. Further, it implies that 56.3% of the coursework mark can be attributed to students attending their lectures and practical's. Figure 1 shows a scatter plot of coursework marks by student attendance.

Feedback from students has been highly positive. This includes students always eager to contribute their understanding of materials and applying it to current news/trends. Wanting to contribute in the lectures on how the topics linked to what is happening with the week. Waiting for lectures to discuss current trends, emailing staff with current trends in cybersecurity and talking to staff in the corridors. Some of the feedbacks include

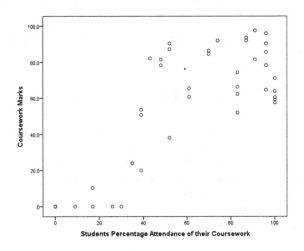

Fig. 1. Correlation between student attendance and coursework marks

– "Lectures and Labs are interesting, I am always engaged, and we cover interesting news which is useful."
– "Good examples used/analogies and interactive in class".
– "Excellent contextualization of materials with real-world scenarios"

5   Conclusion

Very little correlation was found between students' academic performance and their prior use of technology or the results of their aptitude tests. Where correlation was found it tended to relate to student motivation; this agreed with previously published work that student motivation was a key factor in their academic success. Items of interest that linked current topics being taught to current real-world events were gleaned from the news and other sources. Incorporating this material into a new teaching framework for the second-year students has significantly improved their academic performance. This success is attributed to their increased engagement and interest in applying their skills to real-world scenarios.

References

1. Ramsden, P.: Learning to Teach in Higher Education. Routledge, London (2003)
2. Biggs, J.: What the student does: teaching for enhanced learning. High. Educ. Res. Dev. **18** (1), 57–75 (1999)
3. Casey, A.: Models-based practice: great white hope or white elephant? Phys. Educ. Sports Pedagogy **19**(1), 18–34 (2014);
4. Boud, D.: Problem-based learning in education for the professions. Higher Education Research and Development Society of Australasia (1985)
5. Dewey, J.: The need for a philosophy of education (1934). Schools **7**(2), 244–245 (2010)
6. Fook, J., Gardner, F.: Critical Reflection in Context: Applications in Health and Social Care. Routledge, London (2012)
7. Ghaye, T.: Teaching and Learning Through Reflective Practice: A Practical Guide for Positive Action. Routledge, London (2010)
8. Kolb, D.: Experiential Education: Experience as the Source of Learning and Development. Prentice-Hall, Englewood Cliffs (1984)
9. Peterson, K., DeCato, L., Kolb, D.A.: Moving and learning: expanding style and increasing flexibility. J. Exp. Educ. **38**(3), 228–244 (2015)
10. Mezirow, J.: Conclusion: toward transformative learning and emancipatory education. Fostering critical reflection in adulthood: a guide to transformative and emancipatory learning, pp. 354–376 (1990)
11. Schn, D.A.: Educating the Reflective Practitioner: Toward a New Design for Teaching and Learning in the Professions. Jossey-Bass, San Francisco (1987)
12. Hume, A.: Promoting higher levels of reflective writing in student journals. High. Educ. Res. Dev. **28**(3), 247–260 (2009)
13. Boud, D., Walker, D.: Promoting reflection in professional courses: the challenge of context. Stud. High. Educ. **23**(2), 191–206 (1998)
14. Laurillard, D.: Rethinking University Education: A Conversational Framework for the Effective Use of Learning Technologies. RoutledgeFalmer, London (2002)
15. Macfarlane, B., Gourlay, L.: The reflection game: enacting the penitent self. Teach. High. Educ. **14**(4), 455–459 (2009)
16. Comber, C., Colley, A., Hargreaves, D.J., Dorn, L.: The effects of age, gender and computer experience upon computer attitudes. Educ. Res. **39**(2), 123–133 (1997)
17. Wong, H.K., Wong, R.T., Allred, S., David-Lang, J.: The First Days of School: Implementation Guide. Harry K. Wong Publications, Inc. (2016)

18. Turley, R.T., Bieman, J.M.: Competencies of exceptional and non-exceptional software engineers. J. Syst. Softw. **28**(1), 19–38 (1995)

19. Colley, A., Henry, O., Holmes, S., James, L.: Perceptions of ability to program or to use a word processor. Comput. Hum. Behav. **12**(3), 329–337 (1996)

20. Jiau, H.C., Chen, J.C., Ssu, K.-F.: Enhancing self-motivation in learning programming using game-based simulation and metrics. IEEE Trans. Educ. **52**(4), 555–562 (2009)

21. Serrano-Cámara, L.M., et al.: An evaluation of students motivation in computer-supported collaborative learning of programming concepts. Comput. Hum. Behav. **31**, 499–508 (2014)

22. Hawi, N.: Causal attributions of success and failure made by undergraduate students in an introductory-level computer programming course. Comput. Educ. **54**(4), 1127–1136 (2010)

23. Law, K.M.Y., Lee, V.C.S., Yu, Y.-T.: Learning motivation in e-Learning facilitated computer programming courses. Comput. Educ. **55**(1), 218–228 (2010)

24. Feldt, R., Angelis, L., Torkar, R., Samuelsson, M.: Links between the personalities, views, and attitudes of software engineers. Inf. Softw. Technol. **52**(6), 611–624 (2010)

25. Švábenský, V., Vykopal, J., Cermak, M., Laštovička, M.: Enhancing cybersecurity skills by creating serious games. In: ACM ITiCSE 2018 Conference (2018)

26. Byrd, R.: Cybersecurity: 1) what math is necessary and 2) developing ubiquitous cybersecurity in current computing programs. J. Comput. Sci. Coll. **33**(4), 53–59 (2018)

27. Bishop-Clark, C.: Cognitive style, personality, and computer programming. Comput. Hum. Behav. **11**(2), 241–260 (1995)

28. Ranjeeth, S., Naidoo, R.: An investigation into the relationship between the level of cognitive maturity and the types of errors made by students in a computer programming course. Coll. Teach. Methods Styles J.(CTMS) **3**(2), 31–40 (2007)

29. Martin, A., Maria, V., Beena, A., Lucia, T.: Prediction of association among numerical aptitude, programming skills, trait emotional intelligence on students performance. Int. J. Comput. Sci. Eng. **4**, 9 (2012)

Choose Your Pwn Adventure: Adding Competition and Storytelling to an Introductory Cybersecurity Course

Tom Chothia, Chris Novakovic$^{(\boxtimes)}$, Andreea-Ina Radu, and Richard J. Thomas

School of Computer Science, University of Birmingham, Birmingham, UK
{t.p.chothia,c.novakovic,a.i.radu,r.j.thomas}@cs.bham.ac.uk

Abstract. Narrative is an important element of gamification. In this article, we describe the development of a framework that adds a narrative to an 11-week cybersecurity course. The students play the part of a new IT security employee at a company and are asked to complete a number of security tasks, for which they receive flags. As well as being used to assess their performance throughout the course, students can send the flags they find to a number of different characters to progress the storyline in different ways. As the story unfolds they find deceit, corruption and ultimately murder, and their choices lead them to one of three different endings. Our framework for running the story and the exercises is completely self-contained in a single virtual machine, which the students each download at the start of the course; this means that no resource-consuming backend or cloud support is required. We report on the results of qualitative and quantitative evaluations of the course that provide evidence that both the VM and the story contained within it increased student engagement and improved their course results.

1 Introduction

Live security exercises are a popular and fun means of engaging with cybersecurity topics in academia, industry [8], and government [21] alike. The pedagogical benefits of these exercises have been widely reported (e.g., [1,9,12,18,19,29]); participants often cite the enjoyment and satisfaction of competing, their increased motivation to learn about cybersecurity, improved practical knowledge of theoretical aspects of cybersecurity, and the discovery of deficiencies in their knowledge as benefits of taking part.

One common type of live security exercise is the *Capture The Flag* (CTF) competition. The objective is for participants (whether individuals or teams) to defend a host running vulnerable services while simultaneously attacking other teams' hosts running the same services (an *attack/defence-style CTF*). Alternatively, participants can solve standalone challenges from a range of categories, including binary reverse-engineering, forensics, and web security, without the need to interact directly with the other participants (a *Jeopardy-style CTF*). The successful exploitation of a vulnerable service or solving of a challenge

© Springer-Verlag GmbH Germany, part of Springer Nature 2019
Z. Pan et al. (Eds.): Transactions on Edutainment XV, LNCS 11345, pp. 141–172, 2019.
https://doi.org/10.1007/978-3-662-59351-6_12

reveals a secret piece of information known as a *flag*, which scores points for the participant when submitted to a *flag server* operated by the CTF organisers; the submission of flags for more difficult challenges scores a greater number of points for the participant, and the participant that scores the most points over the course of the competition is declared the winner. Some attack/defence-style CTFs also incorporate elements of Jeopardy-style CTFs. In both cases, the exercise typically runs over a short period of time (usually 12–48 h).

Live security exercises commonly have themes or simple linear narratives to give structure to the exercise, connect otherwise-disparate technical challenges, and to amuse or sustain the interest of their participants. The long-running academic CTF, iCTF, has featured a variety of storylines since it began in 2001, from infiltrating and ultimately disarming a terrorist network (with the aim of defeating the terrorists more quickly than the other participants) to running a botnet-based organised crime operation (with the aim of amassing more illicit money from victims than the other participants by the end of the competition) [29]. The 2014 edition of the high-school CTF picoCTF featured a storyline about helping a broken robot to get home [5], while the 2017 edition required participants to locate and rescue a friend who suddenly and unexpectedly disappears [4]. Cybersecurity camps, elaborate exercises requiring participants to be physically present in a given location over a longer period, afford their organisers the ability to form more detailed and immersive narratives than CTFs: Feng et al. developed a camp with a storyline based on the theme of the *Divergent* young-adult science fiction novel series [11], while the industry-led HackFu event hires professional actors to play characters who interact with participants to progress the storyline [20]. Similarly, the theme for the Cambridge-led cybersecurity camps Inter-ACE [28] and Cambridge 2 Cambridge (C2C) [17] 2017 was cybersecurity warfare, placing participants in the scenario of having to defend the nation against a rogue organisation. Participants had to discover and take down strategic assets belonging to adversaries, as well as search for forensic clues on hard drives recovered from behind enemy lines.

Given the pedagogical benefits of live security exercises, instructors may find it desirable to introduce them into the curricula of academic cybersecurity courses. However, there are several potential barriers to doing so.

The funding to run more immersive forms of live security exercise, such as cybersecurity camps, is rarely available for individual academic courses; with their lower operating costs, CTFs are more favourable for inclusion in academic curricula. Even so, CTFs require continuous supervision by their organisers to guarantee the smooth running of the competition; a pool of organisers working intensive shifts can ensure that a 48-h CTF runs successfully, but this is not viable in an academic teaching scenario where courses run over a period of several months.

There are also technical barriers: the infrastructure underpinning a CTF is typically large and complex (e.g., [9,29]), and the computing power (and, for attack/defence-style CTFs, network bandwidth) required for the smooth operation of a CTF is usually not available for teaching purposes. Additionally, CTFs inevitably involve attacking vulnerable network services, and there is a danger that students' malicious network traffic could interfere with other network hosts that are not part of the competition; we (and others [3]) have found university IT support staff hesitant to allow malicious traffic to pass over any network they control.

We have developed a framework for including Jeopardy-style CTF challenges in academic cybersecurity courses, and have integrated it into our own 11-week undergraduate course. The framework takes the form of a virtual machine (VM) containing vulnerable services and challenges devised by the course staff; they can be revealed gradually to students as the relevant cybersecurity topics are taught in lectures, allowing individual exercises to feature particular challenges. Each student runs the VM locally and attempts to solve each challenge inside the VM as it is made available by the course staff. The successful completion of a challenge reveals a flag to the student, which can be submitted to a flag server controlled by the course staff for credit in the exercise; flags are unique to a particular instance of the VM, allowing for the detection of collusion between students.

The framework also features a *narrative engine* with which students may optionally engage with: as well as gaining course credit by submitting discovered flags to the flag server, students may progress a non-linear storyline by emailing the same flags to fictional characters that exist within the VM. The narrative engine is reusable: the narrative is contained in a single file (the *story map*) that defines the identities of the characters, the story that connects them (and the student), and decisions that may be taken by students at particular points during the story to influence the plot. The narrative we have developed for our course follows screen-writing best practice (e.g., [27]), and is designed to be compelling enough that students become attached to the characters and therefore feel invested in progressing the storyline to completion over an 11-week period.

Our framework provides the benefits of live security exercises to cybersecurity students while avoiding the drawbacks discussed earlier: students run the VM on their own hardware (e.g., their laptops), so course staff need not invest time continually maintaining a centralised infrastructure to operate the CTF, and malicious traffic is only routed inside a particular student's virtual network, eradicating the impact that an inexperienced student's actions may have on the university network. Since the framework is reusable, instructors can easily make changes to both the challenges and narrative between iterations of the course (e.g., in order to incorporate student feedback gathered during previous iterations).

Our framework has been used in some form in all four iterations of our course. The framework has driven all of the continuous assessment in each iteration; we therefore expected students to interact with it for 3–4 h per week over 11 weeks. The use of VM-based CTF-style exercises was popular with students, as indicated by high student satisfaction levels reported in the end-of-course anonymous feedback questionnaires. A storyline was added in time for the fifth iteration of the course, where we found that following the storyline led to improved student attainment and overall student engagement, as well as improved development of students' knowledge of cybersecurity issues.

The rest of this article is organised as follows. We provide a brief overview of the structure and content of our undergraduate cybersecurity course at the University of Birmingham in Sect. 2; our own requirements influenced design decisions we made while creating the framework, although it is flexible enough that instructors for cybersecurity courses at other universities can provide their own exercises and narrative within the same framework. We then describe the structure of the framework itself: Sect. 3 describes the architecture of the VM distributed to students at the start of the course, and Sects. 4 and 5 describe the infrastructure that controls progression of the story that takes place within the VM. Section 6 outlines the story we developed for our course and the decisions that students can make in order to influence the plot. In Sect. 7, we provide an evaluation of the framework and story based on an analysis of students' marks for several iterations of our course and feedback we gathered from them after each iteration. We conclude in Sect. 8.

A website with additional information, a downloadable copy of our latest VM, and sample exercise sheets can be found at https://www.cs.bham.ac.uk/ internal/courses/comp-sec/vm_story. Parts of the current work have previously been published in [6, 7].

2 Our Cybersecurity Course

Since the 2013/14 academic year, the School of Computer Science at the University of Birmingham has offered an optional introductory cybersecurity course to second-year undergraduates, with a particular focus on technical skills and understanding. The course runs for 11 weeks, with 2 h of lectures and 2 h of lab sessions per week. It is assessed both formatively (via continuous assessment, worth 20% of a student's final grade) and summatively (via exam, worth the remaining 80%). Topics covered in the course have included cryptography, access control, network and protocol security, web security, buffer overflows, and reverse-engineering of binaries. Students enrolling on the course are expected to arrive with basic programming and networking skills.

Prior to the 2015/16 academic year, the School also offered a graduate-level introductory cybersecurity course. While this course covered many of the same topics as the undergraduate-level course, and also integrated the framework we present in this article into its continuous assessment (with many of the same outcomes), in this article we focus exclusively on the undergraduate-level version of the course. We encourage the reader to refer to our earlier work [7] for an analysis of the graduate-level course.

The continuous assessment for the course is delivered in the form of exercises, lasting for 2–3 weeks each, that are intended to test students' in-depth understanding of the topics covered in lectures; the difficulty of the exercises is set based on experience gained from teaching previous courses and knowledge of other courses that the students have taken.

2.1   Marking and Grading Criteria

Each exercise is marked out of 100; grade boundaries are positioned at intervals of 10 marks between 40 and 70, with a mark above 70 representing high-quality work and a mark below 40 representing failure. Generally, a third of the marks are awarded for a basic solution (e.g., for the protocol security exercise, a working attack against the protocol), another third are awarded for an optimal solution (e.g., a protocol attack with no unnecessary steps), and the final third are awarded for showing a clear understanding of the problem (e.g., a description of each line of the protocol attack, making it clear what each part of the message does, and why the attack works). Students were informed in advance of how marking would take place and were told what was expected of a high-scoring submission, but did not expect to receive top marks for all of their continuous assessment. Marks were not scaled; as shown in Sect. 7, they naturally ended up distributed across all grades.

For all exercises, students were required to submit written answers describing the steps they took to recover flags from the VM, and—where appropriate—a description of what the vulnerabilities were and how they worked, and an explanation of how they could be fixed. Not all questions required the recovery of flags from the VM, and flags were not used to unilaterally prove that the student completed the exercise, but were instead intended to give the marker some degree of assurance that the students' written answers were dependable. There were minor variations to the questions in the exercises for each iteration of the course, to prevent students from simply reusing solutions from a previous iteration. Examples of the full exercise sheets are available from https://www. cs.bham.ac.uk/internal/courses/comp-sec/vm_story.

2.2   Exercise Content

Each iteration of the course has featured continuous assessment consisting of either four or five exercises corresponding to the topics taught in lectures. We now describe how Jeopardy CTF-style challenges are integrated into each exercise, and outline how students are expected to complete the challenges in order to find them.

Exercise 1: Basic Encryption. The first exercise familiarises students with performing cryptographic operations in Java. The students are given the passwords to two user accounts on the VM, `alice` and `bob`. `bob`'s home directory contains incomplete Java source code for an encryption application; the supplied code contains methods for encrypting files using AES (in either CTR or CCM mode) and RSA using a user-defined key. The CTF-style challenges for this exercise involve decrypting AES/RSA-encrypted files in `bob`'s home directory that each contain a flag; students are required to write the corresponding decryption methods for the application and use their compiled code to recover the flags from the encrypted files. Additionally—as an example of a question that is not assessed as part of a CTF-style challenge—a file in bob's home directory contains the message "Pay Tom 1000 pounds" encrypted using AES in CTR mode; students are not given the encryption key, and must therefore manually edit the bits of the ciphertext in the file so that, when decrypted using the code they have written, the corresponding plaintext reads "Pay Bob 9999 pounds".

Exercise 2: Access Control. The VM contains a number of files protected with flawed access controls. One flag is stored in a file hidden in an obscure location in the file system rather than being given appropriately restrictive permissions; others are stored in files with a variety of insecure permissions that allow the file to be read (e.g., via a chained confused deputy attack against two insecure programs with the setuid bit set). The challenges in this exercise require students to bypass these weak access controls and recover the flag contained within each file.

Exercise 3: Protocol Analysis. Students are given two key-agreement protocols in the standard "Alice and Bob" security protocol notation, Java source code of servers implementing these protocols, and raw network packet traces of clients communicating with these servers using these protocols. The protocols are vulnerable to a man-in-the-middle attack and a replay attack respectively. Students must discover and describe the attacks, implement them, and run them against the servers running on the VM; successful exploitation of each server reveals a flag.

Exercise 4: Web Security. The VM runs a web server that hosts what at first sight appears to be an online furniture store; however, hidden inside this furniture store is a black-market website. Students must investigate this website, find the black-market interface and carry out a number of attacks. An SQL injection attack allows them to view all products stored in the backend MySQL database, including the black-market products and a flag. By analysing the cookies set by the furniture store, they can discover how the hidden website authenticates its users and gain access to it. The site displays a flag from a protected file that the students can submit to show that they accessed the hidden website. A file upload attack allows them to recover the MySQL server login details used by the black-market website; logging into the MySQL server using these credentials reveals another database containing a flag. A shell injection attack provides access to a shell running as the www-data user, revealing a final flag in a protected file in the file system. Non-flag questions in this exercise additionally cover XSS and CSRF attacks.

Exercise 5: Reverse-Engineering. For this exercise, students must reverse-engineer four programs: two written in heavily-obfuscated Java and compiled into JDK bytecode, and two written in C and compiled into native code. All of these binaries behave as servers, and are listening on ports on the VM. Students must reverse-engineer the first three programs to recover a password expected to be entered into the program which, when entered into the copy of the program running as a server on the VM, causes the program to output a flag. The final program is an x86 binary for managing PGP keys, which also contains a backdoor; this binary listens on a port on the VM and runs as the root user. Students must find the backdoor by examining the binary in the free edition of the IDA disassembly tool [13] and use it to gain access to a root shell on the VM; a final flag is stored in a file in the /root directory.

3   A VM-Based Framework for CTF-Style Challenges

Our design goal was to create a VM-based framework suitable for use in a university cybersecurity course in which students could complete Jeopardy-style CTF challenges for course credit. While the use of VM-based exercises to support cybersecurity education is common (e.g., [3,24]), our aim was to design exercises that assess the full range of cybersecurity topics taught in the course in a fun and accessible way.

Our framework is based on a single VM that students download on their own hardware (e.g., their laptop) at the start of the course and import into the free and open-source VirtualBox virtualisation software [22]. This VM runs a Linux operating system containing several services, such as a web server, database server, and daemons running purpose-built insecure protocols, as well as many user accounts and complex, flawed access control configurations.

3.1   Flag Generation

When the VM boots for the first time, a *setup script* runs that generates the flags. These flags are written to particular locations (e.g., into the source code of a service which is then compiled, or into a password-protected MySQL database). The setup script then sets appropriate permissions on the generated files and binaries, and deletes any source code it compiled before deleting itself.

The setup script generates a random *VM identifier*, intended to be unique for each VM. To generate a flag for a particular question in an exercise, the function defined in Algorithm 1 is used: the VM identifier is concatenated with the *exercise number* and *question number*, and the resulting string is PKCS#7-padded and encrypted with AES using a 128-bit key (the *course key*) chosen by the course staff; the ciphertext can be represented as a string of 32 hexadecimal characters, and this is the flag that the student is required to submit. The validity of submitted flags is checked on the flag submission server using the inverse of the function in Algorithm 1: when decrypted with the course key, invalid flags will not be correctly PKCS#7-padded, or will be missing the Ex header.

Input: Course key K, exercise number n_e, question number n_q, VM identifier v
Output: Flag
function GENERATE_FLAG(K, n_e, n_q, v)
    $flag\_data \leftarrow$ "Ex" $|| \ n_e \ || \ n_q \ || \ v$
    $plaintext \leftarrow$ PKCS7_PAD($flag\_data$)
    $ciphertext \leftarrow$ AES_ENCRYPT($K, plaintext$)

    ▷ Return *ciphertext* as string of 32 hexadecimal characters
    return BASE16($ciphertext$)
end function

Algorithm 1. Generating a VM-specific flag for a particular exercise and question

3.2   The Flag Submission Server

Students submit flags that are generated by the startup script by logging into the flag submission server (a website operated by the course staff) using their University IT account credentials and pasting the 32-character string into the input box for the appropriate exercise and question.

The flag submission server decrypts the ciphertext and verifies that it is a valid flag for the given question by checking the identifiers contained within the resulting plaintext. The server records details of the flag submission for the markers and instantly informs the student whether the submission was successful. Students are allowed an unlimited number of flag submission attempts for a particular question. To avoid the CTF-style challenges being perceived as competitions, students cannot check whether other students have submitted flags for a particular question.

An administrative page on the flag submission server shows the course staff details of all flag submissions for a given exercise and question, including the identity of the student submitting the flag, when the submission was made, and the identifier of the VM from which the flag originated. Students sometimes complete exercises using multiple copies of the VM (e.g., one on a laptop and one on a desktop computer), so we occasionally detect multiple VM identifiers for a particular student. However, students are explicitly instructed not to share their VMs with other students, so two students submitting flags with the same VM identifier is a possible indicator of plagiarism. The flag submission server does not reveal the results of this check to the student, but instead alerts the course staff of any irregularities on the administrative page; the course staff then follow this up with the implicated students individually (as we discuss in Sect. 7).

It would be possible for good students to download a fresh copy of the VM and reverse-engineer the flag generation program, giving them the ability to generate their own flags. However, we note that doing this would be harder than completing any of the exercises, in particular the existing reverse-engineering exercises. Additionally, we require students to submit descriptions of how they solved each exercise, which would be hard to do convincingly without solving the exercise as intended. A larger concern is students finding a way to gain root privileges on the VM and finding information that makes the exercises trivial; to counter this, we have carefully designed the exercises so that they rely on the secrecy of as few files as possible (e.g., in the web security exercise, the website's PHP code is not considered secret, and students are given access to it along with the exercise sheet).

4   Enhancing Teaching Through Stories

While gamification—in the form of point-scoring, team-based competition, freedom to fail and rapid feedback [16, 23, 26]—is popular in cybersecurity education, one must also consider the importance of storytelling and character development to ensure that the target audience remains engaged [15, 25].

Building on our previous successes, we extended the VM framework described in Sect. 3 with a story for students to discover. The story is told through emails and news updates to a website in the VM, made possible with the integration of a local mail server and a custom-built *story engine* into the existing VM architecture; as the mail server and story engine are contained entirely within the VM, no support or maintenance is required from course staff, and each student controls their own version of the story. The story engine uses a set of XML files defining the content of emails and news updates to reveal to the student, and another XML file defining the conditions that must be met in order to progress along different paths of the storyline; it is therefore easy to change the story without modifying the internal mechanics of the VM. The story language features expressive logic permitting a range of complex scenarios (e.g., mutually-exclusive events, and different responses to different orders of actions taken by the student). If the VM has an Internet connection, we make it possible to provide telemetry for analytic purposes.

Figure 1 depicts the interactions of the components of the VM framework described in Sect. 3 and the story framework described in this section and in Sect. 5. In brief, the process is as follows:

1. The setup script generates the flags and places them in files at the appropriate paths.
2. The setup script deletes itself.
3. The story engine sends the first emails, which can be read by the student from the player space via a mail client.
4. From the player space, the student interacts with the exercises and the web server, with the goal of obtaining the flags.
5. The flags are submitted to the flag submission server, an external website operated by the course staff.
6. The student emails the obtained flags to one of a number of characters, in order to progress the story.
7. The story engine periodically checks for new mail sent to the characters' inboxes on the mail server.
8. The story engine optionally sends the email to an external telemetry server.

9. Depending on which character received the email, the story engine advances the plot, updating the website hosted on the VM with appropriate news postings and sending new emails; the process repeats from step 3 onwards until the story ends.

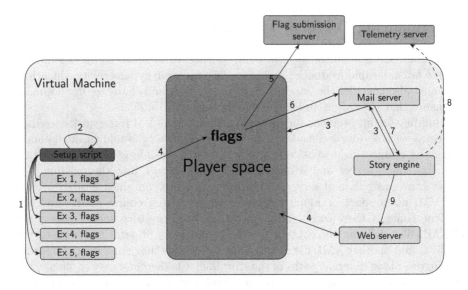

Fig. 1. The framework components: a self-contained virtual machine, a lightweight flag submission server and, optionally, a telemetry server

Students interact with the story engine by sending emails to the VM's mail server, which their mail client in the VM is preconfigured to use. The story engine runs as a `cron` job, periodically checking inboxes on the mail server, posting news updates to the website, and sending emails to the student from different characters in the story. Students advance the story themselves using flags they find by completing the course's regular exercises: after completing an exercise, the student must decide which character to email the recovered flags to. When the story engine receives an email, it will verify the enclosed flag and determine which character's inbox the email was sent to. Based on the choices made by the student, the engine progresses the story by posting further news updates on the website and sending new emails to the student. This feedback loop gives students the ability to control what happens in the story using an approach for increasing player engagement that is commonly found in large-scale computer games.

Our story follows the classic Hollywood story arc structure: a trigger event, crossing a threshold, overcoming obstacles, a setback, and then a final push. Each of these five stages of the story corresponds to a two-week exercise. The students start out as a new security employee at a company, where they are asked by their line manager to complete some decryption code and find some flags, and are warned to keep the flags secret. Meanwhile, the students receive a second email from a mysterious stranger telling them that there is something wrong at the company, and that they should instead send the flags to them. The story engine ensures that the students can only choose one of the two options. As the story progresses, they discover that the company is being used as a front for a black-market website (the Cotton Highway) and, after the police become involved, they must decide what to risk and who to side with.

We introduced the story as a trial extension to the course VM, giving the students the option of following the story or not. The concept of the story and how students could interact with it was described in lectures, and a statistically-insignificant bonus mark was offered for following the story. To evaluate the value of the story, we performed surveys for students who followed it and those who did not. Analysis of the results showed that students who followed the story felt engaged, while those who did not felt that the concept was good, with positive feedback. We also evaluated the difference in obtained marks between the two groups of students, and found that students who followed the story achieved significantly higher marks on average than those who did not. To rule out the possibility that stronger students chose to follow the story and weaker students chose not to, we compared the marks each student achieved on this course with the marks they achieved on other courses. We found that students who followed the story did much better than their marks from other courses would predict, whereas the marks of students who did not follow the story were consistent with their marks in other courses. This suggests that following the story did improve student performance. A more detailed analysis is presented in Sect. 7.2.

Further extensions have been made to the story engine and the way the course is gamified. For example, one extension to the story engine implements *welfare flags*: should a student have mitigating circumstances that prevent them from completing a particular exercise, a special flag can be given to them that progresses the story beyond that exercise; this ensures that students are never put at a disadvantage to their peers. Other extensions to the story engine make it possible to define multiple paths forward for a given set of conditions (providing some randomness to the consequences a student faces for sending flags to a particular character), and artificially delay emails being sent and news stories being posted on the website (simulating a human being on the receiving end of the student's emails, and giving the story an organic nature). This allows self-paced learning, and a more bespoke student experience regardless of whether the student took similar choices to their peers. We also improved the VM's reporting ability such that if the VM was unable to send telemetry data due to a lack of an Internet connection, it would retry when connectivity became available.

5   The Story Engine

In order to convey a story to the students, we required an immersive way of communicating with them. We therefore made the story dynamic, reacting to the actions taken by the student so their experience would feel personalised.

To achieve this, we developed a Java-based story engine that would not only monitor the decisions made by the student, but also tailor its output based on these decisions. To further enhance the immersion, we added a company website (hosted on a web server running locally on the VM), featuring a news section where the story engine would add new updates as the story progressed. These updates could be relevant to the decisions taken, or presented in a more general format.

One aim of this extension to the VM was to make the story easy to write and maintain while requiring no particular programming knowledge. This is achieved through the use of an XML-based configuration file for the story engine, which we refer to as a *story map*. The story map encodes the different paths that can be taken through the story and the objectives that have to be completed in order to progress along each path. State attributes in the story map are used to track progress through the story.

In the event that a student abandons the story before it ends, they can to return to where they left off at any time; alternatively, they may use a welfare flag (an extension to the story engine described in Sect. 4) given to them by the course staff to advance the story to a specific point.

5.1   Story Map

The story map is an XML-encoded file; an overview of its structure is shown in Fig. 2.

The `<exercise>` element provides a logical separation between the different parts of the story; as our course was already written around a series of five exercises, we chose to break our story into five parts, each corresponding to a particular exercise, although this is customisable. Inside each `<exercise>` element are several `<event>` elements defining events that occur within the story, split up into smaller `<tasks>` and the `<required>` conditions that trigger them.

The `<tasks>` element contains a list of tasks that the story engine performs when an event is triggered. These are either `<email>` tasks (instructing the engine to send an email to the student), or `<news>` tasks (instructing the engine to update the website with a new news story). Both task types point to auxiliary XML files containing the text of the emails to be sent and news stories to be posted.

The `<required>` element contains a list of conditions that must be met before the event's `<tasks>` are executed. These can either be `<token>` elements (indicating that a specific flag must have been sent to a specific email address, defined in the `sent_to` attribute), or `<finished>` elements (indicating that a specific event must have already occurred). Nestable `<AND>`, `<OR>` and `<NOT>` elements allow conditions to be combined or negated, allowing for arbitrarily complex requirements for triggering tasks. The story engine can also randomly select an event to trigger if multiple events are triggered by the same conditions; this gives each student a more bespoke experience and allows the otherwise-linear story to appear to progress organically.

```
<story_map>
  <exercise>
    <event>
      <required>
        <!-- Arbitrarily complex conditions, e.g.: -->
        <AND>
          <finished ... />
          <OR>
            <token ... />
            <token ... />
          </OR>
        </AND>
      </required>
      <tasks>
        <!-- Perform these actions when conditions are met -->
        <email ... />
        <news ... />
      </tasks>
    </event>
  </exercise>
  <news_stories>
    <!-- Static news story definitions -->
    <static_story ... />
  </news_stories>
  <extras>
    <!-- Character definitions -->
    <users ... />
  </extras>
</story_map>
```

Fig. 2. Overview of the story map file structure; some element types (e.g., `<users>`, `<news>`, `<static_story>`) additionally rely on external XML files

The `<event>`, `<email>`, `<news>` and `<token>` elements contain a `complete` attribute; these are used to track which events and tasks have already been completed and which flags have already been sent to the story engine, thus tracking the current state of the story. Their values are initially set to `false`, then updated to `true` as appropriate by the story engine as the story progresses.

The `<users>` element points to another auxiliary XML file that defines characters by their account name and password on the VM's mail server; the story engine periodically checks the inboxes of these characters and reacts to emails received from the student, as described below. The `<news_stories>` element defines *static stories* to be posted on the news page at particular times, and is described in more detail in Sect. 5.4.

5.2   Receiving Flags

The students progress the story by emailing the flags they find when solving
exercises to one of the story's characters via a mail server which runs locally on
the VM. The story engine polls the inbox of each character defined in the story
map; received emails are searched for candidate flags (32-character strings of
hexadecimal characters, matching the flag format described in Sect. 3.1). Candidate flags are decrypted using the course AES key to check their validity. When
an email has been processed, and telemetry data logged, the email is deleted
from the inbox; if there is no Internet connectivity, the email is deleted only
after a copy has been sent to the telemetry server. When a valid flag is found,
the story engine extracts which exercise and question number the flag corresponds to and identifies any requirements involving this flag in the story map. If
the flag has been sent to the correct character (as defined in the requirement's
sent_to attribute), the requirement's complete attribute is set to true.

5.3   Sending Emails

The most common task is for the story engine to send an email from one of
the characters to the student via the VM's mail server. Separate XML files
encode the body of each email to be sent, along with its subject, sender and
recipient (for team exercises, where each student is a different character). The
story engine completes an <email> task by reading the XML file defined by its
path attribute and sending an email based on its contents. By taking advantage
of the logical operators available in the <required> element, different emails
can be sent depending on the choices made by the student; a common pattern
is "send email w if flag x was received by user y, but not if event z has been
completed".

5.4   Posting News Stories

The website used in one of the final exercises features a news page containing
a client-side script that populates the page with all news updates encoded as
XML files located within a specific public directory on the web server. The story
engine can post updates to this page as the story progresses (*dynamic stories*)
simply by copying the XML file defined by the <news> element's path attribute
into the public directory; when the student reloads the page, the update becomes
visible.

It is also possible to define *static stories* unrelated to the overall story in
the story map via <static_story> elements, which are posted to the website's
news page at predefined times regardless of how the student is engaging with the
story. Static stories give a sense of realism to the website, and provide a regular
supply of news updates, giving the student a reason to keep checking the news
page.

5.5   Telemetry

To allow the course staff to observe the decisions taken by the students, the story engine sends a copy of any emails sent to the story's characters, along with the student's VM identifier (as described in Sect. 3.1), to an external telemetry server controlled by the course staff.

Given that the student must include flags they find in the emails they send in order to advance the story, it is possible to combine these emails with the telemetry functionality to track which flags have been discovered by the student, rather than requiring the students to submit their flags to a separate flag submission server operated by the course staff. This provides a way of forcing students to interact with the story in order to gain credit for completing exercises; however, this was undesirable for our iteration of the course, which featured the story as a trial extension.

6   The Story

Progression and storytelling, as identified by Stott and Neustaedter [26], are two key concepts of game design that can be successfully applied to teaching and learning. This approach, however, is less prevalent in cybersecurity education. Our objective was to create an exciting, alluring and believable story, with the eventual aim of increasing student engagement with the course.

Our story follows the three-act screenwriting structure [27] commonly used in Hollywood scripts. Each exercise corresponds to a separate stage within the story arc: a call to adventure, crossing a threshold, overcoming obstacles, a setback, and a final push. This ensures that the story arc keeps the students engaged and excited to progress through the story.

One consideration when developing the plot of a story is whether the nature of the events is appropriate for the target audience. We applied the BBFC [2] and ESRB [10] classification schemes to our story, and found that its mild references to drugs and violence and moderate threat would likely cause it to be rated "12" or "Teen" respectively, making it appropriate for undergraduate students. The story engine is agnostic of the story map and its auxiliary files that define the emails and news updates shown to students, so our framework also supports plots that suit alternative audiences, for example younger teenagers or children.

6.1   Setting and Characters

The story takes place at Sensible Furniture, a fictional furniture company with a dark secret that is revealed as the story progresses. The plot features a protagonist—played by the student—and five other characters whose objective is to manipulate the protagonist into carrying out actions that follow their agendas:

Employee 427. Sensible Furniture's new cybersecurity advisor, and the main character and protagonist of the story, played by the student. In defining the protagonist, we chose a number instead of a name in order to (a) ensure all students can identify with the character, and (b) introduce a sense of impersonal coldness to the setting in which the story takes place.

Jak Kinkade. The CEO of Sensible Furniture. They introduce Employee 427 to their new working environment, reappearing towards the end of the story to give Employee 427 a final push towards a dangerous path.

Nik Adler. Employee 427's line manager at Sensible Furniture. Their main role is giving Employee 427 their daily tasks, and keeping them on track.

Charle Garcia, aka Chimp. An employee of Sensible Furniture. At the start of the story, Charle is known by the alias "Chimp" and approaches Employee 427 to convince them to join their side, hinting that the company's bosses are suspicious characters. Chimp's character represents the outcast, the undercover potential ally who will guide Employee 427 along the path of righteousness.

PC Thomson Gazal. A police officer, appearing when Employee 427 experiences a crisis and the available options seem to be limited. Thomson presents a new opportunity for Employee 427 to choose the path of righteousness.

Carol Miller. The IT administrator of Sensible Furniture by day, and a questionable character by night. She appears towards the end of the story, in order to give it a new twist. Carol offers Employee 427 a different perspective on the events that have unfolded and a new opportunity: a role in the criminal underworld.

6.2 Plot

An overview of our story's structure, and how the different stages of the story map to the course's exercises described in Sect. 2.2, can be seen in Fig. 3. It depicts all of the story's characters, and all information—flags, emails and news updates—that can be exchanged between the student and the story engine. The arrows show the possible paths the student can follow at any given point, together with their effects on the story's progression.

The first exercise requires the student to demonstrate an understanding of cryptography by writing code in the VM that decrypts certain encrypted files containing flags. This coincides with the opening stage of the story's plot, in which Employee 427 is welcomed to the company by CEO Jak Kinkade and introduced to Nik Adler, their line manager. Nik instructs Employee 427 to send the decrypted files to him. Moments later, Employee 427 receives another email from a person named Chimp (see Appendix A.1), suggesting that the management should be considered suspicious, and are "in cahoots with the underworld". Chimp requests that Employee 427 sends the decrypted files to them instead, and offers to join forces with Employee 427 to take down the management. This provides the student with the choice of following one of two paths: either be a good employee by sending the files to Nik, or risk trusting Chimp instead.

The second exercise requires the student to demonstrate an understanding of access control on Linux file systems and mount attacks against common access control misconfigurations to recover flags from restricted-access files on the VM. This exercise coincides with the second stage of the plot, in which Employee 427

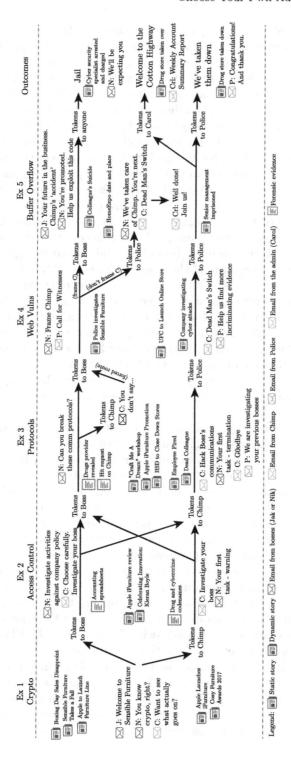

Fig. 3. An overview of our story, and how it fits into the exercise structure of our course

must learn more about the company's other employees by inspecting the contents of their home directories. The home directories contain clues that there is illegal activity occurring within the company, but give no indication of who is involved; this is intended to make the student question their previous decision. They find accounting spreadsheets in Nik's home directory with some suspicious entries: code names for drugs and cybercrime. In Chimp's home directory, some files containing information about drugs and cybercrime transactions can be found. At this point in the story, the student can change paths by emailing their flags to the character they chose not to email in the first stage of the story.

The third exercise involves breaking some encrypted communication protocols and requires the student to launch attacks against implementations of those protocols running on the VM in order to recover flags. This coincides with the third stage of the plot, which begins to seal Employee 427's fate. Employee 427 intercepts and decrypts secret messages being sent over the company's network; the messages reveal who the drugs provider is and, disconcertingly, a request for a hit on Chimp. At this stage of the story, if Employee 427 is cooperating with Nik, they cannot switch sides: if they try to email the recovered flags to Chimp, Chimp will bitterly refuse to accept them and tells Employee 427 to continue on their current path. If Employee 427 is collaborating with Chimp, a setback appears: Employee 427 is fired from Sensible Furniture, and receives an email from Chimp informing them that their activity has been discovered and directing Employee 427 to communicate with PC Gazal. The company website's news page will then display two new updates: one announcing that Employee 427 has been fired, and another reporting that Charle Garcia, a former employee, has "committed suicide".

The fourth exercise focuses on web security, and requires the student to perform a variety of attacks against an interactive website hosted on a web server running on the VM, leading to the discovery of the Cotton Highway, a black-market website hidden behind it. This coincides with the fourth stage of the plot, in which the plot thickens on both paths. On the path where Employee 427 cooperates with Nik, they receive a surprising request: investigate and attack the company website, and, if illegal activity is found, frame Chimp (who is still alive on this path). At the same time, PC Gazal introduces himself, asking Employee 427 to become a confidential informant. Employee 427's situation seems very grim on this path, and Gazal's introduction heralds a chance at redemption: the student can choose to continue down what seems like a dark road and frame Chimp for the illegal activity on the website, or turn to the police. On the path where Employee 427 collaborated with Chimp before their premature death, Employee 427 receives a "dead man's switch" email set up by Chimp to be sent automatically in the event that something bad were to happen to them. The email reveals Chimp's real identity, and contains information incriminating Nik and Jak in drug trafficking and hiring hitmen. At this point in the story, only two courses of action are apparent for Employee 427: either continue working with Nik and Jak and fall in with the criminal underworld, or cooperate with PC Gazal and hope to be exonerated.

The fifth exercise requires the student to reverse-engineer a number of programs, including a service that runs as the `root` user on the VM, and exploit a vulnerability to gain superuser access to the VM. This coincides with the final stage of the plot, which places the spotlight on the heretofore background character Carol, Sensible Furniture's IT administrator. Carol reveals that she operates the Cotton Highway, the company's hidden black-market website. If the student chose to collaborate with PC Gazal in the previous stage, she offers Employee 427 a potential third course of action: use their newfound superuser access to the Sensible Furniture systems to join the criminal underworld and supplant Nik and Jak as the drug kingpin. With the police closing in on Nik and Jak, Carol's offer is the last twist of the story. The news of Charle's apparent suicide appears on the company website. However, it is later revealed that this was a contract killing arranged by Nik and Jak.

The story's ending depends on the decisions made by the student:

- If Employee 427 remains loyal to Nik and Jak, they have no escape and, regardless of who they choose to turn to, they are ultimately sent to jail along with Nik and Jak. Nik menacingly informs Employee 427 that they are expecting his arrival (see Appendix A.2).
- If Employee 427 sides with Chimp and turns over the last set of flags to PC Gazal, a happier ending occurs: Nik and Jak are imprisoned, and the Cotton Highway is shut down. PC Gazal also reveals that Chimp was his fiancée, thanking Employee 427 for their help in apprehending Chimp's murderers.
- If Employee 427 accepts Carol's offer, they take over the Cotton Highway, supplanting Nik and Jak as the drug kingpin. If Employee 427 previously betrayed the managers, they receive a threatening email from Nik, letting them know Chimp had been "taken care of", and that Employee 427 is the next target on the list.

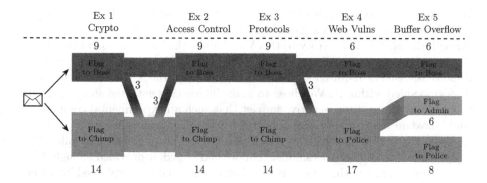

Fig. 4. The decisions taken by students on the course to progress through the story (Color figure online)

6.3   Student Choices

Figure 4 depicts the decisions made by the 23 students who chose to engage with the story, as reported to our telemetry server. The paths are colour-coded as follows: red paths indicate cooperation with Nik, green paths indicate collaboration with Chimp and PC Gazal, and blue paths indicate acceptance of Carol's offer.

At the start of the story, 9 students chose to follow Nik's orders, and 14 chose to trust Chimp. However, in the second stage of the plot, where they are given some clues that illegal activity is occurring within the company, 3 students from each path chose to switch sides. This behaviour substantiated our expectation that students would not blindly follow a specific path to the story's conclusion, but would instead doubt their choices in response to events that occurred within the story, or would simply switch sides just to see what (if any) effect their actions would have on the plot.

Allegiances remain steady for the third stage of the plot, while the fourth stage sees 3 more students shifting from following management orders to refusing to frame Chimp for the illegal behaviour occurring within the company and instead cooperating with the police. At the end of this stage, we see only 6 students remaining loyal to the management, while 17 of them are cooperating with PC Gazal in order to find incriminating evidence on Nik and Jak.

The appearance of Carol in the final stage of the plot divides the students who had previously been cooperating with the police, with 8 choosing to continue cooperating, and 6 choosing instead to become a drug kingpin. We also note that 3 students abandoned the story between these stages. The roughly-even split of story endings emphasises that students felt that all three paths were viable, validating the quality of writing and our story design.

7   Evaluation

We now perform an analysis of the effect of introducing the VM and CTF-style challenges to our cybersecurity course, and then assess the value introduced through the addition of a story to this VM. Unlike the introduction of the story, the introduction of the VM was a major change to the course: all of the continuous assessment required students to interact with the VM and submit valid flags embedded within it. We chose to make interacting with the story optional to avoid any unexpected negative impact that such an experimental component could have on the course's large cohort if it were made compulsory.

From a cohort of 144 students, a self-selected sample of 23 chose to follow the story; while this number was smaller than we had hoped, it provided enough data to carry out an interesting analysis. The low uptake could be explained by a lack of regular promotion of the story, or by students being less inclined to involve themselves in an aspect of the course that was not mandatory. Students who chose to follow the story were not given an inherent advantage in the continuous assessment compared with those who chose not to: as discussed in Sect. 4, we awarded a statistically-insignificant bonus mark for the continuous assessment component of the course as an incentive to interact with the story, and none of the paths in the storyline contained hints about how to proceed with the exercises.

7.1   Assessing the Impact of Introducing a CTF-Style VM

We first consider correlations between flag submissions and continuous assessment marks following the introduction of the VM in the 2013/14 iteration of the course. Recall from Sect. 2.1 that to complete an exercise, students were required to submit not only flags they recovered from the VM, but also written descriptions of vulnerabilities that were exploited to recover the flags and proposals for fixing those vulnerabilities. We leveraged the data submitted to the central flag submission server to compare how successful a student was at recovering flags (which was assessed automatically by the flag submission server) with the quality of their written answers (which was assessed manually by the course staff). From this, we can consider whether it is possible to replace manual marking of exercises with a fully-automated solution based solely on flag submissions.

Figure 5 shows a set of scatter plots of each student's continuous assessment mark compared with the number of valid flags they submitted, across the 2013/14 and 2014/15 iterations of the course. Each point reflects a single student; the number of flags submitted (on the y axis) is weighted for difficulty. We observe a strong correlation between the number of flags submitted and the continuous assessment mark, as shown in Table 1. We note that this correlation is not uniform across all grades: it is weaker for students who achieved the highest grade (awarded for a mark of 70 or greater) than it is for those who achieved lower grades.

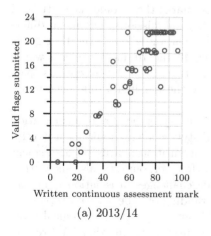

(a) 2013/14

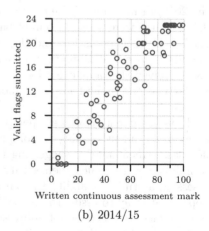

(b) 2014/15

Fig. 5. Scatter plots of students' written continuous assessment marks and the number of valid flags they submitted

Table 1. The correlation between the number of valid flags submitted by a student and their written continuous assessment mark for the course

	Iteration of course	
	2013/14	2014/15
All marks	0.92	0.93
Marks ≥ 70	0.37	0.68
Marks < 70	0.91	0.90

We found that students who submitted a valid flag for a given question also received at least a good mark for their written answer for that question. The difference between good and outstanding marks can be attributed to higher-attaining students demonstrating a deeper understanding of the course content and cybersecurity issues associated with a particular question. For instance, when students were asked to fix flaws in the protocols in Exercise 3, only students with a strong understanding of the protocols could propose and describe adequate solutions, regardless of whether they were able to recover the corresponding flags.

We note that the 2014/15 iteration of the course was simpler than other iterations: the reverse-engineering exercise was unassessed, as were the written questions in the protocol analysis exercise requiring students to propose fixes for the protocol vulnerabilities. For this iteration, we observe a stronger correlation between the continuous assessment marks and the number of valid flags submitted. As with 2013/14, we observe a weaker correlation for students who achieved the highest grade, although it is not as pronounced.

Figure 6 shows the continuous assessment marks that students achieved in the 2013/14 iteration of the course versus the marks they would have attained if the course were assessed purely based on flag submissions. The mean difference between marks is 1.5, and the standard deviation is 2.5. Given that grade boundaries occur at 10-mark intervals between 40 and 70, most students would have received the same overall grade, although there are some exceptions (particularly at the highest grade boundary, where the maximum difference was 9 marks).

From a student attainment perspective, our analysis shows a high correlation between a student's ability to complete CTF-style challenges and their continuous assessment marks, suggesting that flag acquisition is a useful assessment technique for academic cybersecurity courses. However, our data also shows that assessing a student's ability to complete such challenges in isolation is not an appropriate way to assess the level of understanding of cybersecurity topics.

One facet of teaching not addressed by this analysis is the pedagogical value to students of formulating detailed, long-form answers to questions and receiving feedback on the assessments they complete. This requires a degree of self-reflection on behalf of the student. Higgins et al. [14] provide evidence that students are driven by more than just the potential of attaining high marks,

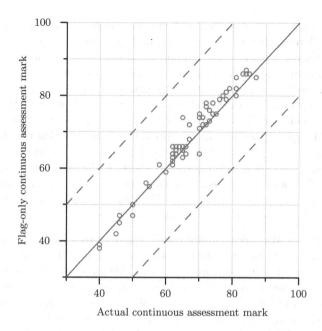

Fig. 6. Comparison of 2013/14 students' actual continuous assessment marks and the marks they would have been awarded had they only been assessed on their valid flag submissions

benefiting from feedback that allows them to further develop their engagement with the subject. In our course we provide detailed, personalised feedback for all written answers, something that students indicated was highly valued and a reason for their overall satisfaction with the course; consequently, our course was ranked third-best for feedback from assessments amongst all courses offered by the School. Using flag-only assessment would both deprive students of this feedback and decrease their satisfaction with the course. However, we must also acknowledge that manually marking submissions and providing this rich feedback is highly labour-intensive on the part of the course staff, and its viability depends heavily on the course's staff-to-student ratio.

In any taught course, there is the potential for students to plagiarise, whether accidentally or intentionally; the same potential exists when utilising flag-based assessment, although we can detect many incidents of such plagiarism automatically thanks to the unique VM identifier built in to the flag structure (see Sect. 3.1). Across all iterations of the course, we encountered three cases where groups of students had submitted flags with the same VM identifier, or the VM identifier was inconsistent with the student's previous flag submissions:

– In the first case, a group of four students submitted the same flag and similar written answers for a particular exercise. When interviewed, they admitted to copying each other's work; each student was given a warning and mark of 0 for the entire exercise.

- In the second case, two students submitted the same flag, but their written answers differed. After review, it transpired that the students were using low-powered devices with a small amount of internal storage, and were sharing the same instance of the VM on an external disk to save space; both students were given advice on how to avoid any potential repercussions.
- In the final case, a student had posted a screenshot of their VM's current state on a social media website showing that they had completed a particularly challenging question, in an apparent attempt to impress their peers; the screenshot included the flag they had managed to recover by completing the question, and some enterprising students had transcribed the flag from the screenshot and submitted it to the flag submission server ahead of the student who had recovered the flag. The students concerned were penalised for their lack of foresight or ethics as appropriate.

Conversely, we also occasionally encountered cases where students submitted different flags but identical written answers. We note that had we employed flag-only assessment, we would have been unable to detect this sort of plagiarism, and would thus have created a favourable environment for plagiarism in which students could feign understanding of the cybersecurity issues underpinning an exercise simply by following instructions for recovering flags from their own instance of the VM from a more knowledgeable student. Overall, we saw much lower rates of plagiarism on our course than on other courses that had a continuous assessment component contributing 20% to the final course mark; when asked informally, some students commented that the requirement to submit written answers alongside flag submissions meant that they saw no benefit to plagiarising flags.

7.2 Assessing the Impact of Introducing a Story

We now consider how the course was impacted in the 2016/17 academic year by the addition of a story that was optional for students to follow.

We first compare the final course marks awarded to students who did and did not follow the story. Table 2 shows a summary of the final course marks (out of 100) for the 2016/17 iteration of the course; a histogram of these marks is shown in Fig. 7. Figure 7 shows that the minimum mark for students who interacted with the story was 50, with the majority achieving a mark of 70–80. We also note that of the 20 students with the highest continuous assessment marks, 15 had interacted with the story rather than completing the exercises solely through flag submission and written answers.

Table 2. Summary of final marks for the 2016/17 iteration of the course

Student category	Population	Average mark
Followed story	23	72.35
Did not follow story	121	61.27
All students	144	63.04

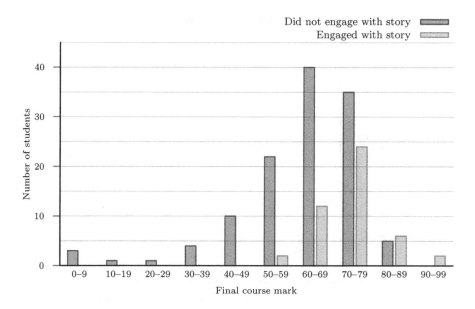

Fig. 7. Histogram of final marks for the 2016/17 iteration of the course

To assess the impact of the VM's story on student engagement with the 2016/17 iteration of the course, we released an additional assignment during the University's "reading week"—when no teaching takes place, and students are expected to engage in independent learning—to research and write a report on current cybersecurity issues. We cross-referenced the report each student wrote with data sent by their VM to the telemetry server, and found that reports written by students who engaged with the VM's story contained on average 74% more words than reports written by those who did not. We note that marks allocated to this assignment were given simply for completing the report; we believe that writing a longer report is a good indicator of greater engagement with the course, and therefore that interacting with the story is correlated with increased engagement.

From the telemetry data, we discovered that students generally submitted their flags to the flag submission server before using them to progress the story via the story engine in the VM. 7 students immersed themselves in the story more than others, and engaged in conversation with the story engine; a sample of the emails they sent can be found in Appendix B. This suggests that the story was believable and engaged students, encouraging them to spend more time on course-related activities.

Finally, to account for individual student ability, we analysed the difference between each student's final mark in our course and their average mark across all courses for the previous year. We removed from the analysis 7 students who did not have an average mark for the previous year (this usually occurs in welfare cases), and 2 students who did not submit any continuous assessment or sit the exam for

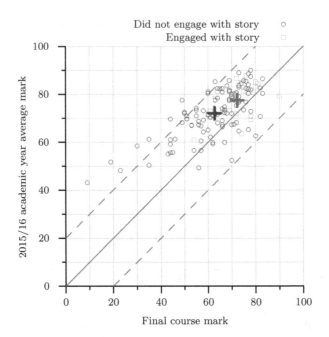

Fig. 8. Scatter plot of students' final marks for the 2016/17 iteration of the course versus their average marks for the previous year

our course. Following this, we tested for any differences between the sets of students who did and did not interact with the story. The results are shown in the scatter plot in Fig. 8; the analysis showed that the mean difference for students who did not interact with the story was -9.22 (i.e., their final mark for our course was on average 9.22 marks lower than their previous-year average mark), whereas the mean was only -5.09 for those who did interact with the story (p-value < 0.05). This shows that interaction with the story did in fact improve student performance, and the difference in means is not likely a result of chance. The lower average mark for both sets of students could be explained by the natural increase in difficulty of courses in successive years of a degree programme.

To gauge how well the story was received by the cohort, we requested the students' participation in an online post-course survey about the story; we received 52 responses. We received excellent feedback: those who interacted with the story gave an average score of 5.5/10 when asked how much the story increased their engagement with the course (with 6% stating that it significantly increased their level of engagement), and gave an average score of 7/10 when asked how fun they found the story (with 12% rating it as extremely fun).

In the same survey, we asked students who began the story whether they saw it to completion; 38% did. The majority of students completed the story in 1 h, and it was, predominantly, the curiosity about how the story would progress that motivated them. Those who did not engage with the story at all gave different reasons for their choice, e.g. more important priorities in other courses. Amongst those who did not engage with the story, there was a variation in the expected time required to compete the story, with most suggesting 2 h to more than 3 h. This disparity—between the perception of how time-consuming it would be to interact with the story amongst those who chose not to, and how time-consuming it actually was amongst those who did—may have influenced take-up; had we informed the students in advance of the expected amount of time it would take to complete the story, it is possible that more students would have participated. Some students were unable to complete the story regardless of their desire to do so, as they had not recovered a sufficient number of flags to advance the plot for at least one of the exercises, and did not have extenuating circumstances requiring us to issue a welfare flag allowing them to advance the plot forcefully. These issues could both be addressed in future iterations of the course.

Overall, the consensus of the concept of the story was very positive, with 97% of students who engaged with it and 84% of those who did not agreeing that the story was a good idea; students commented that it did (or would) make the course more interesting and increase engagement, with an alternative reward to what students would typically expect. When asked if it would be a good idea to add a story framework to other courses taught in the School, 63% of students who engaged with the story and 59% of those who did not agreed, suggesting a list of courses that could benefit from the introduction of a story. This suggests that not only did our story framework add value to our course, it could potentially add value to others too.

Finally, when asked about the story itself and how satisfied they were with its conclusion, the students gave an average rating of 3.3/5, with 17% being extremely satisfied. An average score of 5.9/10 was given for the plausibility of the plot, with 3% considering it extremely believable. When asked how interactive and captivating they found the story, scores of 6.2/10 and 6.3/10 were given respectively, with 13% of students stating that they found the story extremely captivating and were keen to see how the story progressed. When asked to rate the quality of the storytelling, an average score of 7.5/10 was given, with 18% rating the story as very well-written. These factors may have contributed to the level of engagement with the story and the course in general. A sample of the comments we received is given in Appendix C.

From the results of the survey, we conclude that students who engaged with the story were encouraged through their captivation with and curiosity about the story to devote more time to the course and therefore complete it with higher continuous assessment marks. Even those who did not engage with the story considered it a worthwhile addition to the course, so we suspect that, if the expected participation requirements had been made clearer from the outset, we would have observed greater levels of engagement. The survey demonstrates the positive impression of the story on the 2016/17 cohort and sheds light on why only a relatively small number of students completed the story; the reasons for this can easily be addressed, and the survey gives us confidence that interacting with the story could be made compulsory in the next iteration of the course.

8   Conclusion

In this article, we have presented a virtualised framework for integrating Jeopardy-style CTF challenges into cybersecurity courses, along with a narrative extension to this framework. Students run the framework on their own hardware, eliminating the need for course staff to maintain a complex backend infrastructure. The narrative extension is highly parameterisable, making it easy to modify or rewrite the story between iterations of a course. We have evaluated both the framework and the narrative extension by integrating them into the continuous assessment component of our own 11-week introductory cybersecurity course, the former in the 2013/14 academic year and the latter in the 2016/17 academic year; this allowed us to evaluate the impact of the framework and chosen story on students' academic performance and the broader student learning experience.

Through an analysis of the continuous assessment and final course marks obtained by the students over two iterations of our course, we found that a student's ability to recover flags in the CTF challenges correlated closely with their overall performance on the course; as our framework generates and embeds flags and validates flag submissions automatically, this allows for a degree of automated marking to be employed, although we would not advocate this as the sole method of assessing students' level of understanding of cybersecurity topics. Through an analysis of students' marks for both our course and other courses, we found that students who engaged with the story in our course performed better than their average mark in other courses would have predicted, whereas those who did not engage with the story performed no better (or worse); post-course surveys indicated that students valued the plausibility and entertainment value of the plot, thus providing evidence that the introduction of a narrative into the course further improved student engagement and attainment.

As future work, we are considering enhancements that can be made to the framework's story engine to make narratives more realistic and immersive, e.g. the addition of social media communication or pre-recorded videos.

Acknowledgement. This work was supported by grant GEN1214 from the Higher Education Academy.

A   Sample Emails from Our Story

As described in Sect. 6.2, the story engine advances the plot in part by sending emails from various characters in the story to an email account accessible to the student from within the VM. Two emails that form part of the story we created for our course are shown below; the student assumes the role of Employee 427.

A.1   Introduction of Chimp

The story begins with this email to Employee 427 from a mysterious character initially known only as Chimp.

Hey!

I told those guys in IT they need to give you stronger encryption keys
for email. Guess old moneybags decided it's too expensive to actually
care. What do you care, anyway? You're the new cybergeek I see - what a
generic term nowadays which has absolutely no context.

Who am I? You'll find out soon enough, but you need to prove youself to
me first. Why am I emailing you? Well, congratulations smarto - you
bagged last place in the prize list. The guy who sat in your seat was
involved in something big, but he went missing. So... what happens if
one of your best goes 'away'? You replace them with someone better, or
at least that's probably what HR said to you to sell the job.

This is where you come in. The email you just got from Adler? There's
more context than just a simple decryption task to get you started.
Working in 'cahoots' with the underworld is the manager's game, pinning
it on the little people in that bottom 99.99% leaves them grinning like
a cheshire cat. You had better know what I'm getting at or I'm finding
someone else.

So - those files you got for 'decryption'? Giving the answers to the top
0.001% isn't going to go down well for someone. Someone who is
completely innocent and has zero involvement, but they want to get rid
of soooo much.

All you have to do is give me as many cryptographic tokens you can find
inside them instead, and satisfy the idiots upstairs on the 42nd floor
by sending them some junk response a few minutes later - leave it til
your lunch break if you want. I don't really care how you play them off.

Anyway - I'm not going to tell you my life story, and I *really* don't
want to hear how your life story almost became some game. Just do what I
say and I'll make sure you're safe - just don't give me any curve balls,
and remember. *Once you're in, there's no leaving*.

```
 /~\
C oo
 _( ^)
/ ~\
```

A.2 An Epilogue

This email concludes one of the paths through the story, and is sent from Nik to
Employee 427 after the student completes the final exercise if they chose to work
with Nik in the third stage of the plot (represented by the red path in Fig. 4).

427,
Your arraignment is looming - you've been arrested, charged and judge,
jury and (pity!) executioner are sending you for a little 'trip'.
We'll be there with open arms as you are brought into your cell, only to
be known to the inmates as 'the traitor'.

Here's something to think about before you arrive. Sleep with one eye
open. You're mine now.

N.

B Emails Sent by Students to the Story Engine

As discussed in Sect. 7.2, 7 students displayed greater-than-average engagement
with the story by sending (sometimes in-character) prose to the story engine
along with the flags they had recovered. The story engine forwards copies of all
emails sent to it by the student to our telemetry server (refer to Sect. 5.5 for
further details); a sample of the emails these students sent is shown below.

- Hey mate, would you mind putting this key in your
  ~/.ssh/authorized_keys? No particular reason

- Found a token, have fun: 653d72c294c382de153dccce86f63ddb

- Hi there,
  Something big you say? I hope that I can trust you with these...

- Here.
  855e8fb63feed93e2c73785fc83737cf
  65e802467c57f7d0ecac094ad9d496af
  14673f7f3467e826b9f0425b5f14466a
  What is really going on in this place?
  427.

- Subject: HELP!!!
  I have some incriminating evidence on my bosses!
  I don't know who to turn to!
  Here's some statements from my boss' private directory!

- Well I'm just interested to see what happens here, I'll take the red
  pill.
  Here's the first token: 463325b2759dc7d7c901755c6876b187

C Post-course Story Survey Feedback

To evaluate the impact of the introduction of a story to the 2016/17 iteration of
the course (see Sect. 7.2), we surveyed students after the course had ended for
their opinions on the story. We received 52 responses; a sample of the feedback
the students gave is shown below.

- "I loved the story but it seemed to finish abruptly, and it wasn't long enough! "More emails would have been nice too, as we only got to interact with the story five times (one for each exercise).
  "I did like the complicated underground manoeuvres of the Sensible Furniture crowd. The Charles Garcia reveal and discovering the message that led to his demise was also a big moment in the tale.
  "RIP Chimp, may he never be forgotten"
- "Was genuinely upset when Chimp died. RIP."
- "Loved it. Great idea from start to finish!"
- "I found the story more enjoyable after finishing all of the exercises because then the story could be retried and different endings could be found."
- "I liked the opportunity to choose a path, but also be able to change at certain points. Felt involved with the characters and had a fitting ending."
- "The bad guys got what they deserved! Justice yay!"
- "Interesting to see how the story developed from certain situations."
- "I didn't lose (end up in jail), the taste of victory is sweet."
- "It's fun and enjoyable and definitely sets the exercises apart from other courses"
- "Gives context to the exercises, bit of fun to make people want to do them."
- "It gives the exercises meaning, rather than doing them for the sake of doing them"
- "Engages students to pay attention to the exercises, gives them a little real-life context (which often aids understanding) and instils confidence in students that the course is being very well-managed."

References

1. Beuran, R., Chinen, K.i., Tan, Y., Shinoda, Y.: Towards effective cybersecurity education and training (2016)
2. British Board of Film Classification. http://www.bbfc.co.uk
3. Bursztein, E., et al.: Webseclab security education workbench. In: 3rd Workshop on Cyber Security Experimentation and Test (CSET 2010) (2010)
4. Carnegie Mellon University: picoCTF 2017. https://2017.picoctf.com/about
5. Chapman, P., Burket, J., Brumley, D.: PicoCTF: a game-based computer security competition for high school students. In: USENIX Summit on Gaming, Games, and Gamification in Security Education (3GSE 2014) (2014)
6. Chothia, T., Holdcroft, S., Radu, A.I., Thomas, R.J.: Jail, hero or drug lord? Turning a cyber security course into an 11 week choose your own adventure story. In: USENIX Workshop on Advances in Security Education (ASE 2017). USENIX Association (2017)
7. Chothia, T., Novakovic, C.: An offline capture the flag-style virtual machine and an assessment of its value for cybersecurity education. In: USENIX Summit on Gaming, Games, and Gamification in Security Education (3GSE 2015) (2015)
8. Cyber Security Challenge UK. https://www.cybersecuritychallenge.org.uk
9. Davis, A., Leek, T., Zhivich, M., Gwinnup, K., Leonard, W.: The fun and future of CTF. In: USENIX Summit on Gaming, Games, and Gamification in Security Education (3GSE 2014) (2014)

10. Entertainment Software Rating Board. http://www.esrb.org
11. Feng, W.: A "Divergent"-themed CTF and urban race for introducing security and cryptography. In: USENIX Workshop on Advances in Security Education (ASE 2016). USENIX Association, Austin (2016). https://www.usenix.org/conference/ase16/workshop-program/presentation/feng
12. Ford, V., Siraj, A., Haynes, A., Brown, E.: Capture the flag unplugged: an offline cyber competition. In: Proceedings of the 2017 ACM SIGCSE Technical Symposium on Computer Science Education, pp. 225–230. ACM (2017)
13. Hex-Rays SA: IDA: Freeware Version. https://www.hex-rays.com/products/ida/support/download_freeware.shtml
14. Higgins, R., Hartley, P., Skelton, A.: The conscientious consumer: reconsidering the role of assessment feedback in student learning. In: Studies in Higher Education, vol. 27 (2002)
15. Kapp, K.M.: The Gamification of Learning and Instruction: Game-Based Methods and Strategies for Training and Education, 1st edn. Pfeiffer & Company, San Francisco (2012)
16. Logan, P.Y., Clarkson, A.: Teaching students to hack: curriculum issues in information security. SIGCSE Bull. **37**(1), 157–161 (2005). http://doi.acm.org/10.1145/1047124.1047405
17. Massachusetts Institute of Technology, University of Cambridge: Cambridge 2 Cambridge. https://cambridge2cambridge.csail.mit.edu
18. McDaniel, L., Talvi, E., Hay, B.: Capture the flag as cyber security introduction. In: 49th Hawaii International Conference on System Sciences (HICSS), pp. 5479–5486. IEEE (2016)
19. Mirkovic, J., Peterson, P.: Class capture-the-flag exercises. In: USENIX Summit on Gaming, Games, and Gamification in Security Education (3GSE 2014) (2014)
20. MWR InfoSecurity: HackFu: Run your own event, Part 3: creating the theatrics (2017). https://hackfu.mwrinfosecurity.com/run-your-own-event/the-theatrics/index.html
21. National Cyber Security Centre: CyberFirst courses. https://www.ncsc.gov.uk/information/cyberfirst-courses
22. Oracle Corporation: VirtualBox. https://www.virtualbox.org
23. Radu, A.I., Thomas, S.L.: Organising monkeys or how to run a hacking club. In: Workshop on Cybersecurity Training & Education (VIBRANT 2015) (2015)
24. Schreuders, Z.C., Ardern, L.: Generating randomised virtualised scenarios for ethical hacking and computer security education: SecGen implementation and deployment. In: Workshop on Cybersecurity Training & Education (VIBRANT 2015) (2015)
25. Sheldon, L.: The Multiplayer Classroom: Designing Coursework as a Game, 1st edn. Course Technology Press, Boston (2011)
26. Stott, A., Neustaedter, C.: Analysis of Gamification in Education. Surrey, Canada (2013)
27. Trottier, D.: The screenwriter's Bible: A Complete Guide to Writing, Formatting, and Selling Your Script. Silman-James Press, Los Angeles (1998)
28. University of Cambridge: Inter-ACE. https://inter-ace.org
29. Vigna, G., et al.: Ten years of iCTF: the good, the bad, and the ugly. In: USENIX Summit on Gaming, Games, and Gamification in Security Education (3GSE 2014) (2014)

A Virtual Classroom for Cybersecurity Education

Jens Haag[1], Harald Vranken[2,3]([✉]), and Marko van Eekelen[2,3]

[1] Cologne University of Applied Sciences, Cologne, Germany
Jens.Haag@ou.nl
[2] Open Universiteit, Heerlen, The Netherlands
{Harald.Vranken,Marko.vanEekelen}@ou.nl
[3] Radboud University, Nijmegen, The Netherlands

Abstract. Education in general and cybersecurity education in particular can be made more attractive by adding hands-on experience to classrooms. This requires new technology, such as virtualisation, to be developed fully geared towards the needs of educational purposes. Over the years, several techniques have been developed by the authors. In this paper, the authors first give a full account of their earlier work on a distributed virtual computer lab for cybersecurity education. Then, this virtual lab is extended with educational enhancements, such as an intelligent tutoring system, which resulted in a prototype for a virtual classroom for cybersecurity education.

Keywords: Virtual lab · Distributed lab · Cybersecurity · Education

1 Introduction

Knowledge distribution and knowledge acquisition are essentials for educational establishments. Usually they are built on two components: *theory* and *hands-on experience*, where "hands-on" refers to tasks in which learners observe or manipulate real objects or material. We find this in many academic disciplines, amongst others the field of information technology (IT) resp. computer science. Here, the theory is traditionally taught in lessons or by textbooks. The knowledge that students learn, is often illustrated, deepened and anchored by carrying out practical (hands-on) exercises.

While the content of a discipline is usually fixed in the curriculum, a challenge is how to organize the hands-on experience. Especially in the field of communication technology and IT security, which are sub-disciplines of computer science, special requirements occur with respect to the hands-on learning environment, e.g. the isolated real-world character and manageability.

Usually, an exercise is derived from and also targeted at a real-world setting, e.g. setting up and configuring hosts and networks or attacking a system within a network. This requires that the learning environment feels like and behaves

© Springer-Verlag GmbH Germany, part of Springer Nature 2019
Z. Pan et al. (Eds.): Transactions on Edutainment XV, LNCS 11345, pp. 173–208, 2019.
https://doi.org/10.1007/978-3-662-59351-6_13

as close as the real-world setting to the learner. To gather experiences, learners should be able to try out things they learned in theory. This includes doing things right as well as doing things wrong. In the scope of communication technology, this could mean that students will set up a network environment, either with a valid or an invalid configuration. With respect to IT security, this could mean that a student will protect a system and another one tries to attack it. Depending on the aim of a certain task, everything is working fine, the environment gets down or damaged, or something in between can happen. However, this requires that the learning environment is isolated from the real world in order to prevent interferences. Also, the manageability of the hands-on learning environment is crucial for both lecturer as well as learner. E.g. the lecturer may use the environment in different courses with several learners, so a time-saving clean-up and reset process of the environment is required to get an equal initial state for each learner in each course. For the learner, a great user experience as well as a short training period might result in an increased acceptance level which finally can lead to an improved learning outcome.

A common way to organise hands-on experiences is to use a *computer laboratory* or *computer security laboratory* for education. A computer lab in the scope of communication technology and cybersecurity typically consists of a computer or a group of computer systems usually connected into a network. The systems as well as the network behave as in the real world, but they are not connected to it - they are neither part of a critical infrastructure nor can connect to any. In other words the system and also the network are *isolated* from the outside world. Many tasks can be realised using a computer lab which otherwise would not be possible, are forbidden or can cause damage. In the scope of communication technology and cybersecurity, the use of a computer lab is a suitable and common way for hands-on experiences. Nevertheless, this situation still holds challenges and thus can be improved.

This paper introduces a virtualised classroom environment for use in cybersecurity education. We address the technical details of the distributed virtualised computer lab that we developed, and we also show how eduction is organised and supported in this lab. We give a complete overview of our work in this field by including the essential parts of our previous work. Evaluations of students' experiences with our lab show that students enjoy the hands-on experience, which nicely implements the concept of edutainment.

Educational Context

The Open Universiteit (Netherlands) as well as the Cologne University of Applied Sciences (Germany) offer courses in the field of computer networks and cybersecurity. While the Open Universiteit is a university for distance education, the Cologne University of Applied Sciences is a traditional on-campus university. Both universities offer practical courses in networking and cybersecurity, but the setting is mostly different.

Research Challenge

Providing a safe playground is only one requirement of a virtual classroom. An additional challenge is to figure out what environment fits best in a certain learning scenario. This requires to find a balance between technical opportunities, educational requirements and also the demands of the learners.

Overview

Section 2 presents our distributed virtual computer lab, which provides the basis for the virtual classroom to develop. In Sect. 3 an intelligent tutor system is described which extends the basis with an exercise assistant working towards a virtual classroom. With the educational enhancements of Sect. 4 the virtual classroom prototype emerges. In Sect. 5 we briefly discuss implementation and evaluation details. We describe related work in Sect. 6 and we conclude the paper in Sect. 7.

2   A Distributed Virtual Computer Lab

2.1   The Basis: A Virtual Computer Lab

Initially we developed a Virtual Computer Lab (VCL) [18] as a stand-alone environment, composed of two nested software virtualisation layers, that each student can install on his/her computer. The software components to build the VCL are freeware or open source, and are distributed to students through a DVD or the university's cloud storage.

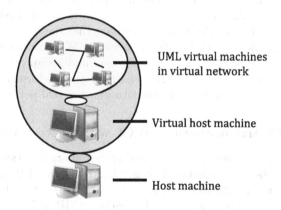

UML virtual machines in virtual network

Virtual host machine

Host machine

Fig. 1. Architecture of the VCL

The VCL is composed of one physical host and two virtualisation layers, as shown in Fig. 1. The host machine is the student's computer, which runs an arbitrary operating system, i.e., the host operating system. The first virtualisation layer creates the virtual host machine. It consists of virtualisation software such as VMware Player (freeware) or Oracle VM VirtualBox (open source), which runs on the host machine just like an ordinary application. Versions of this software are available for a large range of platforms. VirtualBox for instance runs on host machines with either Windows, Linux or Mac OS X. This first virtualisation layer therefore runs on nearly all student computers, regardless of the hardware and the host operating system. The virtual host machine runs the virtual host operating system. For the VCL we selected Linux, since it is open source and can be distributed to students without licensing costs. In fact, we selected Knoppix, a bootable live Linux system containing a collection of GNU/Linux applications and the KDE graphical desktop environment.

The second virtualisation layer is a Linux application, called Netkit [17], that runs inside the virtual host machine. This second virtualisation layer allows to instantiate multiple virtual machines that all run Linux. Netkit applies virtualisation based upon User Mode Linux (UML) [33,34] and allows to setup and configure UML virtual machines with virtual network interfaces, and to connect these into virtual networks.

The hardware requirements for running the VCL are very modest. A few UML virtual machines can already be run smoothly on a PC with a Pentium-4 processor and 256 MB memory. The VCL has been used successfully in our security courses by hundreds of students with only few minor problems.

2.2   Adding Distributivity: A Distributed Virtual Computer Lab

Our next step was to extend the VCL into a Distributed Virtual Computer Lab (DVCL) [26] that enables two or more geographically distant students to connect their local VCLs across an external intermediate network, which is usually the internet. Figure 2 shows such a setup. To preserve the isolated property of a computer security lab, the DVCL system ensures that the intermediate network cannot intercommunicate with the virtual network. Within their VCLs, the students are able to work synchronously in a group, and assign roles and tasks for working on an assignment (e.g. hacker, administrator, and user). As result, the working scenarios are much closer to the situations in real networks.

2.3   Adding Central Authority: DVCL with Central Authority

Our DVCL with central authority [27] optimises the organisation and management when students work together. Initially, the DVCL used Peer-2-Peer (P2P) connections to connect students' VCLs with each other. For that reason, the students need to know the communication endpoint (IP address and TCP port) of their remote partner(s). Furthermore, additional network configuration (e.g. port forwarding) is mandatory. Connecting three or more VCLs is possible, but can lead into infinite circular flow of network packets in the case of a misconfiguration. Overall, our experiences with the DVCL showed that a significant effort was needed by the students to manage their VCL. To optimise the organisation and management, we developed a central administration point ('central

Fig. 2. Architecture of the DVCL

authority') hosted by the university to connect remote VCLs into sessions and to control the packet flow between the VCLs. Now, each VCL must only know the address of the university server which is usually static and therefore can be easily provided by using a configuration file. Figure 3 illustrates two students connecting their VCLs by using the central administration point. Students do not need to know the communication endpoint of each other anymore; they simply join a distributed virtual network session or can create a new one.

Fig. 3. Architecture of the DVCL with central authority

3 Adding an Intelligent Tutoring System

Our evaluation showed that students of a traditional on-campus networking course deem it crucial for their learning success to be able to get support from a course advisor [29]. While an on-campus university will be able to provide course advisors, which can support students in so-called guided learning hours, this support is no longer feasible if students work e.g. at home in the evening hours using a virtual lab.

A common way to resolve this issue is an intelligent tutoring system (ITS). An intelligent tutoring system is a computer system that aims to provide instruction or feedback to learners, usually without requiring intervention from a human advisor [6,7]. We introduced a tutoring system called Electronic Exercise Assistant (EEA) for our DVCL environment. The aim of this EEA is to offer support and guidance for students while working out an exercise, even if a human course advisor is not available.

3.1 A Typical Exercise Example

A very common task for future IT network administrators is to setup, configure, and secure a network. Therefore, an example assignment for students participating in a networking course could be:

"Setup and configure a scenario with at least three hosts (client, router, server). Client and server should be located within different subnets. The client should be able to intercommunicate with the server by using the intermediate router. The routing should be based on static routing tables."

The minimal requirement for this setup is shown in Fig. 4, consisting of at least three hosts. The client and the server have one network interface; the router is equipped with two network interfaces: one interface connects to a network with the server, the other one with the client.

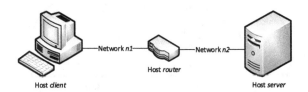

Fig. 4. Example network setup

In this example exercise, students will have to set up hosts and interconnect them accordingly within two different networks. They will have to assign appropriate IP addresses to these hosts and ultimately configure the routing by altering the routing tables on the hosts. Once the setup is configured properly, students can demonstrate the validity of their solution, e.g. by sending network packets between client and server.

While setting up and configuring this scenario, the students can gather several basic and advanced practical experiences, like designing, preparing, and setting up an example network scenario according to the assignment, configuring the hosts and network interfaces, configuring the routing, and discovering different behaviour caused by different configurations.

Solve the Exercise

To solve this exercise, students need to know at least the basic commands to start and to administrate the virtual lab (Netkit). In addition, they have to apply their networking knowledge to configure the hosts according to the assignment. Using the VCL, a valid and straightforward configuration to solve the example assignment may look like stated in Listing 1.1.

Listing 1.1. Valid solution using Netkit

```
1  // Create the hosts and networks in Netkit
   vstart client  --eth0=n1
3  vstart router  --eth0=n1 --eth1=n2
   vstart server  --eth0=n2

   // Assign IP address on the client
7  ifconfig eth0 10.0.0.1 up

9  // Assign IP address on the router
   ifconfig eth0 10.0.0.2 up
11 ifconfig eth1 11.0.0.2 up

13 // Assign IP address on the server
   ifconfig eth0 11.0.0.1 up

   // Set default gateway on the client
17 route add default gw 10.0.0.2

19 // Set default gateway on the server
   route add default gw 11.0.0.2

   // Connection test on client to the server
23 ping 11.0.0.1
```

3.2 Exercise Modelling

In the following we show how the exercises can be transferred into a formal representation, in order to be processed by a computer program. First we will show the partition of our example exercise into activities that will then be organised in a graph structure. This graph will then be extended with conditions that will make the activities verifiable. We also show a way to add feedback attributes to the graph in order to model a certain feedback strategy. Finally we introduce probing, a mechanism to improve the verifiability of activities.

Activities

Typically, exercises will start with an empty lab. Students have to perform activities that result in a working network environment, configured according to the requirements of the given exercise. While Listing 1.1 shows the commands needed to solve the exercise in Netkit, the minimal conceptual activities needed for solving this exercise are listed in Table 1.

Table 1. Activities needed to solve the example exercise

Activity	ID
The client network has to be created	A1
The server network has to be created	A2
The client has to be connected to the client network and an appropriate IP address has to be assigned	A3
The server has to be connected to the server network and an appropriate IP address has to be assigned	A4
One NIC of the router has to be connected to the client network and an IP address from the client network has to be assigned	A5
One NIC of the router has to be connected to the server network and an IP address from the server network has to be assigned	A6
The client has to be configured to use the router's NIC in the client network as default gateway	A7
The server has to be configured to use the router's NIC in the server network as default gateway	A8
Routing has to be enabled on the router	A9
Client and server must intercommunicate via the intermediate router using the IP protocol	A10

While A10 is the final activity, the order of the activities A1 through A9 shows only one possible sequence. The order can vary because some activities are independent from each other (e.g. A1 and A2), while some other activities have interdependencies (e.g. A1 is a precondition for A3).

These activities and their interdependencies can be modelled as an acyclic, directed graph with exactly one sink (node N with *outdegree(N)=0*) and at least one source (node M with *indegree(M)=0*). Activities are represented by nodes. A precondition is modelled as a directed edge from the predecessor to the successor, seamlessly indicating the order of the activities. The final activity will be represented by a sink. Activities without a precondition will be represented by sources.

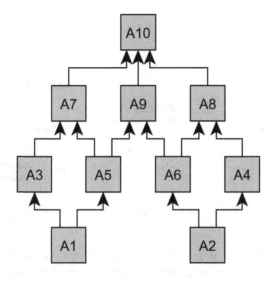

Fig. 5. Example graph

A valid graph for our example exercise is shown in Fig. 5. This graph is based on the activities stated in Table 1. The interdependencies and thus possible sequences of activities show a valid example. These can of course vary, depending on the exercise and the author's intent, too.

Conditions

In order to process the graph, the activities have to be verifiable. That means that a condition is needed to detect or to decide, whether an activity is deemed passed, i.e. whether the student has successfully solved a part of the exercise.

Network packets, obtained from the student's Netkit lab, can be used to detect and verify network properties and behavior of an Ethernet based network [28]. By modelling network specific expert knowledge as predicates and verifying these predicates using the captured network packets, it is possible to detect e.g. the presence of certain hosts and also routing behaviour. While our first prototype demonstrated the technical feasibility of that approach by using SQL queries to model predicates, we improved on it by using description logics [30].

For the terminological box (TBox) we created a network ontology for Ethernet based networks, representing the network layers 2 and above [31], including but not limited to the header and payload fields of the most commonly used protocols, e.g. Ethernet (RFC1042), ARP (RFC826), IP (RFC791), TCP (RFC793), and UDP (RFC768). In addition, we added a unique identifier for each packet and the network origin. An excerpt of our ontology for Ethernet networks is shown in Fig. 6.

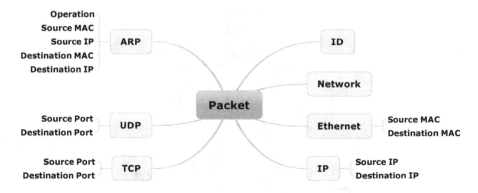

Fig. 6. Ontology excerpt for ethernet networks

Using this ontology it is possible to model expert knowledge as predicates using a logic programming language, e.g. Prolog [19]. For example, the expert knowledge to describe the network behaviour "routing" is:

> *"Routing occurs if an OSI layer 3 IP transmission of a network packet between two hosts is based on more than one OSI layer 2 transmissions."*

The technical background is shown in Fig. 7. The client wants to communicate with the server using the IP protocol, but the server is located in a different network segment. Direct intercommunication between client and server is not possible, because the underlying Ethernet protocol does not support communication over network borders. The client has to use a known router located in the same network as itself, and thus reachable by Ethernet. The client now sends an

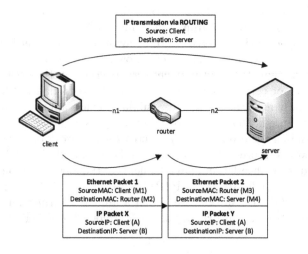

Fig. 7. Routing packet flow example

IP packet addressed to the IP address of the server, but the underlying Ethernet packet will be addressed to the router. When the router does receive such a packet, it will forward it to the server. While the two packets that the client and the router send do not differ on the IP layer (both are sent from the client, and addressed to the server), both differ on the Ethernet layer, with different source and destination MAC addresses.

Based on the Ethernet network ontology, this behavior can be expressed as the Prolog predicate in Listing 1.2.

Listing 1.2. Prolog predicate for routing

```
1 routing  :-
     ip_packet(X,A,B),
3    ip_packet(Y,A,B),
     ethernet_packet(X,M1,M2),
5    ethernet_packet(Y,M3,M4),
     M1 \= M3,  M2 \= M4.
```

This predicate can be read as *"routing occurs, when there are two IP layer packets X and Y, both sent from IP address A to IP address B, for which the source and destination addresses differ on the Ethernet layer."*

Predicates can be used as conditions to detect activities. E.g. the predicate "routing" can be used to verify the activity A10. We extended the graph, so that every activity can be associated with a condition to verify that activity.

Routing is only one example. We successfully created predicates describing e.g. the presence of hosts and networks, the network behaviour NAT or routing, and also higher level usage. E.g. ARP spoofing behaviour can be detected if two hosts within the same subnet having different MAC addresses, pretend to own the same IP address using the ARP protocol. However, this behaviour can also be caused by a misconfiguration of the hosts. For that reason this condition requires preconditions to verify a valid and error-free setup.

We also found a trade-off between the shape of an assignment and the capabilities to design predicates. If the assignment is more tightly controlled (e.g. predefined network names and IP addresses), more precise predicates can be designed to detect activities. If the assignment is more generic, the predicates also have to be designed in a more generalised manner.

Feedback

There are various types of feedback strategies which can be used to support students working on the exercise, e.g. suggestions, complete guiding, or an exam mode. The specific shape will be either customised to match the author's aims or customised to the learning style of the learner or a combination. Usually recent progress the student has made in the exercise graph should trigger interaction with the student according to the feedback strategy.

Therefore we extended the graph with feedback attributes. The graph as a whole can be associated with an attribute containing the exercise description; all activities can be associated with different attributes for feedback control, i.e. text messages that give hints about what the next activity might involve (pre messages), or text messages that give feedback about detected activities (post messages). An example for activity A1 from our example exercise looks like Listing 1.3.

While our message mechanism provides the technical means for the implementation of various feedback strategies, the evaluation and choice of an appropriate strategy resides with the exercise author.

Listing 1.3. Example feedback attributes

```
  pre_message = "You will need at least one host connected
      to network 'n1'."
2 post_message = "Network 'n1' detected."
```

Probing

While the verification of activities based on passively observed network packets works for many activities, there still are limitations. One such limitation occurs when an activity needs to be verified that does not have immediate results in the form of network packets.

An example for that would be A9 from our example exercise: the routing functionality has to be activated on the router. Students can do that by setting the appropriate kernel flag on the router if this flag is not enabled by default (Enable IP Forwarding: echo 1 > /proc/sys/net/ipv4/ip_forward). This however will not result in the occurrence of observable network packets, until packets are sent to the router for being routed. A possible solution would be to ask the student to send appropriate network packets himself. We followed a different approach. For detecting certain activities we inject special predefined network packets into the Netkit environment to provoke a certain predictable behavior. This behavior can also be expressed as a predicate. In the routing example we inject an Ethernet packet addressed to the router into the client network that is addressed to a host in the server network (which does not have to exist) on the IP level. If routing is enabled in the router, the router will try to reach that host in the server network using ARP requests. These packets can be used to verify that routing is indeed enabled on the router.

Such a "probing" packet can be assembled by strictly following the network stack, starting with an Ethernet frame. The destination MAC address must be the router's NIC connected to network n1. In Netkit, the MAC address of a network interface is bound to the name of the client, resulting in a predictable MAC address for the router'+ s first NIC eth0: 0aab64910980. The source MAC address can be virtual, e.g. eeba7b99bca5, followed by an

IPv4 ethertype identifier (0x0800). The encapsulated IP packet starts with the version identifier (0x4), followed by mandatory header fields, e.g. length and checksum. The source IP address can be virtual but should be located within the IP range of network n1. The destination IP address can also be virtual but must be part of subnet n2. The IP packet encapsulates an ICMP echo request just to get a complete and valid network packet. This customized packet layout can be represented by a hexadecimal character array, e.g. 0aab6491 0980eeba 7b99bca5 08004500 001c1234 4000ff01 549c0a00 00010b00 00100800 f7fd0001 0001. Tools, e.g. PackEth, can help authors to design and validate such packets.

We extended the graph, so that every activity can be associated with a custom network "probing" packet to be sent once before verifying its condition. While that actively alters the environment, it enables the verification of additional activities.

3.3 The Electronic Exercise Assistant

In order to support a student while working on an exercise, we developed an exercise assistant, which can be used in the VCL. As shown in Fig. 8, the exercise assistant is composed of three components: reasoning engine, feedback engine, and an interface to the student's working environment called Netkit interface.

The reasoning engine itself is composed of a reasoner and a knowledge base, which contains a TBox ("terminology box") and an ABox ("assertion box"). The TBox contains knowledge about the domain, i.e. our ontology, in the form of predefined predicates that can be extended by the author with exercise specific extensions, while the ABox contains the concrete instantiations.

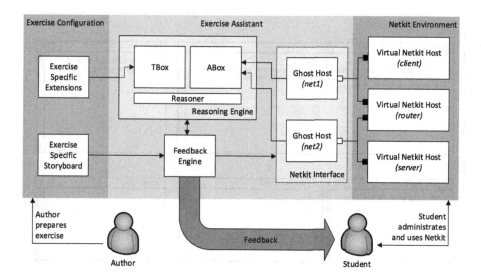

Fig. 8. Architecture of electronic exercise assistant

The data in the ABox is obtained through an interface to the "real world", in our case the Netkit interface. The Netkit interface consists of one or more Ghost Hosts [26] that record network packets from their respective Netkit network, extract the information in them and store that information in the ABox. The Ghost Hosts can also be used to inject special network packets into the environment.

The feedback engine is the part where the activity graph will be processed. Our exercise assistant is able to read an exercise graph stored in the GraphML format [32]. Once read, the activities are continuously processed according to their interdependencies, starting at the source nodes which represent activities without preconditions. Processing the activities in this case means verifying their conditions and giving the student feedback according to the feedback attributes of that activity. Once the activity is completed it will be removed from the graph and thus as a precondition for its successors. The feedback engine can also use the Netkit interface, respectively the Ghost Hosts, to insert custom network packets into the environment in order to provoke certain network behaviour to verify an activity's condition using the reasoning engine.

The Exercise Assistant is a software program written in the programming language C using SWI-Prolog [25] as the reasoning engine.

Using the VCL, the window layout of the desktop presented to the students looks like Fig. 9. The exercise assistant shell is a window where the student can keep track of the feedback generated by the feedback engine. The linux shell is a window where the student is able to administrate and use Netkit in order to e.g. create hosts and networks. Once a host is started, it will open a respective shell enabling the student to administrate the host itself. Further hosts, e.g. the router and the server, will open respective shells too.

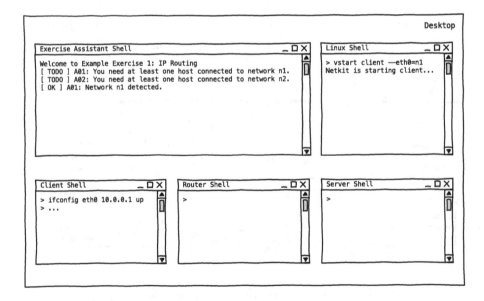

Fig. 9. DVCL desktop draft

Example

The Figs. 10, 11, 12, 13, 14, 15, 16, 17 and 18 show the exercise assistant shell, guiding the example exercise in which we replaced the linux desktop window by a sketch to improve the readability. We authored the activities of Table 1 according to the exercise graph of Fig. 5 and added verbose feedback. The introduced routing predicate is used to verify the final activity (A10). The intermediate activities too have been modeled using our ontology, partially by utilising probing packets. Once started, the exercise assistant introduces the exercise by displaying the exercise description (see Fig. 10). Starting with the activities without precondition (A1 and A2), the exercise assistant will prompt the student using the respective pre_messages.

The student can start solving the exercise according to Listing 1.1. After the first command **vstart client --eth0=n1** is entered using the linux shell, the exercise assistant is able to confirm this valid activity (see output in Fig. 11).

While A1 is being marked as verified, using the respective **post_message** of A1, the remaining independent activities without preconditions will be displayed again, superseding the preceding messages. According to the exercise graph, the

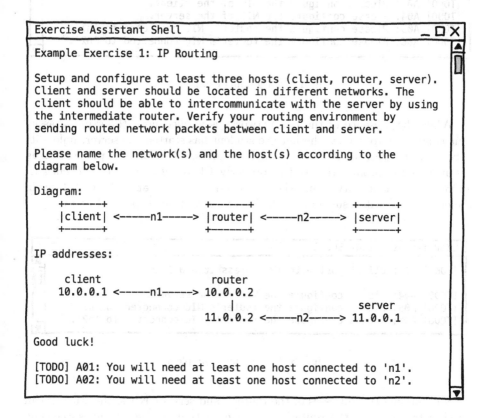

Fig. 10. EA guiding example 1

student is now able to choose A2, A3 or A5 as the next activity. Starting the router connected to network n1 and n2 results in a verified presence of n2 (see output in Fig. 12).

```
┌────────────────────────────────────────────────────────────────────┐
│ Exercise Assistant Shell                                  _ □ ✕     │
├────────────────────────────────────────────────────────────────┬───┤
│                                                                │ ▲ │
│ [ OK ] A01: Network n1 detected.                               │ ▯ │
│                                                                │   │
│ [TODO] A02: You need at least one host connected to network 'n2'. │   │
│ [TODO] A03: Please configure the NIC of the client.            │   │
│ [TODO] A05: Please configure the router's NIC connected to 'n1'. │ ▼ │
└────────────────────────────────────────────────────────────────┴───┘
```

Fig. 11. EA guiding example 2

```
┌────────────────────────────────────────────────────────────────────┐
│ Exercise Assistant Shell                                  _ □ ✕     │
├────────────────────────────────────────────────────────────────┬───┤
│                                                                │ ▲ │
│ [ OK ] A02: Network n2 detected.                               │ ▯ │
│                                                                │   │
│ [TODO] A03: Please configure the NIC of the client.            │   │
│ [TODO] A04: Please configure the NIC of the server.            │   │
│ [TODO] A05: Please configure the router's NIC connected to 'n1'. │   │
│ [TODO] A06: Please configure the router's NIC connected to 'n2'. │ ▼ │
└────────────────────────────────────────────────────────────────┴───┘
```

Fig. 12. EA guiding example 3

While the presence of the two networks is verified now, the exercise assistant is not able to detect whether the student has started the server, unless its network interface card is assigned an IP address. Therefore the pre_messages are authored to prompt the student properly. Choosing to assign the client's IP address as next activity, using the command ifconfig eth0 10.0.0.1 up in the client shell, will result in a verified activity A3 (see output in Fig. 13).

```
┌────────────────────────────────────────────────────────────────────┐
│ Exercise Assistant Shell                                  _ □ ✕     │
├────────────────────────────────────────────────────────────────┬───┤
│                                                                │ ▲ │
│ [ OK ] A03: Client host with IP address 10.0.0.1 detected.     │ ▯ │
│                                                                │   │
│ [TODO] A04: Please configure the NIC of the server.            │   │
│ [TODO] A05: Please configure the router's NIC connected to 'n1'. │   │
│ [TODO] A06: Please configure the router's NIC connected to 'n2'. │ ▼ │
└────────────────────────────────────────────────────────────────┴───┘
```

Fig. 13. EA guiding example 4

Still missing IP addresses of the router's and server's NICs, the student can proceed to configure the router's NICs (see output in Fig. 14 and succeeding output in Fig. 15).

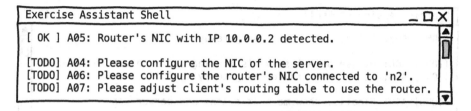

```
Exercise Assistant Shell                                    _ □ X
[ OK ] A05: Router's NIC with IP 10.0.0.2 detected.

[TODO] A04: Please configure the NIC of the server.
[TODO] A06: Please configure the router's NIC connected to 'n2'.
[TODO] A07: Please adjust client's routing table to use the router.
```

Fig. 14. EA guiding example 5

Having verified that the two NICs of the router are present, the exercise assistant is able to verify A9 using a probe packet. For the simple reason that routing is enabled per default for hosts in the Netkit environment, the condition of A9 can be verified immediately (see output in Fig. 16).

After assigning an IP address to the remaining NIC of the server, the student has to alter the routing table on the client and on the server. The exercise assistant is also able to verify these activities by using probing packets (see output in Fig. 17).

Finally, the student is asked to demonstrate the routing functionality by sending packets between the client and the server using the intermediate router. One valid solution is to use the command **ping**.

Once the final activity is verified, the exercise assistant congratulates the student and then quits (see output in Fig. 18).

```
Exercise Assistant Shell                                    _ □ X
[ OK ] A06: Router's NIC with IP 11.0.0.2 detected.

[TODO] A04: Please configure the NIC of the server.
[TODO] A07: Please adjust client's routing table to use the router.
[TODO] A09: Ensure, that the router is able to route packets.
[ OK ] A09: Router acts as a router between n1 and n2.

[TODO] A04: Please configure the NIC of the server.
[TODO] A07: Please adjust client's routing table to use the router.
```

Fig. 15. EA guiding example 6

```
Exercise Assistant Shell                                    _ □ X
[ OK ] A04: Server's NIC with IP 11.0.0.1 detected.

[TODO] A07: Please adjust client's routing table to use the router.
[TODO] A08: Please adjust server's routing table to use the router.
```

Fig. 16. EA guiding example 7

```
┌─────────────────────────────────────────────────────────────────┐
│ Exercise Assistant Shell                            _ □ X │
├─────────────────────────────────────────────────────────────────┤
│                                                              ▲   │
│ [ OK ] A07: Client uses router as gateway to 'n2'.          ▯   │
│                                                                  │
│ [TODO] A08: Please adjust server's routing table to use the router. │
│ [ OK ] A08: Server uses router as gateway to 'n1'.              │
│                                                                  │
│ [TODO] A10: Finally, show me that client and server can        │
│             intercommunicate.                               ▼   │
└─────────────────────────────────────────────────────────────────┘
```

Fig. 17. EA guiding example 8

```
┌─────────────────────────────────────────────────────────────────┐
│ Exercise Assistant Shell                            _ □ X │
├─────────────────────────────────────────────────────────────────┤
│                                                              ▲   │
│ [ OK ] A10: Setup verified, exercise completed.             ▯   │
│                                                                  │
│ [DEBUG] Solved in 7 minutes and 42 seconds.                    │
│ [ OK ] Finished! Well done!                                 ▼   │
└─────────────────────────────────────────────────────────────────┘
```

Fig. 18. EA guiding example 9

4   Applicability and Educational Enhancements

4.1   Security

The DVCL with Central Authority (CA) is able to connect students' local labs, even if they are distant from each other. The system ensures, that no other hosts will be harmed by malicious network packets. The topic, that was not covered so far, is, that there is always a risk that third parties will try to unauthorized use, interfere or attack *our* system.

This risk will increase by the importance of the system. If our system, meaning the DVCL client and the CA server, is actually used in a real-life educational setting, additional requirements appear. If the system is e.g. used to grade a student's work, it will be likely that someone will try e.g. to influence the results.

Use Case Scenario

The DVCL with CA system allows that remote students can work together. While the students will use their own computer, the university has to provide the CA. In our use case scenario we assume that a student uses the DVCL client outside the university (e.g. at home) utilising an internet connection to connect to the CA. A mobile environment using a cellular data plan is also possible.

Figure 19 shows a corresponding use case diagram of the DVCL with CA. The left side represents the student's home, connected via internet (cloud in the middle) to the university's CA on the right side. A student, as a user of his desktop or laptop computer, uses the DVCL client to interact with a university's CA using a control channel connection. An additional data channel connection will be established for each remotely connected virtual network.

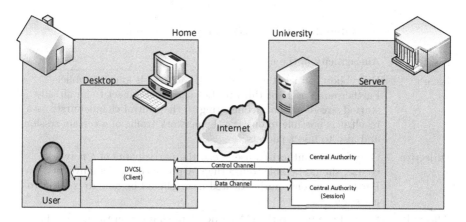

Fig. 19. Use case diagram of the DVCL with CA

Security Issues

During the development of the DVCL with CA system some security issues appeared [65]. Details for each issue are listed in Table 2. This table first describes the security **issue**. E.g. the first issue addresses the fact that everybody is able to use the CA if the IP address is known. This may be the desired behaviour for a general public learning environment, but the security **objective** for a university would be to limit the access, e.g. to their own students. **Affected** by this issue is the control channel which is open for everyone to connect to. An appropriate counter **measure** is to add a mechanism that users have to authenticate using a previously issued username and password first. If the credentials are valid, the CA authorises the user, otherwise the user will be rejected.

Security Measures

According to Table 2, four security issues were identified. These issues can be resolved by adding (resp. implementing) the following seven measures to our DVCL client server architecture.

Measure 1: Credentials. There are already existing, common concepts to issue and verify user credentials. For a university it could be wise to use existing directories, e.g. via Lightweight Directory Access Protocol (LDAP) or Network Information Service (NIS), to authorise students and to keep the administration effort low. For our prototype, we decided to issue and use a combination of username and password, stored and verifiable using a text file on the CA. Once a student will connect to the CA, a valid credential will be required first. For security reasons, it is recommended for final productive systems to store the passwords hashed rather than in plain text. Equipped with a **username** and a **password**, the DVCL CA tries to find a matching combination using the database. Once a valid combination is found, the user is authenticated, otherwise rejected. We successfully added this measure to our DVCL with CA prototype.

Table 2. Security issues and counter-measures

No. 1	Authenticity of the user
Issue	Everybody can use the CA if the IP address is known/public. Furthermore, users or third parties can also connect to an already started session without connecting to the control channel first. As a result it is possible to observe the network traffic of a certain session and also to inject packets
Objective	Only certain authorised users, e.g. the participants of a network course, should be able to use the CA provided by the university. Furthermore, only authenticated users should be able to connect to a session
Affected	Control channel on the CA's side, data channel on the CA's side
Measure 1	The CA shall require a username and password first to access the control channel
Measure 2	The CA shall issue an access token for authenticated users on the control channel, which will be required to use a data channel
No. 2	Authenticity of the CA and a CA session
Issue	The source code of the DVCL with CA will be public, because everybody should be able to serve a CA
Objective	The university's CA as well as their sessions should be authentic
Affected	CA, CA session
Measure 3	A verifiable certificate shall be added to the CA
Measure 4	A verifiable certificate shall be also added to the CA sessions
No. 3	Confidentiality of the control and session data
Issue	Data sent between the client and the CA resp. session can be read and also reused (e.g. the credentials) by third parties, if they are in a privileged position
Objective	The data transmitted between client and CA resp. sessions should be confidential
Affected	Control channel and data channel
Measure 5	The data transmitted on the control channel should be encrypted
Measure 6	The data transmitted on the data channel should also be encrypted
No. 4	Integrity of the control and session data
Issue	Data sent between the client and the CA can be modified by third parties, if they are in a privileged position, e.g. within the same local network using a man-in-the-middle attack
Objective	Nobody should be able to modify commands or packets from or to a student's lab. This is essential if the DVCL with CA will be used for an exam
Affected	Control channel and data channel
Measure 7	A verifiable signature for the transmitted data shall be added

Measure 2: Token. The control and the data channel are separated, independent channels and rely on different transport protocols (TCP and UDP). An authorised connection on the control channel does not involve the data channel. We decided to issue an access token on the control channel when a user is successfully authorised. This token will be required to authenticate on the data channel. Since the token will be issued and verified using an encrypted connection (see Measure 5 and 6: Encryption), it can not be captured and reused by third parties.

Measure 3 and 4: Certificate. A common concept to be able to verify the authenticity of a certain host is to use a certificate based on a public key infrastructure (PKI). A PKI involves a private and a public key pair, based on strong mathematical algorithms. A message encrypted with a private key, can only be decrypted using the corresponding public key, and vice versa. For server authentication, the client uses the server's public key to encrypt a secret key. The server can get access to this secret key only if it can decrypt the data from the client with the correct private key. A common software package that is able to deal with a PKI is Open Secure Socket Layer (OpenSSL). Using OpenSSL, it is possible to create a private key and a certificate for the server. The key `server.key` has to be private and stored on the server while the certificate `server.crt` is public and will be used by the server to identify itself, and also by the client to verify the server's authenticity.

Using and verifying a certificate can be added with some lines of code to the DVCL environment. When the DVCL client connects to the server, it is able to verify the server's authenticity. In case of an unexpected or faked certificate, a message will be printed to the student and the connection will be aborted.

Measure 5 and 6: Encryption. A common method to use encryption in software components is to use an existing, public software library, for example the Open Secure Socket Layer (OpenSSL), which provides different symmetric and asymmetric cryptography algorithms and adjustable key sizes. The implementation of such a library into an application is rather simple, compared to a self-made library. We decided to use TCP-based Transport Layer Security (TLS) [22–24] for the control channel and UDP-based Datagram Transport Layer Security (DTLS) [20, 21] for the data channel.

Measure 7: Signature. The use of OpenSSL for encryption and decryption does also ensure data integrity by calculating and verifying a message digest. This digest of the message will be calculated and appended to the encrypted data before it is sent to the network. When the message arrives at the destination node, OpenSSL recalculates the digest based on the data and compares that digest to the digest appended to the message. If the values do not match, the data has been corrupted and will not be processed. This is a built-in process of the TLS specification.

4.2 GUI

Initially the DVCL client was designed as a tool to be used in a command line interface (CLI) environment. The CLI is a text-based input-output system provided by the operating system, where a user can interact with the system or a service by entering certain commands including parameters and receiving textual responses. The DVCL client requires providing different parameters, e.g. the IP and the port of the DVCL's Central Authority (CA). The benefits include a flexible and easy way to add, remove and change parameters, the re-usability in other programs (batch-mode), and low development effort. A shortcoming however is that students first have to learn utilising the CLI including certain parameters in order to learn with the DVCL. One possibility would be to predefine values as far as possible, but this will not be feasible for certain parameters, e.g. the name of the local network. A way to improve the usability of the DVCL can be the introduction of a graphical user interface (GUI) to control the DVCL client [65]. Since the students are usually more familiar with using a GUI instead of using a CLI, a lower training period can be expected. This can result in an increased acceptance level, enables more time for learning, and finally can lead to an improved learning outcome. In order to reduce the training period, the GUI should support typical DVCL use cases. Also common misconfigurations should be prevented.

Table 3 lists typical use cases, which can occur while utilising Netkit and the DVCL client. The table starts with different cases on working with Netkit, followed by major cases occurring while administrating the CA using the client, and closes with cases originated by the interaction of Netkit and the client, respectively

Table 3. Use cases

No.	Case	GUI
1	Create a host without a network connection	☐
2	Create a host with a network connection	☒
3	Create a host with more than one network connection	☒
4	Login to the CA with username and password	☒
5	List available remote sessions	☒
6	Create a new remote session	☒
7	Delete a remote session	☒
8	Create a local network without a remote connection	☒
9	Connect a local network to a remote session	☒
10	Connect a local network to more than one remote session	☐
11	Connect more than one local network to one remote session	☒
12	Disconnect a local network from a remotely connected session	☒

Explanation:
☒ This case should be supported via GUI.
☐ This case should not be supported via GUI.

a remote connection. All use cases, except 1 and 10, should be supported in a GUI. Creating a host without a network connection does not make sense in a learning environment which focuses on networking practices. Connecting a local network to more than one remote sessions is technical possible, but increases the risk of a circle, which can lead to a failure of all involved systems.

We developed an example GUI for the DVCL client, which supports the use cases listed in Table 3. This GUI can be started as usual by clicking on a program icon. This can also be an automatic process within the DVCL environment using the autostart feature of the underlying operating system. The screenshots shown in Figs. 20, 21, 22 and 23 were captured using an Ubuntu Linux distribution. The look, fonts and the colors were set by the Ubuntu theme and will look different on other desktop environments.

At first, a logon screen will appear as shown in Fig. 20.

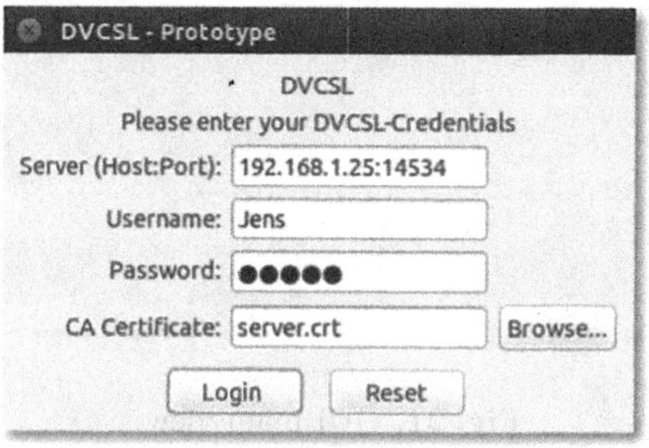

Fig. 20. GUI login

This screen is responsible to support use case no. 4. The address of the CA and also the path to the certificate are predefined but still editable. Also a username and a password have to be entered in order to continue. The button "Login" establishes a connection to the given CA and sends username and password for verification. The certificate will also be validated. If one of these processes fails, the connection will be aborted and the GUI will report an error.

If the credentials and also the certificate are successfully validated, the main screen will appear as illustrated in Fig. 21. This screen consists of three essential areas: The **local area** on the left, the **remote area** on the right, and the **status area** at the bottom.

The **local area** can be used to administrate local Netkit hosts and networks and thus is responsible for use case no. 2 and 3. Using the button "Create virtual Host/Network" will present a dialog shown in Fig. 22a. This dialogue can be used to create a new virtual host connected to at least one virtual network. A hostname and at least one named network are required, fulfilling use case no. 1. It is also possible to add and name additional networks, for example to create a router. The host will run in a new window, this is identical to a start via CLI (e.g. `vstart client --eth0=net1`). The new network(s) will appear in a list at the left area. This list also captures virtual networks, which are not started

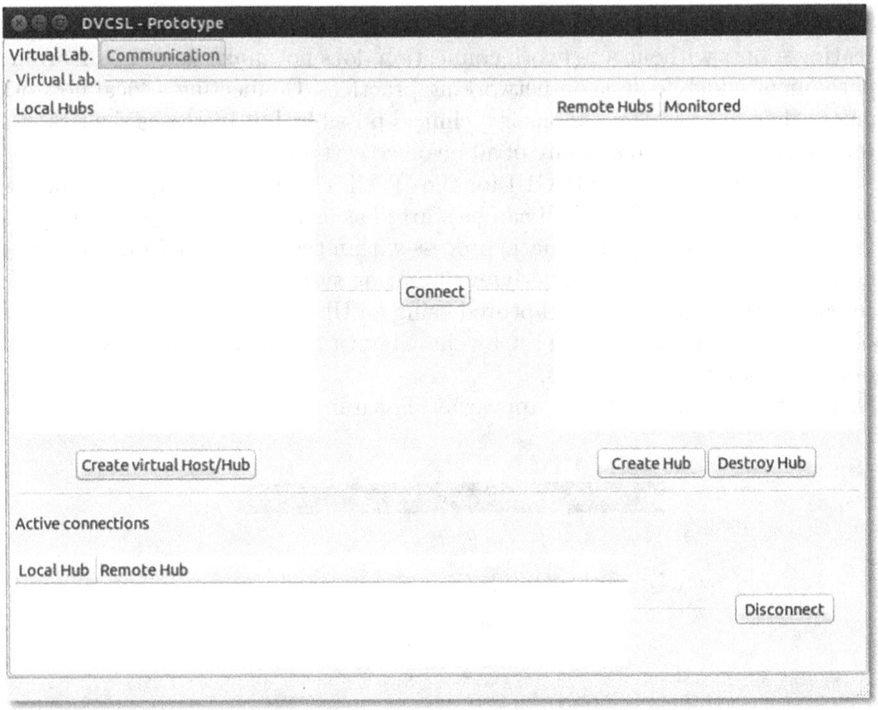

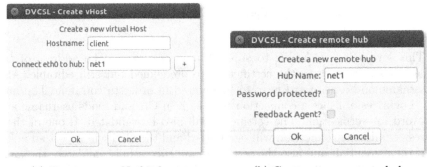

Fig. 21. GUI main view

(a) Create a new Netkit host   (b) Create a new remote hub

Fig. 22. GUI options

using the GUI but the CLI. We utilise a function of the Linux kernel called *inotify* to observe a certain directory and to detect if something has changed. If a Netkit network was started, a file handle will be placed in a certain preconfigured directory. This file handle will be used by the virtual hosts to connect to a certain virtual network.

An example screen can be found in Fig. 23.

The **remote area** can be used to administrate sessions of the CA. In the GUI, the term *session* is mapped to the closer matching network term *Hub*. Already existing sessions will be listed directly after the login, according to use case no. 5. A new session can be created with the "Create Hub" dialogue, which is presented in Fig. 22b. The session first requires a name. Additionally, the creator of the session as the "owner" is able to set a password. Other participants, e.g. the learning group members, have to know and also have to enter this password in order to connect to this session. Finally, a new remote session will be created on the CA. This session will appear immediately in the remote area. An example screen can also be found in Fig. 23.

Local networks can stay local, according to use case no. 8. A local network can also be connected to a remote session (use case no. 9). This requires to select a previously created network in the local area and an existing session in the remote area first. An established connection between a local network and a remote session will be displayed in the **status area**. This connection can be terminated by selecting the related entry and using the button "Disconnect" (use case no. 12). It is possible to connect more than one local network to the same remote session (use case no. 11). An additional connection attempt from an already connected local network will be aborted and a message will pop up (use case no. 10).

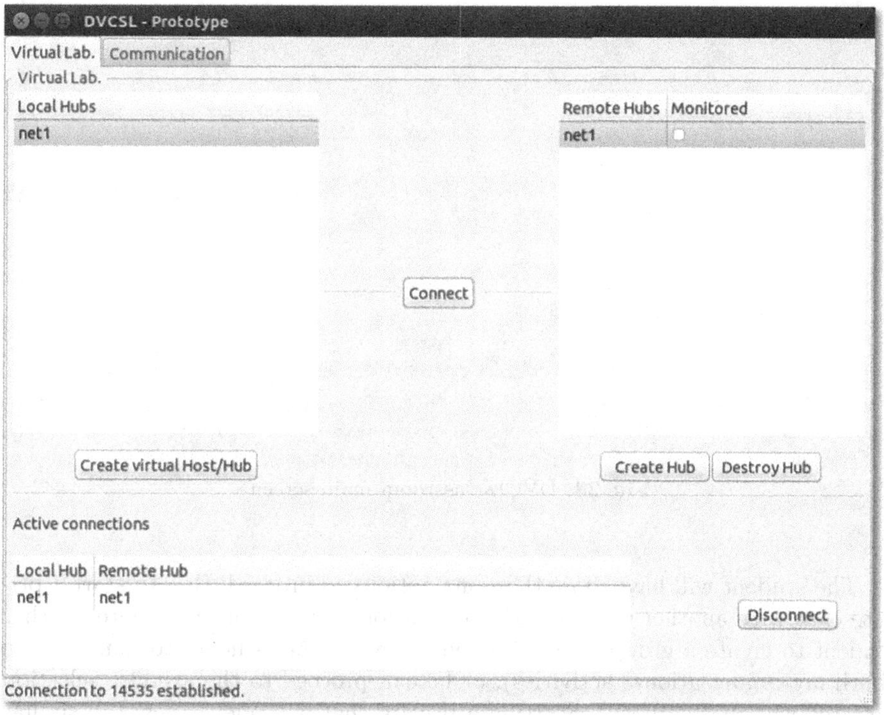

Fig. 23. GUI showing a connected network

4.3   Virtual Classroom Prototype

Our virtual classroom prototype [65] is based on, utilises and extends our existing DVCL (cf. Sect. 2.2) with Central Authority (cf. Sect. 2.3), including the Intelligent Tutoring System (cf. Sect. 3), security enhancements (cf. Sect. 4.1), and the GUI (cf. Sect. 4.2).

A student has first to login to use the DVCL (see Fig. 20). Once logged in, the main screen with the 'lobby', resp. the classroom chat will be presented as illustrated in Fig. 24. The lobby consists of three areas: An area where messages will appear to the left, an area with a list of users currently logged in to the right, and an area with a text input box to create and send own messages at the bottom.

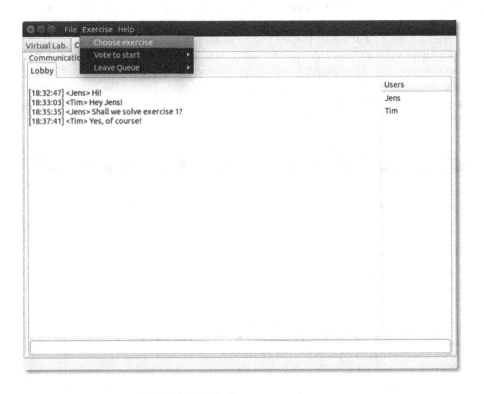

Fig. 24. DVCL classroom main screen

The student will have more than one options to proceed. He can start a private chat with another student (communication activity), he can invite another student to create a group or will be invited by another student to join a group (both are organisational activities), or he can proceed to the exercise selection area (educational activity). Starting a private chat will open a new tab similar to the lobby chat, except that messages will only be readable by the selected dialogue partner. A private chat is independently of other states. For manual group forming, the student can select another student to invite him into a group (see Fig. 25a), or he will be invited to join a group. A pending invitation has to be accepted or rejected in a dialogue prompt (see Fig. 25b). If a group with at least two students is formed, a new tab will appear for the group chat. This tab is similar to the lobby chat, except that messages will only be readable by the group members.

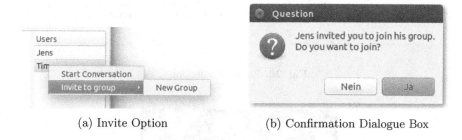

(a) Invite Option   (b) Confirmation Dialogue Box

Fig. 25. Manual group forming

Despite a group already exists or not, the student can access the exercise selection area (see Fig. 24). In Fig. 26, one exercise titled *Basic Networking A1* is included with a desired group size of 3. After selecting the exercise, the student has to decide to work alone or to search for a group. If the student is already a member of a group, which does not have an exercise selected yet, a third option will be available to assign the selected exercise to this pre-existing group.

Work alone means that the exercise will start immediately without waiting for group members. By selecting *Search a group*, the DVCL environment will look for an already existing group, where at least one group member is still missing and the group decided to solve the same exercise. If such a group is found, the student will be assigned to this group. If no suitable group can be found, the student will be assigned to a waiting queue (see Fig. 27). In case that the queue already holds a suitable student (who has selected the same exercise), a new group will be created for them. Finally, the group size will be checked. If the group is already complete, which means that the group has the predefined group size, the exercise will be started. If the group is still incomplete, the group members can vote to start the exercise anyway (see Fig. 28), but this action will requires the approval of all other group members (see Fig. 29).

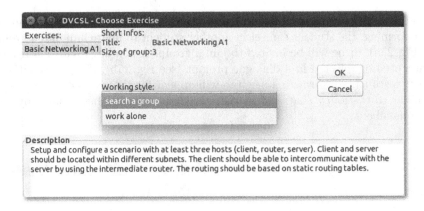

Fig. 26. Exercise selection

Fig. 27. Student is assigned to waiting queue

Fig. 28. Overwrite a predefined group size

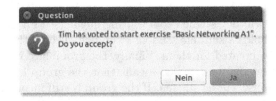

Fig. 29. Confirmation dialogue

5   Implementation and Evaluation

5.1   Implementation

The VCL in Sect. 2.1 make use of Netkit[1], User Mode Linux[2], Knoppix[3], and the virtualisation layer VMware Player[4] or VirtualBox[5].

The DVCL in Sect. 2.2 is based on a software component, consisting of a Ghost Host and a Remote Bridge. The Ghost Host provides an interface to the virtual network, where Ethernet frames can be extracted and injected. The Ethernet frames that are extracted by the Ghost Host, are first encapsulated in the IP/UDP protocol (acting as transport protocol), and next sent to the Remote Bridge endpoint of a fixed distant destination. For incoming data, the IP/UDP protocol is removed by the Ghost Host and the Ethernet frames are injected into the local network. We developed both components using the programming language C.

The DVCL with Central Authority in Sect. 2.3 makes use of our developed components Ghost Host and Remote Bridge, extended by a new software component called Central Authority. We developed the Central Authority also using the programming language C using threads, shared memory, and TCP/UDP sockets.

Our Intelligent Tutoring System in Sect. 3 is also a software program, written in the programming language C. It makes use of Ghost Hosts to connect to Netkit's virtual networks, and a file reader interface to load and parse the exercise configuration. The reasoning engine is included by the software package SWI-Prolog[6].

The Security Measures in Sect. 4.1 improve the DVCL with Central Authority. Security measure 1 and 2 are based on source code extensions of the pre-existing C code, measures 3 to 7 additionally make use of the software package OpenSSL[7].

The Graphical User Interface (GUI) in Sect. 4.2 and also the Virtual Classroom Prototype in Sect. 4.3 are developed using the programming language C. We use GTK[8], a multi-platform toolkit for creating graphical user interfaces.

5.2   Evaluation

Before we started the development of our DVCL with CA system, we evaluated [29,35] an on-campus practical networking course at the Cologne University

---

[1] Netkit, http://wiki.netkit.org, Online, accessed April 2018.

[2] The User-mode Linux Kernel Home Page, http://user-mode-linux.sourceforge.net, Online, accessed April 2018.

[3] KNOPPIX, http://www.knopper.net/knoppix, Online, accessed April 2018.

[4] VMware Player, http://www.vmware.com, Online, accessed April 2018.

[5] VirtualBox, http://www.virtualbox.org, Online, accessed April 2018.

[6] SWI Prolog, http://www.swi-prolog.org, Online, accessed April 2018.

[7] OpenSSL - Cryptography and SSL/TLS Toolkit, https://www.openssl.org, Online, accessed April 2018.

[8] GTK+, https://www.gtk.org/, Online, accessed April 2018.

of Applied Sciences, where students have to work out and solve assignments. They also have to defend their solutions. A special property of this course is that the students are given a high degree of flexibility during their assignment preparation time. We wanted to discover the learning behaviour of students who are free to choose their learning environment in order to successfully complete the course. In addition, we wanted to determine the success of the course. The results were used as a justification and also as motivation for our work with respect to an optimised alignment of our technical implementation and practical course concepts in place.

249 students signed up for the practical course "Communication technology and networks". 191 students passed, i.e. they worked out the assignments, and demonstrated and defended their solutions successfully. Most of the 23% unsuccessful students registered but did not participate at all; some seemed to have other shortcomings; a few tried but could not defend their solution properly. 178 of them (71%) participated in our evaluation process.

While the preferences for learning environments and behaviour were fairly distributed, a predominant majority of the students thought of *working in groups* as well as *receiving guidance and feedback* as crucial to their learning success. Students are also interested in new and innovative learning environments. It is important that these new environments do not replace more traditional ones, but rather add on to them.

One way of modernising the practical course would be the introduction of an e-learning system, which would be explicitly welcomed by 49% of the students. In addition to that, nearly half of the students said that they would like to work independently from the lab at least partially, which they would be enabled to do by the introduction of such a system.

Given the students' preference for group working and guided learning, one should take these two key factors into account when introducing an e-learning system. This means that, in order to gain the students' acceptance, an e-learning system should enable collaboration as well as guidance, and shouldn't be limited to simply providing an environment for solving assignments online.

6 Related Work

The idea of using an isolated network as an environment to perform IT related tasks for the purpose of research or education is widely recognised [36–40]. There are two general approaches to create such an environment:

The first approach is to create or use an isolated, physical network with physical hosts that is separated from an operational network such as a campus network [36,41]. This isolation may be achieved by physical separation of the networks or by using components like firewalls to restrict data flow between network areas [42]. Within this isolated network the students can perform exercises and work with a real-world like network setup. Remote access to such a network may be granted by using remote access technologies such as Virtual Private Network (VPN) [43]. Administration and maintenance of such a lab however is labour-intensive. Students work in the lab with super-user rights and can modify system configurations at will. After a session, it is necessary to clean up system configurations, which may even require reinstalling operating systems.

The second approach makes use of virtualisation technologies to create an isolated, virtual network with virtual hosts. Literature refers to such an environment in the context of education or e-learning usually as a virtual lab [47,50–54]. This approach significantly reduces the amount of physical hardware resources (e.g., switches, routers, hosts), since the required resources are created by virtualisation. Cleaning up or reinstalling a virtual lab simply means reloading the virtual environments, which can even be an automated task.

Literature also reports two main approaches to provide an isolated network. In the first one, the environment is located at a central place, usually at the university [44–49] and students can get physical or remote access by using a secured network connection. A central place could also be a cloud [55–57] or a federated lab [58,59]. Although such labs may be accessed remotely at any time from any place, they are generally not easily scalable. Allowing an arbitrary number of students to participate at the same time requires students to reserve timeslots in advance for working in the lab. This may impose restrictions for students in distance education, who usually study in evening hours and weekends. Provisioning a remote lab for peak access outside office hours, may result in a largely over-dimensioned lab with a low average degree of utilisation and hence a waste of resources.

Second, the environment is provided as a preconfigured, stand-alone software package which can be installed and used by students on any computer, usually their private computer [18,60–62]. This gives the students the opportunity to safely carry out assignments wherever and whenever they want to. We used the Virtual Computer Security Lab [18] as base for our research work.

Literature also reports many scopes where intelligent tutoring systems (ITS) were developed or applied, e.g. in the scope of teaching mathematics [8,9,63,64], databases [10–12], programming languages [13] like JAVA [14,15] or Haskell [16], IT security [1,3,5], and physics [2,4]. We added an ITS to model and also to verify networking exercises.

7   Conclusion

Step by step we developed a virtual classroom for use in different educational contexts for cybersecurity network education. The classroom has been realised both in a distance learning context and in an on-campus context. This was made possible by extending a basic virtual security lab (VCL) with distributivity, a central authority, tutoring by an exercise assistant, and finally security and educational enhancements.

Starting from the VCL as a basis, which we had designed as an isolated system, we first enabled group work for students by connecting two VCLs on the network level. In the resulting Distributed Virtual Computer Lab (DVCL), remote students are able to work synchronously together, using an intermediate connection, e.g. the internet. The DVCL system ensures that the isolated network stays isolated and cannot intercommunicate with the internet. We next extended and improved the DVCL by providing a central authority (CA). The CA simplifies the usage of our DVCL for the students (and also for academic staff) and - in addition to it - avoids administrative configuration errors while connecting remote labs.

When working on practical exercises in a lab environment, students need guidance and feedback. It is challenging to provide such feedback and guidance in a virtual lab when human course advisors are not available. This is e.g. the case when students use the DVCL at home outside office hours. We showed that network traffic captured in a lab can give some indication of what a student has already configured according to a certain exercise. We used this insight to develop an Electronic Exercise Assistant. This software program is able to recognise the progress of students in an exercise and can provide appropriate feedback and support, based on preloaded rules and conditions. This significantly improves the learning situation for students. Besides this automatic support, the exercise assistant can also verify intermediate and complete solutions of an exercise.

In order to turn our DVCL into a virtual classroom, we made several enhancements. A first enhancement is to resolve security issues and prevent misuse of the DVCL. Such security requirements are necessary when using the DVCL in an actual, real-life learning environment. A second enhancement is to add a GUI which supports students in connecting to the lab and joining sessions with other students. Our final enhancement was to extend our virtual classroom with facilities to support social interactions, such that students e.g. can meet, form learning groups, talk, and discuss. These enhancements allow students to communicate, organise, and carry out educational activities in our virtual classroom in a similar way as in an on-campus classroom setting.

We described in this paper the technology behind our virtual classroom, including both the technical implementation details and the educational principles on which it is based. It is now up to the educators to use the virtual classroom and to evaluate its impact on the learning of students. We intend to use the virtual classroom in practice at the Cologne University of Applied Sciences and the Open University in the Netherlands, and to continue our research on the application of DVCLs in distance education.

References

1. Hu, J., Meinel, C., Schmitt, M.: Tele-lab IT security: An architecture for interactive lessons for security education. In: Proceedings of the 35th SIGCSE Technical Symposium on Computer Science Education, SIGCSE 2004, pp. 412–416. ACM, New York (2004)
2. Albacete, P.L., VanLehn, K.: The conceptual helper: an intelligent tutoring system for teaching fundamental physics concepts. In: Gauthier, G., Frasson, C., VanLehn, K. (eds.) ITS 2000. LNCS, vol. 1839, pp. 564–573. Springer, Heidelberg (2000). https://doi.org/10.1007/3-540-45108-0_60
3. Mahdi, A.O., Alhabbash, M.I., Naser, S.S.A.: An Intelligent Tutoring System for Teaching Advanced Topics in Information Security (2016)

4. Vanlehn, K., et al.: The andes physics tutoring system: lessons learned. Int. J. Artif. Intell. Educ. 15(3), 147–204 (2005)
5. Hu, J., Schmitt, M., Willems, C., Meinel, C.: A tutoring system for IT security. In: Irvine, C., Armstrong, H. (eds.) Security Education and Critical Infrastructures. ITIFIP, vol. 125, pp. 51–60. Springer, Boston, MA (2003). https://doi.org/10.1007/978-0-387-35694-5_5
6. Corbett, A.T., Koedinger, K.R., Anderson, J.R.: Intelligent tutoring systems. Handb. Hum. Comput. Interact. 5, 849–874 (1997)
7. Psotka, J., Massey, L.D., Mutter, S.A.: Intelligent Tutoring Systems: Lessons Learned. Psychology Press, Hillsdale (1988)
8. Melis, E., Siekmann, J.: ACTIVEMATH: an intelligent tutoring system for mathematics. In: Rutkowski, L., Siekmann, J.H., Tadeusiewicz, R., Zadeh, L.A. (eds.) ICAISC 2004. LNCS (LNAI), vol. 3070, pp. 91–101. Springer, Heidelberg (2004). https://doi.org/10.1007/978-3-540-24844-6_12
9. Canfield, W.: ALEKS: a web-based intelligent tutoring system. Math. Comput. Educ. 35(2), 152 (2001)
10. Yang, F.-J.: A virtual tutor for relational schema normalization. ACM Inroads 2(3), 38–42 (2011)
11. Kenny, C., Pahl, C.: Automated tutoring for a database skills training environment, vol. 37. ACM (2005)
12. Suraweera, P., Mitrovic, A.: An intelligent tutoring system for entity relationship modelling. Int. J. Artif. Intell. Educ. 14(3, 4), 375–417 (2004)
13. Queirós, R.A.P., Leal, J.P.: PETCHA: a programming exercises teaching assistant. In: Proceedings of the 17th ACM Annual Conference on Innovation and Technology in Computer Science Education, ITiCSE 2012, pp. 192–197. ACM, New York (2012)
14. Sykes, E.R., Franek, F.: A prototype for an intelligent tutoring system for students learning to program in Java (TM). In: Proceedings of the IASTED International Conference on Computers and Advanced Technology in Education, pp. 78–83 (2003)
15. Vesin, B., Ivanović, M., Klašnja-Milićević, A., Budimac, Z.: Ontology-based architecture with recommendation strategy in java tutoring system. Comput. Sci. Inf. Syst. 10(1), 237–261 (2013)
16. Jeuring, J., van Binsbergen, L.T., Gerdes, A., Heeren, B.: Model solutions and properties for diagnosing student programs in ask-elle. In: Proceedings of the Computer Science Education Research Conference, CSERC 2014, pp. 31–40. ACM, New York (2014)
17. Pizzonia, M., Rimondini, M.: Netkit: easy emulation of complex networks on inexpensive hardware. In: Proceedings of the 4th International Conference on Testbeds and Research Infrastructures for the Development of Networks & Communities, TridentCom 2008, pp. 7:1–7:10, ICST, Brussels, Belgium. ICST (Institute for Computer Sciences, Social-Informatics and Telecommunications Engineering) (2008)
18. Vranken, H., Koppelman, H.: A virtual computer security lab for distance education. In: Proceedings of the 5th IASTED European Conference on Internet and Multimedia Systems and Applications, EuroIMSA 2009, pp. 21–27. Acta Press (2009)
19. Colmerauer, A., Roussel, P.: The birth of prolog. In: The Second ACM SIGPLAN Conference on History of Programming Languages, HOPL-II, pp. 37–52. ACM, New York (1993)
20. Rescorla, E., Modadugu, N.: Datagram transport layer security (2006). http://www.ietf.org/rfc/rfc4347.txt. Accessed 22 July 2014

21. Rescorla, E., Modadugu, N.: Datagram transport layer security version 1.2 (2012). http://www.ietf.org/rfc/rfc6347.txt. Accessed 22 July 2014
22. Dierks, T., Allen, C.: The TLS protocol version 1.0 (1999). http://www.ietf.org/rfc/rfc2246.txt. Accessed 22 July 2014
23. Dierks, T., Rescorla, E.: The transport layer security (TLS) protocol version 1.1 (2006). http://www.ietf.org/rfc/rfc4346.txt. Accessed 22 July 2014
24. Dierks, T., Rescorla, E.: The transport layer security (TLS) protocol version 1.2 (2008). http://www.ietf.org/rfc/rfc5246.txt. Accessed 22 July 2014
25. Wielemaker, J.: Logic programming for knowledge-intensive interactive applications. PhD thesis, University of Amsterdam (2009)
26. Vranken, H., Haag, J., Horsmann, T., Karsch, S.: A distributed virtual computer security lab. In: Proceedings of the 3rd International Conference on Computer Supported Education, CSEDU 2011, pp. 110–119. SciTePress (2011)
27. Haag, J., Horsmann, T., Karsch, S., Vranken, H.: A distributed virtual computer security lab with central authority. In: Proceedings of the Computer Science Education Research Conference, CSERC 2011, pp. 89–95. Open Universiteit, Heerlen (2011)
28. Haag, J., Karsch, S., Vranken, H., Van Eekelen, M.: A virtual computer security lab as learning environment for networking and security courses. In: Proceedings of the 3rd Annual International Conference on Computer Science Education: Innovation and Technology, CSEIT 2012, pp. 61–68. Global Science & Technology Forum (2012)
29. Haag, J., Witte, C., Karsch, S., Vranken, H., Van Eekelen, M.: Evaluation of students' learning behaviour and success in a practical computer networking course. In: Proceedings of the 2nd International Conference on E-Learning and E-Technologies in Education, ICEEE 2013, pages 201–206. IEEE (2013)
30. Baader, F., Calvanese, D., McGuinness, D.L., Nardi, D., Patel-Schneider, P.F. (eds.): The Description Logic Handbook: Theory, Implementation, and Applications. Cambridge University Press, New York (2003)
31. Tanenbaum, A.S.: Computer Networks. Prentice Hall PTR, Upper Saddle River (1985)
32. Brandes, U., Eiglsperger, M., Herman, I., Himsolt, M., Marshall, M.S.: GraphML progress report structural layer proposal. In: Mutzel, P., Jünger, M., Leipert, S. (eds.) GD 2001. LNCS, vol. 2265, pp. 501–512. Springer, Heidelberg (2002). https://doi.org/10.1007/3-540-45848-4_59
33. Dike, J.: User Mode Linux. Prentice Hall, Englewood Cliffs (2006)
34. Dike, J.: A user-mode port of the linux kernel. In: Proceedings of the 4th Annual Linux Showcase & Conference, ALS 2000, vol. 4, p. 7. USENIX Association, Berkeley (2000)
35. Haag, J., Witte, C., Karsch, S., Vranken, H., Van Eekelen, M.: Evaluation of students' learning behaviour and success as a prerequisite for modernizing practical on-campus networking courses in higher education. Yükseköğretim Dergisi/J. High. Educ. 4(2), 83–90 (2014a)
36. Bishop, M., Heberlein, L.: An isolated network for research. In: Proceedings of the Nineteenth National Information Systems Security Conference, pp. 349–360 (1996)
37. Agarwal, K.K., Critcher, A., Foley, D., Sanati, R., Sigle, J.: Setting up a classroom lab. J. Comput. Sci. Coll. 16(3), 281–286 (2001)
38. Taylor, K.D., Honchell, J.W., DeWitt, W.E.: Distance learning in courses with a laboratory. In: Proceedings of the 26th Annual Frontiers in Education, FIE 1996, vol. 01, pp. 44–46. IEEE Computer Society, Washington (1996)

39. Lo, D.C.-T., Qian, K., Chen, W., Shahriar, H., Clincy, V.: Authentic learning in network and security with portable labs. In: 2014 IEEE Frontiers in Education Conference (FIE), vol. 00, pp. 1–5 (2014)
40. Bardas, A.G., Ou, X.: Setting up and using a cyber security lab for education purposes. J. Comput. Sci. Coll. **28**(5), 191–197 (2013)
41. Jakab, F., Janitor, J., Nagy, M.: Virtual lab in a distributed international environment - SVC EDINET. In: Fifth International Conference on Networking and Services, ICNS 2009, pp. 576–580 (2009)
42. Yang, T.A., et al.: Design of a distributed computer security lab. J. Comput. Sci. Coll. **20**(1), 332–346 (2004)
43. Yoo, S., Hovis, S.: Remote access internetworking laboratory. In: Proceedings of the 35th SIGCSE Technical Symposium on Computer Science Education, SIGCSE 2004, pp. 311–314. ACM, New York (2004)
44. Drigas, A.S., Vrettaros, J., Koukianakis, L.G., Glentzes, J.G.: A virtual lab and e-learning system for renewable energy sources. In: Proceedings of the 1st WSEAS/I-ASME Conference on Educational Technologies, EDUTE 2005, pp. 149–153 (2005)
45. Border, C.: The development and deployment of a multi-user, remote access virtualization system for networking, security, and system administration classes. In: Proceedings of the 38th SIGCSE Technical Symposium on Computer Science Education, SIGCSE 2007, pp. 576–580. ACM, New York (2007)
46. Hu, J., Cordel, D., Meinel, C.: Virtual machine management for tele-lab "IT-security" server. In: Proceedings of the 10th IEEE Symposium on Computers and Communications, ISCC 2005, pp. 448–453. IEEE Computer Society (2005)
47. Keller, J., Naues, R.: Design of a virtual computer security lab. In: Proceedings of the IASTED International Conference on Communication, Network, and Information Security, CNIS 2006, pp. 211–215. Acta Press (2006)
48. Krishna, K., Sun, W., Rana, P., Li, T., Sekar, R.: V-NetLab: a cost-effective platform to support course projects in computer security. In: Proceedings of 9th Colloquium for Information Systems Security Education. The Printing House Inc. (2005)
49. Lahoud PhD (ABD), H.A., Tang PhD, X.: Information security labs in IDS/IPS for distance education. In: Proceedings of the 7th Conference on Information Technology Education, SIGITE 2006, pp. 47–52. ACM, New York (2006)
50. Brian Hay, K.L.N.: Evolution of the ASSERT computer security lab. In: Proceedings of the 10th Colloquium for Information Systems Security Education (2006)
51. Bullers Jr., W.I., Burd, S., Seazzu, A.F.: Virtual machines - an idea whose time has returned: application to network, security, and database courses. In: Proceedings of the 37th SIGCSE Technical Symposium on Computer Science Education, SIGCSE 2006, pp. 102–106. ACM, New York (2006)
52. Damiani, E.: The open source virtual lab: a case study. In: Proceedings of the Workshop on Free and Open Source Learning Environments and Tools, FOSLET 2006 (2006)
53. O'Leary, M.: A laboratory based capstone course in computer security for undergraduates. In: Proceedings of the 37th SIGCSE Technical Symposium on Computer Science Education, SIGCSE 2006, pp. 2–6. ACM, New York (2006)
54. Li, P.: Exploring virtual environments in a decentralized lab. SIGITERes. IT **6**(1), 4–10 (2009a)
55. Ellabidy, M., Russo, J.P.: Using the cloud to replace traditional physical networking laboratories. In: Proceedings of the 45th ACM Technical Symposium on Computer Science Education, SIGCSE 2014, p. 729. ACM, New York (2014)

56. Mhd Wael Bazzaza, K.S.: Using the cloud to teach computer networks. In: Proceedings of the 2015 IEEE/ACM 8th International Conference on Utility and Cloud Computing (UCC), UCC 2015, pp. 310–314 (2015)
57. Salah, K.: Harnessing the cloud for teaching cybersecurity. In: Proceedings of the 45th ACM Technical Symposium on Computer Science Education, SIGCSE 2014, pp. 529–534. ACM, New York (2014)
58. Peterson, L., Anderson, T., Culler, D., Roscoe, T.: A blueprint for introducing disruptive technology into the internet. SIGCOMM Comput. Commun. Rev. **33**(1), 59–64 (2003)
59. Berman, M., Chase, J.S., Landweber, L., Nakao, A., Ott, M., Raychaudhuri, D., Ricci, R., Seskar, I.: GENI: a federated testbed for innovative network experiments. Comput. Netw. **61**, 5–23 (2014)
60. Li, P.: Exploring virtual environments in a decentralized lab. SIGITERes. IT **6**(1), 4–10 (2009b)
61. Li, P.: Centralized and decentralized lab approaches based on different virtualization models. J. Comput. Sci. Coll. **26**(2), 263–269 (2010)
62. Seeling, P.: Labs@home. SIGCSE Bull. **40**(4), 75–77 (2008)
63. Heeren, B., Jeuring, J., van Leeuwen, A., Gerdes, A.: Specifying strategies for exercises. In: Autexier, S., Campbell, J., Rubio, J., Sorge, V., Suzuki, M., Wiedijk, F. (eds.) CICM 2008. LNCS (LNAI), vol. 5144, pp. 430–445. Springer, Heidelberg (2008). https://doi.org/10.1007/978-3-540-85110-3_36
64. Gerdes, A., Heeren, B., Jeuring, J.: Properties of exercise strategies. In: Proceedings International Workshop on Strategies in Rewriting, Proving, and Programming, IWS 2010, Edinburgh, UK, 9th July 2010, pp. 21–34 (2010)
65. Haag, J.: DVCL: A Distributed Virtual Computer Lab for security and network education. Ph.D. thesis, Open Universiteit (2018)

The Cyber Security Knowledge Exchange: Working with Employers to Produce Authentic PBL Scenarios and Enhance Employability

Chris Beaumont[✉] and Peter Hartley

Centre for Learning and Teaching, Edge Hill University, Ormskirk, UK
`Chris.Beaumont@EdgeHill.ac.uk`

Abstract. The shortage of professionals to combat the growth of cyber-attacks demands a response from universities to equip students with relevant skills and knowledge. Furthermore, the small and medium enterprise (SME) sector in the UK particularly lacks information security expertise. This paper explains and critically evaluates innovative approaches which address both problems. Our innovations include open-access adaptable Problem-based learning (PBL) scenarios, developed with industry partners to ensure authenticity. Full resources are available at https://www.cyberedge.uk/cske/index.php. PBL was found to be well-aligned with the multi-disciplinary challenge of information security - it develops essential professional skills and can model the consultancy process. To address the SME skills issues, teams of students, conducted consultancy-based work-placements to address SME-identified problems. Evaluation showed PBL scenarios and consultancy work placements received strongly positive responses from participants. The educational design, processes of development and engagement with partners, and the evaluation methods are readily transferable to other subject domains.

Keywords: Cybersecurity · Problem-based learning · Knowledge exchange

1 Introduction

The growing magnitude of threats from cyber security breaches is well known. In 2016, cyber-attacks were estimated to cost businesses as much as $450 billion a year globally [1] and Lloyd's of London [2] estimated that a major, global cyber-attack could cost an average of $53 billion in economic losses, as much as a catastrophic natural disaster. Lloyds raised the position of cyber security to a ranking of third in their business risk index. Given this growing threat level, it is perhaps unsurprising that there is a severe shortage of professionals with adequate skills to effectively combat cyber security threats with Frost & Sullivan [3] forecasting an increasing trend in the global shortage of professionals, rising to 1.8 million by 2022.

Thus, there is an urgent and compelling need for education and training that will produce suitable professionally competent graduates to fill the gap. Furthermore, the challenge is made even harder because of the rapid rate of change in cyber-attacks: it is

© Springer-Verlag GmbH Germany, part of Springer Nature 2019
Z. Pan et al. (Eds.): Transactions on Edutainment XV, LNCS 11345, pp. 209–228, 2019.
https://doi.org/10.1007/978-3-662-59351-6_14

imperative that education not only encompasses well-established security principles, but also is relevant to the current types of attack.

There is also a second pressing challenge: Small and Medium Enterprises (SMEs) comprise over 99% of the number of UK businesses [4] and they are especially at risk as they possess less expertise and resources than large corporations [5]. Thus, it is critical to explore ways to improve the cyber-security capability of SMEs, so that they are well-prepared to assess and control the risks that they face.

The Cyber Security Knowledge Exchange project (CSKE) used a collaborative approach to develop two interventions that address these problems. It involved working with students and employers as partners to:

1. Create a series of adaptable, open-access, online, problem-based learning (PBL) scenarios and multimedia resources for learning topical aspects of Cyber-security. The innovative feature of this approach is that the PBL scenarios were designed in conjunction with industry partners, whose expertise provided authenticity, depth and currency in the scenarios, whilst the university academics provided the pedagogical expertise to construct effective learning experiences.
2. Develop a student-focused knowledge exchange (KE) model for disseminating good cybersecurity practice to SMEs. This work involved students from the university's MSc Information Security and IT Management course undertaking supervised consultancy-style assignments via a flexible, tested KE model.

This paper provides a critical reflective evaluation of the project so that readers can determine if they wish to use any of the freely-available PBL resources that were developed and/or incorporate some of the other novel features of the project into their own practice. All of the following innovative features are discussed in turn before we conclude with some comments on the overall progress and subsequent developments:

- PBL – a pedagogy for professional learning,
- the consulting/learning model, and the implications for employability,
- the Cyber Security Knowledge Exchange (CSKE) model of professional education,
- integration with work placements,
- the collaborative approach to evaluation.

Whilst the subject domain is cybersecurity, the methodology and processes are more widely applicable. For example, the collaborative approach to develop scenarios with industry partners could be used in any subject discipline where the students typically enter careers in industry; the consulting/learning model can be adapted to any subject where the design of learning environment can mirror professional practice; and the approach to evaluation has already demonstrated its value in projects with a very different context.

The paper is structured as follows: we start by explaining the rationale for PBL, and provide a brief review of the literature to establish the features that make it particularly appropriate for professional learning and relate this to cyber-security. The next section discusses how PBL develops employability attributes and aligns particularly well with a model of consultancy, so students gain much more than subject knowledge. A brief introduction to one of the PBL scenarios then illustrates the approach and underpinning models - all the scenarios are freely available online and can be downloaded and re-purposed/adapted if necessary. Next, we describe and explain the CSKE model for integrating employers, students, PBL and knowledge exchange, and this leads into discussion of the collaborative approach to evaluation and final comments on our overall evaluation.

2 PBL – A Pedagogy for Professional Practice

Developing a pedagogy to improve professional competency requires a paradigm shift from a transmission model of learning to one that more closely matches professional practice. For this reason, the CSKE project was based on Problem-based Learning (PBL). PBL is both a curriculum and a process [6]. The curriculum consists of carefully selected and designed problems that demand that the learner acquires essential knowledge, problem-solving proficiency, self-directed learning strategies and team participation skills [7]. The processes replicate common approaches to solving problems encountered in real life.

There are various models of PBL [8, 9] which tend to differ in terms of the degree of structure in either or both task and process. More recently we have seen a rise in teaching techniques which focus on problem-solving but use a very structured sequence of tutor input and group interaction, such as Team-Based Learning [10] and SCALE-UP [11]. These more structured approaches can demonstrate improvements in student learning and satisfaction but may disguise some of the uncertainties and ambiguities which students will have to confront in their future careers. As a result, the approach adopted within CSKE is a very deliberate attempt to mirror common features of contemporary professional practice and is characterized by the following:

- Students are presented with a messy real-world problem scenario and one that they do not have the knowledge to solve at the outset.
- Students work in small teams (4–5 students) to identify learning issues and a strategy to solve or manage the problem.
- Students carry out individual research/learning and teach others in the team.
- Students collaboratively evaluate the new knowledge and apply it to solve/manage the problem.
- Students reflect on the solution and process.
- The role of the tutor is to act as facilitator to challenge and guide the learning process.

Wilson and Cole [13] suggest that the attributes of PBL provide a framework for future learning, a claim that is reinforced by professional and funding bodies which promote PBL as an appropriate strategy for professional education and it is increasingly becoming the method of choice [14]. Furthermore, Ellis et al. [15] suggest that "the computing discipline lends itself to PBL" in ways which exemplify the current environment for Cybersecurity professionals:

- It is, for the most part, problem driven;
- Problems are typically ill-defined and ambiguous and may even be misunderstood or 'misdiagnosed' by users and clients;

- Lifelong learning is a necessity due to the rapidity and continually changing nature of the industry;
- Practitioners must constantly update their skills and competencies in order to keep abreast of new technology;
- The project group is the predominant mode of operation within the industry; and
- Computing crosses discipline boundaries [15].

A key theme in this paper is authenticity: PBL was originally used to shift teaching in medical schools from a collection of subjects representing individual disciplines to an integrative programme of study, engaging students in problem formulation and solving [7]. PBL has also been adopted in many other areas such as Architecture, Law, Engineering, Psychology, English Literature, Social work, Computer Science, Education and Business, demonstrating its applicability in a variety of domains – particularly those with an emphasis on professions and competencies that are now labelled 'employability skills'.

Whilst we have established that PBL provides a suitable approach for professional learning, it is also worth exploring whether PBL meets the conditions for effective learning that have been established through systematic pedagogic research. In summary, relevant evidence emphasizes the importance of activity that is community (team) and learner centred and takes account of existing understanding, pushing students into their 'zone of proximal development' (ZPD) [16, 17]. In PBL, teams identify learning issues which are relevant to their own needs, thus building on their current understanding and challenging them to advance their knowledge further.

An additional condition is for learning to be knowledge-centred, [17] and PBL aligns well with this requirement since students identify the key concepts and relationships between them, developing a rationale for their solution.

Formative assessment, extended dialogue and feedback are also widely acknowledged as essential for learning [18–21]. Once again, PBL achieves this, through frequent (timely) verbal feedback, that relates to task performance; there is an emphasis on dialogue and argumentation between facilitators and peers.

One important and widely used method for helping to achieve validity of learning, teaching and assessment systems is 'constructive alignment'. John Biggs first coined the phrase to describe the design of a system of teaching and assessment that achieves consistency between desired learning outcomes, teaching approaches and assessment methods. As Biggs and Tang [22] stated "All components in the system address the same agenda and support each other" so that students engage in a deep approach to learning. PBL is a learning system that exemplifies constructive alignment and consequently is regarded as good practice [22]. Thus, we suggest that the combination of authentic problems, together with a process that is aligned with currently perceived good practice for learning can lead to both high levels of engagement with the task and effective development of students' skills and knowledge.

If PBL is so good, the obvious question is why isn't it more widely used? PBL is not without its difficulties, which can be summarised in 3 categories. Firstly, there are student expectations, commonly expressed as "you are the teacher" and/or "I can't trust what my peer says". PBL is often a radical change from students' prior experiences. Secondly there are usually student skill and confidence issues, for example where students can feel uncertain of their capabilities in teamwork, in critical evaluation of the problem, and/or in research techniques. In our experience, some students think that the Google search engine is the answer to every problem. Often they are weak at synthesizing learning issues, which are really research questions. Articulating well-formed specific research questions is not intuitive. This is a critical point: if the student's research is not focused on relevant issues, the problem cannot be effectively solved. These two categories of issue can be addressed through specific skills training and gradually introducing PBL, so that initially students receive considerable guidance and tackle fairly straightforward, well-bounded problems. Subsequently, as students gain confidence and expertise, guidance can be reduced and messier, complex problems can be used.

In order to further scaffold critical analysis and evaluation, a useful technique requires students to produce 'research handouts'. These are brief 2-page summaries (in their own words) which contain their learning issue/research question, summary of research findings and finally the possible application of the findings to the scenario. The handout can be used when sharing their research within the team, but most importantly, a portfolio of such 'handouts' (one for each research question) can comprise an individual part of the assessment. With a suitable weighting (e.g. 70%) we have found that this approach effectively addresses any 'freeloader' issues in the team.

The third and final barrier is often the attitude and skill level of academic tutors; PBL requires the tutor to relinquish a good deal of control (to the students). In our experience, this causes significant anxiety, similarly moving to a facilitator role from that of a teacher requires a different skill set [9]. These problems are not insurmountable, but do constitute barriers to adoption.

Beyond the barriers, there is also the question of how effective PBL is, compared to more traditional pedagogies. Evaluation is not straightforward. What do you evaluate? Any of 'accumulation of knowledge'; 'improvements in practice'; 'approaches to learning'; 'satisfaction with learning environment' are valid. Research to evaluate the effectiveness of PBL has shown that it promotes deeper approaches to learning [23, 24] in an environment that is more stimulating and enjoyable [25, 26]. It enables students to enhance and retain self-regulated learning (SRL) skills [7, 27, 28] and helps students develop employability attributes [9] which are discussed in the next section.

However, it cannot be claimed that there is general consensus regarding the advantages of PBL over traditional teaching. PBL medical programme evaluations conducted by Koh et al. [28] revealed an improvement in students' ability to inquire and learn in a self-directed manner, and the development of a more holistic view of the patient. It produced positive effects on physician competencies after graduation, especially in the social and cognitive dimensions. However, there was no evidence of positive effects of PBL on physician competencies in the technical and teaching dimensions which require psychomotor skills and which are more effectively instilled using deliberate practice methods including formal procedural skills training.

In summary, research evidence analysed in this section has shown that PBL offers significant benefits for self-regulated learning, retention of knowledge, and in developing a systemic view of a situation. What's more, the subject of Cybersecurity is particularly well-suited to PBL, since it abounds with messy, complex and interdisciplinary problems, encompassing strategy, organizational culture, and ethics as well as technical competency and knowledge application. This interplay of technical and management issues is critical for effective information security, and avoids the pitfall of regarding cybersecurity as just a 'technical fix' issue. Such benefits have been recognised by our students, with sustained attendance rates of more than 95% in PBL modules – much higher than the average lecture.

However, technical skills are better learned in a more traditional (structured) way-so we would not expect PBL to be the most effective way for a student to learn technical procedures such as configuring a router or firewall.

Thus, we conclude that PBL is a suitable and effective pedagogy for professional learning and that it enables students to effectively learn to deal with the complexities of messy systems – typified by the cybersecurity subject domain. In the next section we show how it aligns with a consulting model of professional practice, and also develops the employability attributes which are the focus of much current attention.

3   PBL, Employability and the Consulting/Learning Model

PBL aims to produce independent learners who are motivated, engaged in deep learning, work as part of a team, and develop effective strategies, skills and knowledge for lifelong learning and professional work – attributes which align with the concept of employability. There are many models of employability, and even more lists of employability attributes [29–37]. Whichever model and list are adopted, there is general agreement that *interpersonal skills* (listening, verbal communication, teamwork, leadership), *intellectual skills* (problem-solving, creativity, criticality, planning, decision making, prioritizing, metacognition), and *personal qualities* (commitment, initiative, self-efficacy) are included.

PBL provides a suitable environment for the development of these attributes, and there is supporting research evidence of success [7, 9, 27, 28]. For example, complex and messy real-world scenarios provide an excellent vehicle for developing students' analytical and problem-solving skills. Researching and evaluating whether knowledge is relevant and sufficient provides them with significant challenges and uncertainty (and some stress). It also demands managing information, planning & organization, creatively and reflection.

Successful PBL requires effective interpersonal skills for a variety of different purposes. These include social and team maintenance, problem solving, constructing understanding relating to the PBL case and task/process oriented related to organizational aspects. A PBL team without commitment, motivation and time management will fail.

An innovative aspect of CSKE further reinforced the authenticity of the PBL approach by making an explicit link between the PBL process and a model of consultancy. Table 1 shows this applied to a particular scenario involving public Wi-Fi security. This model was developed from early discussions in the project evaluation where questions emerged on the relationships between different components of the project. We recognised that the process of working through the stages of the PBL scenarios could be explained to students in the same terms that we use when planning and implementing a consultancy intervention. This increases students' awareness of the

Table 1. The CSKE Consulting/Learning model.

Consulting model	What PBL normally includes	What you will be doing at each stage in the specific CSKE scenario
Understanding organizational history and context	Scenario analysis Socio-technical organizational analysis Clarification of ambiguities	Individual and team review of scenario text and video resources Team discussion Clarification of ambiguities with tutor/facilitator
Determining the problem to be resolved	Analysis: Identify key issues Simulated consultation with stakeholders (e.g. role-play and/or online interaction) Reviewing technology/processes in use Identifying learning goals Facilitator Guidance	Team review of scenario: identifying key issues Identifying learning goals Team publish action list & summary in forum
Identifying/learning necessary knowledge	Individual research & learning to resolve knowledge gaps Summarising & reflection. Teams share learning	Individual research & learning Individually summary of learning and how it applies to the scenario Team sharing learning/teach each other
Identifying alternative solutions	Determining and agreeing evaluation criteria and process Identifying technical possibilities, considering acceptance issues and organizational fit Facilitator Guidance	Determining evaluation criteria through team discussion Team identification of options for the pentest Facilitator Guidance
Choosing optimal solution	Deciding on best technical, organizational and social outcomes Proposing solution with justification	Team decision and justification Presentation to tutor in role of main stakeholders
Planning the implementation	Applying planning and scheduling techniques Proposing plan and deadlines	Review Scenario text and resources Produce Report/Flyer/video Produce plan/schedule
Implementation	Building the solution (if appropriate) Deploying the solution (if appropriate)	Not applicable to this scenario
Final evaluation	Formal evaluation methods re project success Personal reflection and evaluation	Team evaluation of performance and project success Individual reflection on personal learning & development

processes they will need to conquer 'real-world' problems in their future professional career and reinforces the parallel between the activities of a typical professional consulting model, generic PBL and the specific PBL case. The aim was to systematically embed the generic concepts and stages of consulting, through repeated application in different circumstances.

In summary, this section has demonstrated that PBL provides a learning environment that enables students to practise and develop skills and abilities that are now considered to be essential for employability. Whilst the scale of this project did not justify the claim that all students acquire all these attributes, it is noteworthy that when we asked them about their experiences of learning through the CSKE PBL scenarios, the very first point they raised was that it was particularly effective for enhancing their employability.

3.1   Example PBL Scenario – Public Wi-Fi Security

To illustrate the process in more detail, this section outlines a relatively simple example which uses a scenario of a public Wi-Fi hotspot in a café. The trigger for the problem is the concern of the café owner, having read an article about the dangers of a 'Hot-spot Honeypot', 'Evil Twin', 'Wi-Fi Pineapple' and identity theft. By introducing (but not explaining) terms in this way, students are prompted towards appropriate learning issues.

The scenario is designed to enable students to achieve the following learning issues:

- Identify and explain the security threats and vulnerabilities to using Wi-Fi hotspots.
- Explain how hackers can exploit these vulnerabilities and the tools they can use.
- Explain approaches to mitigating the threats.
- Explain good practice in securing devices and web communications to ensure secure connections when using public Wi-Fi.

Students would be expected to have prerequisite knowledge of Information Security concepts including threat, vulnerability, risk, control, confidentiality, integrity and the basic concepts of encryption.

The task was presented as a small piece of consultancy, mapped against the stages shown in Table 1, which delivered a report containing an explanation that can be understood by the café owner and her staff (a lay audience) and potential solutions and implementation plan which will be understood by technical specialists. A second deliverable was a flyer (for customers) that can be left on tables and/or a short video which can be played in the café so customers can quickly gain the information and know how to stay safe.

Typical learning issues generated were:

- What is a Wi-Fi Pineapple and what can it do?
- What vulnerabilities can a Wi-Fi hotspot have?
- What are the potential threats to customers' devices?
- What hacking software tools are available to exploit the vulnerabilities in open Wi-Fi locations?

- How can the problems be mitigated by the Café and by the customers?
- How can you spot hackers?
- What should/could you do if you suspect someone?

Students worked in teams of 4/5; each team would research around 4 learning issues and create a research handout for each as described above. Each learning issue is explored by at least 2 students, which mitigates against reliance on one individual. The facilitator ensures adequate detail is provided by asking probing questions (for example around protocol weaknesses). Links to possible resources are provided as part of the scenario documentation. The full scenario can be viewed (after registration) at https://www.cyberedge.uk/cske/pbl-scenarios/pbl-1.php.

4 Cyber Security Knowledge Exchange Model

The previous sections show that PBL is a suitable vehicle for developing both professional knowledge and employability attributes. However, a critical issue in Cyber Security is to ensure that that students are dealing with realistic and modern situations.

Thus, a major innovation in CSKE is a model to create authentic scenarios and provide an opportunity for students to deploy their skill/knowledge in the workplace. This section explains the holistic process of creating and using scenarios, together with the CSKE approach of facilitating students to use their skills and knowledge in small supervised consultancy work-placements.

The holistic CSKE model is shown in Fig. 1. The first (capture) phase comprises recruitment of cyber security expert professionals. In our project, these came from web development services, financial (bank) services, emergency (fire & rescue) services and a consultancy group. These professionals were volunteers who responded to an approach from the university to participate. The Computing department had previously developed strong relationships with these organizations, so recruitment was not difficult. They were asked to create brief outlines of scenarios based on real events. This was followed by a knowledge elicitation workshop at which they discussed their outlines with the academic team to elaborate and refine the scenarios. A key function of the workshop was to analyse the scenarios to identify appropriate learning outcomes, possible solutions, knowledge needed, and resources required. The scenarios were subsequently developed into paper-based descriptions and verified by the original authors.

In the second (create) phase, multimedia resources were constructed to support the scenarios. In our funded project, we employed students to work on this part-time. If no funding is available this could be done by organizing the work as a formal student project. The teams were supervised by a Technology Enhanced Learning (TEL) specialist. In the embed phase PBL scenarios were reviewed and tested in an MSc module. Normally, this would be the end of the learning process, but in CSKE we wanted to enable students to put their knowledge into practice in work placements, discussed next.

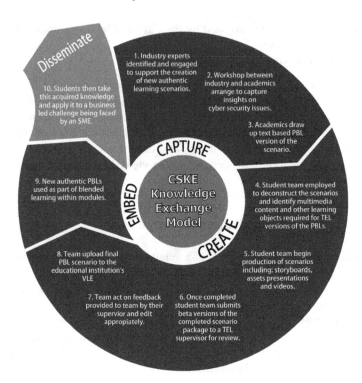

Fig. 1. CSKE model.

4.1 Integrating PBL and Work Placements

In this section, we return to the 'disseminate' stage of the CSKE model (Fig. 1). This innovation was to employ MSc Information Security Students as supervised 'trainee' consultants in 20-day work placements with SMEs. The aim was twofold: to provide students with authentic consultancy experience and to assist SMEs to control cyber-security risks. The process involved the following stages:

1. SME Recruitment.
   The university invited SMEs within the region to participate. The project provided free consultancy on a security project of their choice, requiring some time from their staff.
2. Initial visit to the SME.
   This visit was designed to understand the organizational context and determine/scope the problem. The students, academic (as consultant) and the CSKE Project Manager attended.
3. Agreed Specification.
   The academic and project manager created the specification and contract which were agreed with the SME client.

4. Student placement to complete the work.
   Students worked in pairs, each completing 10 days' work, some of which would be at the university, and some on customer premises.
5. Handover of deliverables.
   Typically, this comprised presenting a report, such as a risk assessment or penetration test report.

It is worth emphasising the differences between this type of placement and conventional student work placements. For example, in the latter, the student is usually supervised by a workplace member of staff who possesses the expertise to ensure that the student completes the work satisfactorily. In the CSKE placements the SME staff did not have that expertise, and it was provided by the university academic. Consequently, the level of supervision by the university was more frequent and detailed than usual. We also placed students in pairs, to reduce their levels of anxiety, and provide peer support for these challenging tasks.

As an illustrative example, one SME requested an information security risk assessment with recommended controls (including policies). The company trains teachers to deliver literacy teaching using phonics. The company had expanded rapidly over the last 18 months, now delivering in 17 regions within Nigeria together with numerous other African states and India. The company had no knowledge of Information Security, despite its widespread use of laptops, mobile phones and tablet computers, and shared data using Dropbox©. It had no policies or security controls in place. The risk assessment carried out by the students followed ISO 27001/ISO 27005 processes, and their recommendations (including policies and online training) were adopted.

5 Project Evaluation

The evaluation strategy used in the Cyber Security Knowledge Exchange (CSKE) project is a further development of an innovative strategy that has been used successfully in national educational projects over the last few years, such as the Jisc-funded Digital Literacies in Transition project at the University of Greenwich [45]. The strategy is designed to engage the project team throughout the project. Its main features are:

- Focus questions with an emphasis on impact and future development.
- Use of concept mapping as a device for both data capture and communication.
- A collaborative and iterative process which runs throughout the main project (and potentially beyond as it can then be 'adopted' and further refined by the project team).

As well as the benefits suggested above from collaboration, where the project team can take on and further develop the evaluation after the formal project is completed, this approach is particularly useful in highlighting the essential features and issues in a project. A concept map provides an overview of the project on 'one side of A4' which can be a more effective stimulus to dialogue than a lengthy formal report and can be especially useful in suggesting links (or the lack of links) between different aspects of the project. It was through this sort of questioning and discussion that the CSKE project team moved towards the learning/consulting model described above (see 3 above).

5.1   The Evaluation Process

The starting point is the series of questions which are summarized in Fig. 2, organized under the following main sub-headings:

- Main outcomes, to include both the outcomes which were specified/planned at the beginning of the project and any emergent or unanticipated outcomes,
- Impact, to include both the impact of whatever the project produced and any impact on the teams and institutions involved which were direct or indirect consequences of the project process,
- Main issues and resolutions, to allow the project to record the major barriers and pitfalls which the project encountered and allow reflection on how (and how far) these were resolved,
- Plans for embedding and sustainability, to focus on what is planned to follow after the project funding/schedule has run its course. One of the problems of the project approach is that this aspect can be neglected and may not be given sufficient attention until it is too late to make meaningful plans. As a result, the long-term impact of a specific project may be diluted or even nullified [38].

Another key feature of this approach is its collaborative nature. Rather than relying on the external evaluator to observe and 'pronounce' on outcomes and impact, he/she operates according to the principles of 'Critical Friendship' which emerged from the CAMEL Project [39] and were later codified for later Jisc and HEA projects [40].

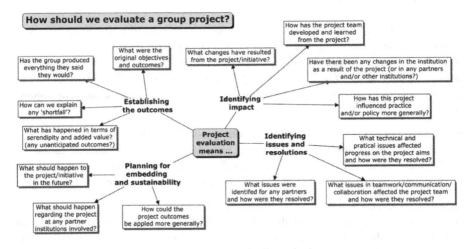

Fig. 2. Project evaluation criteria

5.2   Recording and Reviewing the Outcomes

Following this model, the evaluator engages in regular open discussion with the project team. This discussion produces updates of the concept map which records progress and developments and which can be colour-coded to reflect different degrees of progress, as in Fig. 3. In this figure, different colours/shades have been used to highlight the areas where the project did not fully meet the criterion by the formal end of the project (for example, the timescale was not sufficient to enable much use by SMEs or other institutions), and where the project delivered outcomes above and beyond the initial project aims (for example, the consulting/learning model was not specified as an outcome in the initial project application). The main tasks of the evaluator are to ensure that the map accurately reflects progress (and that there is sufficient evidence to support each point on the map). As a technique, concept mapping is underused in education which is unfortunate as it can support dialogue and exploration about levels of understanding which are difficult to achieve in other ways [41].

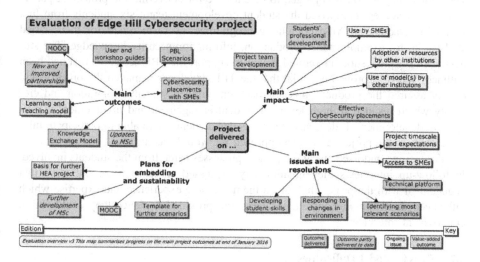

Fig. 3. Final evaluation map

Depending on the complexity of the project, individual maps can be produced for each of the four main sub-heads which can include further details of the evidence for each point.

The ultimate success of the CSKE project will not become apparent until the resources and approaches we have demonstrated have been used repeatedly, both in the educational context (at Edge Hill and other HE institutions) and by SMEs as part of their efforts to combat cybersecurity threats. From this perspective, there is a significant challenge in terms of embedding the outcomes in ongoing practice, a challenge which is confronted (and often not met) by all projects of this type where there is a limited timescale and where the project team may not continue to work together after the funding ceases [38].

6   Evaluation Results

The final overview concept map (Fig. 3 above) identifies those aspects of the project plan which were fully realised as well as areas where there needs to be further long-term analysis and/or development. Each point on the map is supported by relevant evidence and we can illustrate this by focusing on the two principal interventions in this paper: The CSKE Model of creating PBL scenarios and the Consultancy placement model.

6.1   CSKE Model Successes

The CSKE model of working, involving collaboration between academics, industry experts, technology enhanced learning developer, students and a project manager, together with an iterative development method, yielded the target number of scenarios, broadly on schedule with the expected supporting learning resources (videos etc.). Thus, the collaboration was judged to be effective for delivering the project. A particular area of success comprised the student development team: six students from first year undergraduate to MSc computing programmes were recruited for their varied skillsets in, for example: video production, information security knowledge. The student team scripted, shot, and edited videos to support the PBL scenarios that had been outlined. Whilst it proved essential that the TEL developer managed the process, and quality assured the products, this approach encouraged student exploration and creativity which resulted in high levels of student engagement and involvement in curriculum development. It demonstrated to us that students were able to participate fully as partners in the project and is an approach we would recommend.

Very strong endorsement of the project processes came from the students involved. In follow-up interviews they unanimously expressed enthusiasm for the ways that engagement with the project had given them valuable experience and expertise which influenced their thinking on future careers and provided evidence they could use in employment interviews.

6.2   CSKE Model Difficulties

Whilst the process of developing multimedia scenarios was successful in the create phase, significant difficulties were experienced in the capture phase. Despite the long-standing relationships with partner organizations, knowledge elicitation was difficult: we asked partners to arrive with draft scenarios, using a template, but partners provided very variable amounts of detail, not in a consistent format, reflecting the variety of situations and different partner perspectives and expectations. In the most successful cases, technical experts had provided very detailed information about cases with which they were very familiar. In the least successful, the partner had less (and indirect) knowledge of a scenario, which required follow-up meetings with further contacts. Some scenarios were not possible, for example because insufficient information was available, or the suggestions such as web code inspection were unsuitable for PBL. In those cases, alternatives were created through follow-up meetings with partners. The lesson from this experience is an old one: we needed to prepare more fully and have further discussion with prospective partners to clarify their expectations and assumptions and ensure we were working with individuals who had appropriate detailed knowledge of the potential scenarios. Clear, consistent and specific expectations are needed with all stakeholders well in advance.

6.3 CSKE Scenarios

A total of 9 scenarios were developed, addressing diverse and topical aspects of Cyber security. Table 2 provides a brief summary of each. They are freely available with facilitator guides from the project website: https://www.cyberedge.uk/cske/index.php. Scenarios were well-received by students at Edge Hill University, during evaluation interviews, respondents identified that they enjoyed and benefitted from 'solving real-world problems', 'soft-skills development', 'deeper understanding than from lectures' and they highlighted the benefits for employability, both in skill development and in 'providing a framework to discuss those skills at interview'. Five scenarios have also been adapted internationally, in Brazil, where feedback indicated that, after initial resistance to the method, classroom discussion was 'dynamic around different views' with 'clearer learning'. Knowledge assessment was at the same level, but skills had been enhanced significantly.

Table 2. The CSKE PBL scenarios.

Scenario	Aim:
Wi-Fi network security	Enables students to explore the security issues that occur at open Wi-Fi hot spots. See Sect. 3.1 above
Secure software development	Enables students to explore the security risks in rapid application development, methods of mitigating the risks, threats to particular software apps and secure registration
Cryptography	Enables students to explain, justify and select appropriate encrypting software/algorithms to make online applications secure
SME governance	Enables students to explore the security governance, risk assessment, culture and Return on Investment issues that occur in SMEs
Incident management	Enables students to explore a fairly complex cyber attack and the consequent incident management process for a financial institution with approximately 350,000+ users, situated both nationally and internationally. Potential role-play
Web form attacks	Enables students to understand how web forms are attacked, their vulnerabilities and how people/bots exploit them. Risk control through coding best practices, data storage issues and understanding hacker mentality
SME risk assessment	Enables students to explore and develop a sound understanding of ISO27001, particularly the risk assessment, and apply it to an SME context

(continued)

Table 2. (*continued*)

Scenario	Aim:
Social engineering	Enables students to explore the concepts, and methods of Social Engineering. This scenario is based on a real attack that is provided by Ian Mann (2013, pp. 73–86 by agreement)
Information security in fire and rescue service	Enables students to identify risks associated with adopting mobile technology and controlling them whilst maintaining alignment with standards including ISO27001. This scenario involves a large emergency service whose financial resources are subject to external and political decisions

6.4   CSKE Placements Successes

The CSKE model worked well (as judged by clients, students and the academics) in all 3 projects conducted and this suggests that the process is both effective and transferable, whereby the academic ensured the scope of the consultancy was appropriate, the project manager drew up the contract and negotiated details with the client, and the students completed the assignment. This part of the project required a high level of expertise from the students, the placement primarily focused on them applying knowledge and skills in a new environment and demonstrating a professional approach to clients. Again, supervision and checking of work by the academic, as lead consultant, was essential. In the follow-up interviews conducted as part of the project evaluation, all the students confirmed that they particularly valued learning in a real-world scenario, working in a supervised team and the frequent feedback they received. They also found the experience valuable as a basis for discussion during subsequent job interview situations.

In our view the CSKE model is a useful complement to a 'standard' placement: it provides beneficial placements where small organisations have neither the time nor expertise to provide job descriptions and supervision. The CSKE approach involved students, client, university academic and project manager in capturing requirements to produce comprehensive project initiation documents. The benefit of this approach was the depth of process by which we diagnosed the problem and defined the deliverables with the company before the placement.

Furthermore, the task itself required the student to act as consultant, stretching not only their technical, subject specific skills, but also their transferable skills. It positioned the student in a different light from the standard employer-employee relationship and allowed them to take more ownership, responsibility and management of the placement.

6.5   Difficulties

Somewhat surprisingly, the primary difficulty experienced was the very limited response from SMEs. We expected the offer of free consultancy in a clearly important area of Information Security would be very popular. Whilst SMEs acknowledged their need for improved Information Security processes, they indicated that the economic pressures they are now facing meant that they were reluctant to commit to the time needed. Further exploration of the issue revealed that they were extremely focussed on short term objectives and had little spare resource capacity. In our view, this potentially reveals a reactive (rather than proactive) culture with a mind-set that accepts rather than controls information security risks. It is a subject that affords further research, since the consequences of incidents can be very significant, even leading to closure of the business.

7   Conclusions

The need for universities to produce competent graduates to address the global shortage of cyber security professionals is urgent. Furthermore, the SME sector is particularly weak in their cyber security expertise. This article has explained and critically evaluated an innovative approach to cybersecurity education which is designed to help address both of these issues.

Firstly, we drew together the strong research evidence to show that PBL is effective for professional learning. Building on this evidence, we demonstrated that it is well-suited to the complexities of cyber security, and that it aligns with current concepts of good practice for learning, developing students' employability attributes.

Given that Cyber Security threats are changing rapidly, in order to ensure authentic and topical scenarios, the CSKE project developed a model to engage with local industry experts to transfer their 'real world' experience into materials that could be used in the university. Whilst the knowledge-elicitation process was more problematic than envisaged, we found that companies were open and willing to share their expertise and time. We learned that in order to make the process most effective, we needed to invest more time at the start, discussing with prospective partners their expectations and assumptions and ensure we were working with individuals who had appropriate detailed knowledge of the potential scenarios.

The CSKE resources that were produced are freely available for use by other institutions/organizations. There is also significant scope for other institutions to 'pick up the baton' and use our templates to develop new resources as new threats emerge. There is also the potential to use elements of our approach in other areas of the Computing curriculum and in other subject disciplines.

Initial responses from students and tutors experiencing the CSKE scenarios have been positive and while the evidence base so far is small, our previous experience of success with PBL in Computing for more than 15 years [9, 42–44] provides confidence in their utility. We would therefore encourage readers to adopt and adapt them as part of their curriculum. PBL is particularly effective for integrating concepts and skills, complimenting traditional approaches for learning detailed technical skills and knowledge.

Our second innovation was the consultancy project, which shifted the supervision expertise from the placement provided to the university, and promoted the role of the student to 'apprentice consultant'. The response from clients, students and academic participants in this small sample suggests that students step up to the challenge and produce work of professional standard when supported appropriately. In our view this has great potential, both for the benefit of SMEs and in preparing students to be work-ready.

In summary, we have demonstrated that it is possible to engage successfully with industry to develop current and authentic teaching resources. Universities have a long history of engagement through Knowledge Transfer Partnerships (KTP) and research, but partnerships for learning are more rare, and the full-cycle approach of CSKE, where industry provided scenarios to educate students who transferred back benefits to SMEs through short term placements demonstrates the effectiveness of the professional education - addressing the critical need highlighted at the start of this paper.

Perhaps the most important educational conclusion from this project relates to the processes we developed over its lifespan in terms of the engagement of students with the urgent technical and organizational problems which are now evident in cybersecurity. Both processes of scenario development and placement integration engaged students in 'real-life' problem-solving in ways which significantly enhanced their learning and professional confidence. At the end of the day, it will be those professional skills in our students which will enable organizations to successfully combat the significant and growing threats we can now see in cybersecurity.

8 Sponsor

The project was funded by the UK Government Department for Digital, Culture Media & Sport, through the UK Higher Education Academy's (HEA) learning and teaching in cyber security grant scheme.

References

1. Graham, L.: Cybercrime costs the global economy $450 billion (2017). http://www.cnbc.com/2017/02/07/cybercrime-costs-the-global-economy-450-billion-ceo.html. Accessed 11 Jul 2017
2. Lloyds of London: Counting the cost Cyber exposure decoded (2017). https://www.lloyds.com/news-and-insight/press-centre/press-releases/2017/07/cyber-attack-report. Accessed 11 Jul 2017
3. Frost & Sullivan: Global Information Security Workforce Study (2017)
4. House of Commons Library. http://researchbriefings.parliament.uk/ResearchBriefing/Summary/SN06152. Accessed 13 Apr 2019
5. Ashford, W.: SMEs failing to address cyber threats despite risks. http://www.computerweekly.com/news/450423715/SMEs-failing-to-address-cyber-threats-despite-risks. Accessed 11 Jul 2017
6. Vernon, D.T., Blake, R.L.: Does problem-based learning work? a meta-analysis of evaluative research. Acad. Med. **68**(7), 550–563 (1993)

7. Barrows, H.S., Tamblyn, R.M.: Problem-based Learning: An Approach to Medical Education. Springer, New York (1980)
8. Savin-Baden, M.: Problem-based Learning in Higher Education: Untold Stories. Society for Research into Higher Education and the Open University Press, Buckingham (2000)
9. Uden, L., Beaumont, C.: Technology and Problem-based Learning. IGI group, London (2006)
10. Dearnley, C.A., Rhodes, C.A., Roberts, P., Williams, P., Prenton, S.: Team based learning in nursing and midwifery higher education; a systematic review of the evidence for change. Nurse Educ. Today. **60**, 75–83 (2018)
11. North Carolina State University PER&D Group: SCALE-UP (2011). http://scaleup.ncsu.edu/. Accessed 13 Apr 2019
12. McNeil, J., Borg, M., Kennedy, E., Cu, V.I., Puntha, H., Rashid, Z.: SCALE-UP Handbook (2018). https://www4.ntu.ac.uk/adq/document_uploads/teaching/181133.pdf. Accessed 13 Apr 2019
13. Wilson, B.G., Cole, P.: Cognitive teaching models. In: Jonassen, D.H. (ed.) Handbook of Research for Educational Communications and Technology, pp. 601–621. Simon and Schuster Macmillan, New York (1996)
14. Newman, M.: A pilot systematic review and meta-analysis on the effectiveness of problem-based learning (2003). http://citeseerx.ist.psu.edu/viewdoc/download?doi=10.1.1.133.6561&rep=rep1&type=pdf. Accessed 07 Nov 2017
15. Ellis, A., Carswell, L., et al.: Resources, tools, and techniques for problem based learning. In: 3rd Annual Conference on Integrating Technology into Computer Science Education in Computing ITiCSE 1998. ACM/SIGCSE (1998)
16. Vygotsky, L.S.: Mind in Society: The Development of Higher Mental Processes. Harvard University Press, Cambridge (1978)
17. Bransford, J.D., Brown, A.L., Cocking, R.R.: How People Learn: Brain, Mind, Experience, and School. National Academy Press, Washington (2000)
18. Gibbs, G., Simpson, C.: Conditions under which assessment supports students' learning. Learn. Teach. High. Educ. **1**(1), 3–31 (2004)
19. Alexander, R.J.: Towards Dialogic Teaching: Rethinking Classroom Talk, 4th ed. York: Dialogos (2008)
20. Hattie, J.A.C.: Identifying the salient facets of a model of student learning: a synthesis of meta-analyses. Int. J. Educ. Res. **11**(2), 187–212 (1987)
21. Black, P., Wiliam, D.: Assessment and classroom learning. Assess. Educ. **5**(1), 7–74 (1998)
22. Biggs, J.B., Tang, C.: Teaching for Quality Learning at University, 4th edn. Open University Press, Buckingham (2011)
23. Dolmans, D.H.J.M., Loyens, S.M.M., Marcq, H., Gijbels, D.: Deep and surface learning in problem-based learning: a review of the literature. Adv. Health Sci. Educ. **21**, 1087–1112 (2016). https://doi.org/10.1007/s10459-015-9645-6
24. Newble, D.I., Clarke, R.M.: The approaches to learning of students in traditional and an innovative problem-based learning school. Acad. Med. **67**, 557–565 (1986)
25. O'Grady, G., Yew, E.H.J., Goh, K.P.L., Schmidt, H.G.: One-Day, One-Problem. Springer, Singapore (2012). https://doi.org/10.1007/978-981-4021-75-3
26. Albanese, M.A., Mitchell, S.: Problem-based learning: a review of literature on its outcomes and implementation issues. Acad. Med. **68**(1), 52–81 (1993)
27. Loyens, S.M.M., Magda, J., Rikers, R.M.J.P.: Self-directed learning in problem-based learning and its relationships with self-regulated learning. Educ. Psychol. Rev. **20**, 411–427 (2008)
28. Koh, et al.: The effects of problem-based learning during medical school on physician competency: a systematic review. CMAJ **178**(1), 34–41 (2008)

29. Finch, D.J., Hamilton, L.K., Baldwin, R., Zehner, M.: An exploratory study of factors affecting undergraduate employability, Education + Training **55**(7), 681–704 (2013)
30. Redmond, P.: The Graduate Jobs Formula: How to Land your Dream Career. Trotman, Richmond (2010)
31. Maher, A., Graves, S.: Graduate Employability: can Higher Education Deliver?. Threshold Press, Newbury (2008)
32. Kreber, C.: Setting the context: the climate of university teaching and learning. New Dir. High. Educ. **133**, 5–11 (2006)
33. Andrews, J., Higson, H.: Graduate employability, 'soft skills' versus 'hard' business knowledge: a European study. High. Educ. Eur. **33**(4), 413–422 (2008)
34. Abraham, S.E., Karns, L.: Do business schools value the competencies that businesses value? J. Educ. Bus. **84**(6), 350–356 (2009)
35. Archer, W., Davison, J.: Graduate employability: What do employers think and want? The Council for Industry and Higher Education (2008). http://www.cihe-uk.com. Accessed 18 June 2011
36. Cumming, J.: Contextualised performance: reframing the skills debate in research education. Stud. High. Educ. **35**, 1–15 (2010)
37. Yorke, M., Knight, P.: Embedding employability into the curriculum. ESECT (2004)
38. Hartley, P., Turner, N.: Managing and leading projects and project teams. In: Baume, D., Popovic, C. (eds.) Advancing Practice in Academic Development. Routledge, London (2016)
39. JISC: CAMEL approach (2014). https://www.jisc.ac.uk/guides/change-management/camel-approach. Accessed 29 Nov 2017
40. JISC: Critical friends (2014). https://www.jisc.ac.uk/guides/change-management/critical-friends. Accessed 29 Nov 2017
41. Kinchin, I.M.: Visualising Powerful Knowledge to Develop the Expert Student: A Knowledge Structures Perspective on Teaching and Learning at University. Sense Publishers, Rotterdam (2016). ISBN 978 946300625 5
42. Beaumont, C., Sackville, A., Chew, S.C.: Identifying good practice in the use of PBL to teach computing. ITALICS **3**(1), 17–37 (2004)
43. Beaumont, C.: Using problem-based learning in M-level computing module. In: Kneale (Ed.) Perspectives on Masters Level Teaching, Learning and Student Experience. Palgrave (2015)
44. Beaumont, C.: Problem-based learning in Computing A pedagogy for employability. HE Academy (2015). https://www.heacademy.ac.uk/system/files/chris_beaumont_final.pdf
45. University of Greenwich: Digital Literacies at the University of Greenwich (2015). https://jiscinfonetcasestudies.pbworks.com/w/page/76452875/Digital%20Literacies%20at%20the%20University%20of%20Greenwich. Accessed 29 Nov 2017

Virtual Training and Experience System for Public Security Education

Zhigeng Pan[1,2,3(✉)] and Yi Zong[3]

[1] China Academy of Art, Hangzhou, China
[2] Institute of VR, NINED LLC, Guangzhou, China
[3] Digital Media & HCI Center, Hangzhou Normal University, Hangzhou, China
zgpan@hznu.edu.cn

Abstract. Public security is a major problem facing our country at present. Frequent public security accidents have become a great hidden danger affecting social stability. The public security consciousness of our people is generally scarce. When facing such disasters as earthquake and fire, we often do not know how to avoid danger and save ourselves. With the most advanced virtual simulation technology, to popularize public safety knowledge to the whole people, improve public security awareness, has become an urgent task of today's society. This paper designs and implements a virtual simulation system for public security education based on Unity3D engine and virtual reality technology. The system combines earthquake escape and fire fighting. The experiencer can not only experience the horror and ruthlessness of public safety disasters in the virtual world, but also learn how to save himself in the event of disasters without risk. It is an effective scheme to popularize safety knowledge to citizens.

Keywords: Public security · Virtual reality · Earthquake simulation · Human-machine interaction

1 Introduction

The public security awareness of Chinese nationals is generally poor, and they often suffer heavy losses in the face of earthquakes, fires and other disasters. It has become the top priority of public safety work to carry out basic public safety knowledge popularization of the general public, actively carry out corresponding exercises and practical drills, and improve people's ability to cope with public security incidents [1]. There are several main measures for popularizing public security knowledge:

(1) Holding a series of public safety knowledge lectures [2].
(2) Schools with conditions will hold earthquake and fire escape drills from time to time [3].
(3) Popularization through media tools such as public safety knowledge manuals, videos and TV programs.

Although these measures have been widely used, they have many limitations, and the effects received are not obvious [4].

© Springer-Verlag GmbH Germany, part of Springer Nature 2019
Z. Pan et al. (Eds.): Transactions on Edutainment XV, LNCS 11345, pp. 229–237, 2019.
https://doi.org/10.1007/978-3-662-59351-6_15

Today, the wave of Virtual Reality (VR) is sweeping the globe. In the three-dimensional virtual environment constructed by virtual reality technology, users interact with objects in the virtual environment in a natural way, interacting with each other, greatly expanding the ability of humans to understand the world, simulate and adapt to the world [5]. The VR system is an extremely complex system involving graphics and image processing, speech processing, audio pattern recognition, artificial intelligence, intelligent interfaces, sensors, databases, parallel processing, system modeling, etc. [6]. This paper uses virtual reality and human-computer interaction technology to design and produce a virtual training and experience system for public safety education. The scene of the system is produced by 3D MAX software, then imported into the Unity3D engine for scene construction, and uses HTC VIVE virtual head display and handle for virtual roaming and interaction. The experiencer can operate the handle to move and interact in the virtual scene, as if watching and walking in the real world, enhancing the authenticity of the experience.

2   System Design

We divide the public security education system into two modules (seismic science and escape modules, fire and escape modules) for demand analysis. Determine what features the system needs to implement. Figure 1 is the overall architecture of the system.

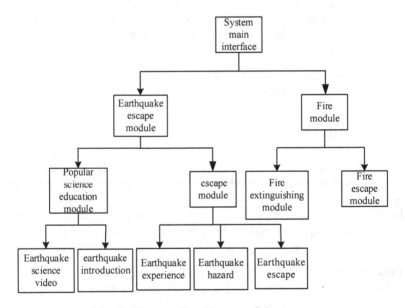

Fig. 1. The overall architecture of the system

3   Scene Design

In order to let the experiencer understand what the earthquake is, the cause of the earthquake and how to save itself from the earthquake, the system contains a science education room. The actual operation diagram of the popular science room is shown in Fig. 2.

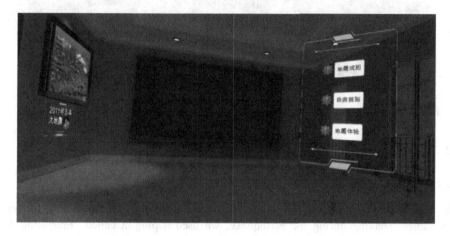

Fig. 2. Science education room operation diagram

The effect we want to achieve is that the user can roam freely in the room. There are three buttons in the menu bar at the center of the room: earthquake cause, self-rescue measures and earthquake experience. Click on the first two buttons to view the relevant science videos on the virtual screen in front of the popular science room. The third button seismic experience will allow the experiencer to move on to the next module: the earthquake experience and the escape module. On the four walls of the room, there are photos of some famous earthquakes in history. The user clicks the round button below the photo, and a text about the earthquake appears next to the photo.

The Earthquake Escape Module is the second module of the Earthquake Subsystem, in which the experiencer can experience earthquakes, temporary houses and ground shaking, falling and fragmentation of items. To enrich the system content and enhance the experience of the experience, we offer three different earthquake magnitudes for the user experience. The three magnitudes are: mild, moderate, and severe. The degree of shaking of the ground and the degree of fragmentation of indoor objects will increase as the magnitude increases. Figure 3 is a schematic diagram of the operation of an apartment scene during a moderate earthquake. It can be seen that indoor furniture such as chairs, chandeliers, decorative paintings and other items have been broken and damaged, and the glass on the windows has been shattered and scattered.

Fig. 3. Schematic diagram of the operation of the apartment scene during the earthquake

4 Earthquake Science and Escape Module Implementation

4.1 Indoor Scene Simulation During Earthquake

In order to achieve the effect of furniture, doors and windows, etc., which were broken by violent shaking during the earthquake, we used a plug-in called "Fracturing & Destruction" for auxiliary development. The plugin contains a script file called "Fractured Object" that is first hung on the object that you want to achieve. The script settings are shown in Fig. 4. Among them, the Source Object selects the object you want to break. Number Of Chunks can be used to input the number of fragments that are fragmented. After setting the above properties, click the Compute Chunks button to calculate and generate the fragments. In order to perform collision detection, each piece of the calculated piece needs to add the Rigidbody component and the Collider component. Because the fragmentation is generated after the earthquake, the isKinematic property in the Rigidbody component that sets all the fragments at the beginning is false, indicating that the rigid body is not affected by the kinetics and will remain stationary. The effect of the crushing can be achieved by setting the value to true after the start of the earthquake. The crushing effect of the four objects after the earthquake is shown in Fig. 5. The four broken objects are: windows, photo frames, porcelain bottles and cabinets.

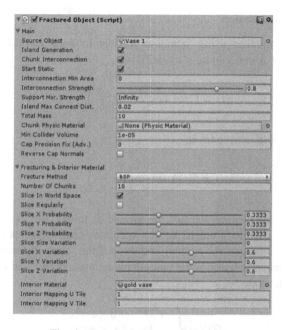

Fig. 4. Fractured object script settings

Fig. 5. Schematic diagram of the object crushing effect after the earthquake

4.2   Vibration Simulation

We simulate earthquakes using vibration models in both vertical and horizontal directions. The horizontal vibration model is:

$$x(t) = f(t)A \cos\left[\omega\left(t - \frac{x}{u_s}\right) + \varphi\right] \tag{1}$$

The vertical vibration model is:

$$x(t) = f(t)A \sin\left[\omega\left(t - \frac{x}{u_p}\right) + \varphi\right] \tag{2}$$

Where $x(t)$ is the displacement of the ground at time t, and $f(t)$ is the envelope function, which is used to simulate the non-stationary characteristics of seismic wave strength. A is the amplitude, the angular frequency is the source distance, us is the wave velocity of the transverse wave, is the random phase angle in (0,), and t is the time. The envelope function model is:

$$f(t) = \begin{cases} t^2/t_1^2 & 0 \le t < t_1 \\ 1 & t_1 \le t < t_2 \\ e^{-\alpha(t-t_2)} & t_2 \le t < t_3 \end{cases} \tag{3}$$

The u_s is 3090 $m * s^{-1}$ and the u_p is about 5470 $m * s^{-1}$.

The function of simulating different earthquake magnitudes can be achieved by modifying the amplitude A in Eqs. (1) and (2). When the experiencer just enters the earthquake escape module, the system will prompt the experiencer to choose the magnitude of the earthquake magnitude. A schematic diagram of the UI interface for selecting the magnitude is shown in Fig. 6.

Fig. 6. Schematic diagram of earthquake magnitude selection

5   Fire and Escape Module Implementation

The function to be implemented by the fire education module is mainly that the experiencer uses the fire extinguisher in the virtual scene to extinguish the flame in the scene and escape after the disaster. In order to reflect the fidelity of the system, the burning object needs to make a Shader similar to the ablation effect. If the fire is too large due to untimely rescue, the user can also choose to escape directly. Figure 7 shows the development flow chart of the fire protection module.

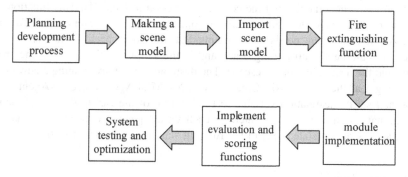

Fig. 7.   The development flow chart of the fire protection module

5.1   Combustion Effect Production

The Shader can achieve the ablation effect when the object is burned. The focus of the Shader is to set a threshold. If a pixel segment value is less than the threshold, then the pixel segment is removed, and the clip(x) function in ShaderLab can perform the above functions. When the incoming x value is less than 0, the pixel where x is located is removed. The actual code in Shader is clip(noiseMap.r-_BurnValue), where noiseMap is the texture image obtained by texture sampling the noise picture, and _BurnValue is

Fig. 8.   Schematic diagram of ablation effect operation

a value that gradually becomes larger with time. We choose the value of the R channel of the noise texture image minus _BurnValue, and if the result is less than 0, then the pixel is culled. The general flame burning effect is to spread from the middle to the periphery. The actual effect of the ablation effect is shown in Fig. 8.

5.2   Personnel Escape Module

In the safe escape route of fire escape, many AI people who escaped from each room escaped to the escape exit. We made a prefab of multiple virtual people (Prefab). The escape group is generated using the coroutine function in Unity3D. This function will generate random characters at the refresh point of each room every time. The Nav Mesh Agent component needs to be mounted at the virtual person's refresh point to implement automatic path finding. Each and in the script sets the speed of the crowd escape and the destination of the escape. The destination is set by creating a new empty object target at the escape exit. Create a new NavMeshAgent object nvAgent in the script, and set its destination variable to the location of the cart in the Start function. The Animator component is mounted on each virtual person to control the character action, and its action state is set to the running state in the Update function.

6   Conclusion

This paper designs and implements a virtual training and experience system for public safety education. The two sub-modules of the system: the earthquake escape module and the functions implemented by the fire-fighting experience and escape module are introduced in detail, and the flow chart and code of some key functions are given.

The article first introduced the research background of the system. It is pointed out that at present, citizens' awareness of safety is low, safety knowledge is generally scarce, and the method of popularizing safety education is not effective. Then combined with the research status at home and abroad, a solution proposed in this paper is proposed. Next, the demand analysis and structural design of the solution given in this paper are mainly divided into two large modules: fire module and earthquake escape module for analysis and design. Then the functions of the two modules are separately subdivided and each function is developed with reference to the requirements analysis. Both modules use HTC VIVE virtual head display and handle to interact, and use VRTK plug-in for auxiliary development of interactive operation. The UI interface of the two modules is developed using the GUI system UGUI that comes with Unity3D. In the earthquake escape module, the wave velocity formula of the shear wave is used to calculate the wave velocity of the shear wave and is substituted into the displacement function generated by the shear wave. Similarly, the displacement function of the longitudinal wave is calculated. The superposition of the two can simulate the vibration of the earthquake. The ShaderLab shader is used in the fire module to achieve the ablation effect of the object burning.

Acknowledgments. We would like to acknowledge the support of the Guangzhou Innovation and Entrepreneurship Leading Team Project under grant CXLJTD-201609.

References

1. Zhu, Z., Zhang, Y.: A review of public safety concepts in developed countries. J. Shenzhen Univ. (Humanit. Soc. Sci.) **01**, 21–25 (2006). 朱正威, 张莹. 发达国家公共安全理念述论. 深圳大学学报(人文社会科学版) **01**, 21–25 (2006)
2. Zhou, W.: On the construction of public security system for large-scale aggregation activities. J. Henan Police Coll. **2**, 120–124 (2017). 周文峰. 论大型聚集活动公共安全体系的构建. 河南警察学院学报 **2**, 120–124 (2017)
3. Zeng, J.: Problems in current high school safety evacuation drills. Ping An Campus **03**, 68–70 (2018). 曾建洪. 当前高中安全疏散演练中存在的问题. 平安校园 **03**, 68–70 (2018)
4. Huang, X., Bai, H.: Risk prediction of rural public security environmental carrying capacity based on the risk entropy. Nat. Hazards **90**(1), 157–171 (2018)
5. Zhou, Z., Zhou, W., Xiao, J.: Overview of virtual reality enhancement technology. Chin. Sci. Inf. Sci. **45**(02), 157–180 (2015). 周忠, 周颐, 肖江剑. 虚拟现实增强技术综述. 中国科学: 信息科学 **45**(02), 157–180 (2015)
6. Fischbach, M., Wiebusch, D., Latoschik, M.E.: Semantic entity-component state management techniques to enhance software quality for multimodal VR-systems. IEEE Trans. Visual Comput. Graphics **23**(4), 1342–1351 (2017)

Intelligent Coach Avatar Based Virtual Driving Training

Mingliang Cao[1(✉)] and Lvjie She[2]

[1] Guangdong Academy of Research on VR Industry, Foshan University,
Foshan 528000, China
merlin.cao@connect.polyu.hk
[2] VR Research Institute, NINEDVR Corp., Guangzhou 310036, China

Abstract. This paper presents an intelligent coach avatar based training system for one-to-one automatic guidance in virtual driving training. Compared with previous training methods, the intelligent coach avatar embodies a combination of more interest and knowledge, and provides a reference for exploring the deep integration of the intelligent behavior mode.

Keywords: Virtual Reality · Intelligent coach avatar · Virtual driving training

1 Introduction

According to data from 2011 to 2016 reported by the National Bureau of Statistics of China, the number of new drivers has grown from about 174 million to 303 million. Driving training schools use traditional methods; however, with more learners, there are not enough cars for them to learn in, which has led to many learners lacking sufficient training time, not accepting the training well, and experiencing high psychological stress. All of these, in turn, affect the learning effects and test results.

With the development of Virtual Reality (VR) technology, learners can use head-mounted displays (HMD) to observe scenes [1]. VR-based driving training can provide a user with a virtual 3D driving scenario to learn the knowledge and skills of driving. This system is designed as a supplement to the driving school training. Therefore, we assume that the users already understood the basic theoretical knowledge, hence the purpose of the virtual system is to address difficulties encountered in the practical driving training and have a sufficient and proper review process. Drivers need to know how to cope with situations like fog or unexpected errors made by themselves or other road users. They have to assess each situation and react in a responsible way [2]. Throughout the guidance of an intelligent coach avatar, the user is given the opportunity to experience such situations and to receive guidance and feedback about how to react.

© Springer-Verlag GmbH Germany, part of Springer Nature 2019
Z. Pan et al. (Eds.): Transactions on Edutainment XV, LNCS 11345, pp. 238–245, 2019.
https://doi.org/10.1007/978-3-662-59351-6_16

2   Intelligent Coach Avatar Based Virtual Driving Training

An avatar is a virtual person based on digital technology, used widely in the Internet and digital platforms, in education, entertainment, medical treatment, training and other fields [3–6]. An avatar can affect a user's self-efficacy and plays a role of empathy from the perspective of users' cognition [7]. The personified expression is generally accepted easily by users, thus, a coach avatar adds a new dimension to a virtual system, making it a more interesting teaching tool.

2.1   Features of the Intelligent Coach Avatar

The intelligent coach avatar (ICA) has several features: (1) immersion – life-experience based interaction, which enables the user to gain real training experience; (2) target – ICA-based user cognitive model which helps the user to understand the training purpose; (3) technique – ICA-based expert system which links knowledge databases and store user behavior data and gives feedback; and, (4) architecture – through user interface design to actualize the function of guide teaching.

2.2   Framework of an ICA-Based Virtual Driving Training System

Figure 1 shows the framework of an ICA-based virtual driving training system. In this system, the biggest problem that users face is to understand quickly where they are and how to make decisions about their next actions. By putting forward a behavior system based on a cognitive model and combined with the information-highlighting mechanism in a three-dimensional scene, the ICA reasoning logic and its interactions with users can be better described, so as to achieve effective perceptual interaction.

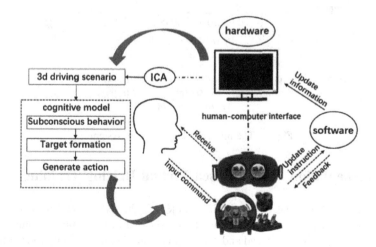

Fig. 1. Framework of ICA based virtual driving training system

Currently, ICA follows the mainstream method of intelligent tutoring system to structure the knowledge database using the generation rule. According to the framework of the intelligent coach avatar, the target content is divided into five steps: (1) knowledge learning, (2) environmental learning, (3) mock examination, (4) learning evaluation and (5) experience feedback.

2.3   ICA-Based User Cognitive Model

The ICA learning module consists of four layers (see Fig. 2): (1) the learning module layer, (2) the reasoning layer, (3) the knowledge description layer, and (4) the knowledge-generation layer. In the first layer, there are also three modules, the knowledge base, the user cognitive model and the corresponding target strategy. This extends upward to the inference process and system framework of the second layer, reorients the resource model, and forms a dynamic and flexible organizational structure. Then the third level of knowledge-description content is differentiated, and the fourth level of knowledge-generation expression is finally obtained.

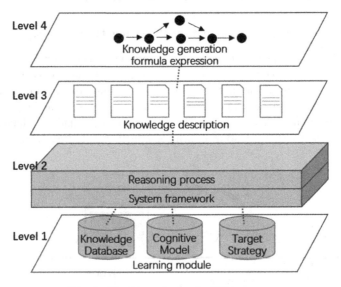

Fig. 2. The hierarchy level of ICA system

3   Implementation of ICA-Based Virtual Driving Training

To meet the teaching goal of car driving Subject 2, the user should master the basic operation skills of driving and have the ability to drive in the simulated sites proved, and to control the vehicle's speed and route. This system describes only four of the five test items based on the driving test syllabus (Fig. 3).

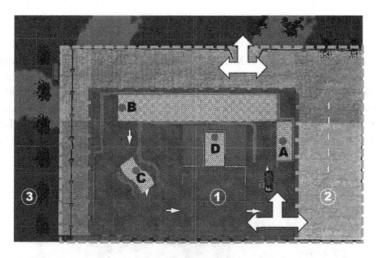

Fig. 3. The map of training site and distribution of four test items

3.1 ICA-Based Virtual Training Item Design

ICA, as a knowledge-based driving instructor, includes a knowledge-acquisition library that meets the specific set of knowledge points, in order to optimize the user's grasp of procedural knowledge. Four items addressed are flank parking, quarter turning, curve driving and reversing into a garage. According to the rules, common knowledge nodes, rule premises and rule conclusions can be extracted, which matches the user's behavior and can be adjusted by feedback. These four items are practiced sequentially and continuously according to site order, and the knowledge nodes in each item are checked in order. If no operation record of relevant knowledge node is detected, the ICA will appear in the user's vision, and the system will give corresponding prompts (Table 1).

Table 1. Knowledge description and linkage of training rules

Number	Item	Rules	Knowledge nodes
A	Flank parking	Stop right in front of the garage, reverse to garage at once, and wheels do not press down on side lines	Reverse → Turn on/off the light detection Edge → Collision detection
B	Quarter turning	Driving straight and turn left, no stopping halfway, no wheel rolling lane edge	Turn → Turn on/off the light detection Edge → Collision detection
C	Curve driving	Control steering and speed smoothly during driving. No parking on the way, the wheels must not touch the lane sideline	Sideline → Collision detection
D	Reverse into garage	Stop close to left on right sideway of the garage, reference to the extension of the garage corner on the right side for once reverse the car	Reverse → Turn on/off the light detection Sideway → Collision detection

3.2   ICA Access and Feedback Interface

The ICA system was developed on the Unity3D platform using Microsoft Visual Studio compiler and can run on Microsoft Windows. The design and implementation details of ICA are discussed below. The access interface (see Fig. 4) introduces the basic requirements and functions of the training system, in the form of text and sound, in the first person of the Avatar. There are three command buttons in the user access interface, where the "START" button corresponds to the event of entering the scene training, "BACK" corresponds to the event reintroduced by the Avatar, and "EXIT" corresponds to the events ending system.

Fig. 4. ICA access interface

This system has been developed to support driving training in the real world. The ICA system has designed two levels: (1) training level – after the user enters the training, only instant information prompts and feedback are provided, no behavior records are saved, and the error feedback is unqualified or all of them are directly restarted or returned to the main menu; and, (2) examination level – in order to enable users to strengthen their theoretical cognitive learning. Users have only one chance to pass all the projects, and will enter the final panel after the training. The system displays the degree of project completion and give suggestions through evaluation.

During the problem-solving phase, the user gets text descriptions of the requirements. After the user cognitive model is constructed through analysis of personal information data, once the user completes the problem or needs systematic guidance, the intelligent virtual coach system will evaluate and give feedback. Based on the results of the evaluation, the system can congratulate the user through ICA and provide information on the record board about the user's mistakes. Users can request more detailed feedback about their needs. After completing the training goal, the user can choose to return to the main menu and exit, use the record board to view the error information, or review the process.

Users interact with ICA through the user interface to build a learning objective framework and view feedback. The ICA feedback interface (see Fig. 5) is presented by the visual information of the Avatar image plus text, supplemented by voice. There are three areas in the interface, from top to bottom: user login area, Avatar dynamic display area and a blank workspace to be expanded by three command components.

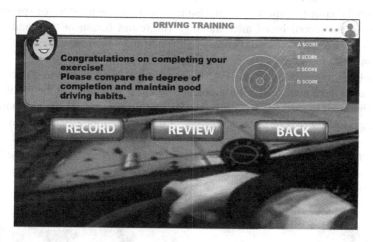

Fig. 5. ICA feedback interface

3.3   ICA-Based One-to-One Guidance

The interface is equipped with an Avatar voice message that provides guidance and uses it animation to display a strong visual presentation, which is expected to contribute to improving understanding and motivation levels. The avatar provides advice, encourages the user, and enhances the credibility of the system by using emotions. The appearance of images and sounds is intended to attract users. The ideal solution is to guide users to follow the system solution path while using interest points to transfer to shallow learning, but to avoid becoming distracted enough to reduce the attainment of the learning goal. The system helps users to find solutions when solving problems, and provides feedback for each user according to the individual's cognitive model to provide the correct solution library.

ICA system feedback is divided into six categories: (1) correct – simply indicates whether the input is done correctly or incorrectly; (2) error – represents a behavior prompt that contains an error; (3) prompt – usually a reminder message, such as "notice the right turn ahead"; (4) detailed prompt – provides more specific messages, such as "keep speed and direction steady", "turn right" etc.; (5) all errors – a series of dashboards that expand error action points for the user to see clearly; and, (6) solution – provides details of the error-handling demonstration. Detailed prompts provide feedback messages generated from the first constraint violation. Initially, the feedback level is set to the right level when the user starts working on the problem. As a result, a simple message is displayed the first time the test results are submitted, and this initial feedback level is low. To encourage users to solve their own problems, the feedback level increases with each submission, until the feedback level reaches the detailed prompt level. The auto-incrementing feedback is stopped at the detailed prompt level to encourage students to focus on one error at a time instead of all the wrong exercises.

ICA provides feedback that is related closely to animation for people in virtual learning environments. The red warning character in the interface contains buttons for requesting solutions, and users can get feedback on their answers to the questions by clicking on the error prompt. Users can also use the drop-down list to see specific level feedback on the record board after training. The restart button in the middle of the interface can be used to clear the history and restart the new training, while the return below can jump to the main menu interface.

To help users adapt better to ICA, the workspace is intuitive and flexible. Most people usually take notes about the problem or the text emphasizing the problem, and use the highlighting method to deepen the relationship between the special points and the corresponding words or phrases. The use of the highlighting mechanism in the user interface is very important for the purpose of helping the user to understand training. From the teaching point of view, many users offer incorrect solutions because they do not read and understand the problem fully. Figure 6 shows some ICA-based virtual training interfaces.

Fig. 6. ICA-based virtual training interface

4   Conclusion

This paper has discussed the design and implementation of ICA to help users get better driving training. It shows that ICA can be used to express knowledge of open tasks. To date, the collaborative learning environment of ICA has not been fully developed [8, 9], and the key to determining ICA as an effective teaching system is the logical top-level design of knowledge-base links, enriching system retrieval, query, and how to deal with decision-making. In future work, we will study the applicability of ICA to other design tasks and explore a variety of ways to enhance the system, such as running a new network-based system.

Acknowledgments. We would like to acknowledge the support of the Guangzhou Innovation and Entrepreneurship Leading Team Project under grant CXLJTD-201609.

References

1. Ropelato, S., Zünd, F., Magnenat, S., Menozzi, M., Sumner, R.: Adaptive tutoring on a virtual reality driving simulator. In: Proceedings of the 10th International Workshop on Semantic Ambient Media Experiences (SAME 2017), Artificial Intelligence MEETS Virtual and Augmented Worlds (AIVR), in Conjunction with SIGGRAPH Asia, 10 November 2018
2. Kopciak, P.A., Kolar, P., Dollfuss, M., et al.: Virtual reality driving simulator prototype for teaching situational awareness in traffic. In: Forschungsforum der Österreichischen Fachhochschulen (2016)
3. Andrade, A.D., Anam, R., Karanam, C., et al.: An overactive bladder online self-management program with embedded avatars: a randomized controlled trial of efficacy. Urology **85**(3), 561–567 (2015)
4. Lerouge, C., Dickhut, K., Lisetti, C., et al.: Engaging adolescents in a computer-based weight management program: avatars and virtual coaches could help. J. Am. Med. Inform. Assoc. **23**(1), 19–28 (2015)
5. Braun, A., Stocklöw, C., Hanke, S., et al.: Summary of the workshop Affective Interaction with Avatars @ Ambient Intelligence 2015. In: Workshop and Poster Papers of the European Conference on Ambient Intelligence, pp. 284–286 (2015)
6. Baylor, A.L.: Promoting motivation with virtual agents and avatars: role of visual presence and appearance. Philos. Trans. R. Soc. B: Biol. Sci. **364**(1535), 3559–3565 (2009)
7. Gratch, J., Rickel, J., André, E., et al.: Creating interactive virtual humans: some assembly required. IEEE. Intell. Sys. **17**(4), 54–63 (2002)
8. Shih, Y.C., Yang, M.T.: A collaborative virtual environment for situated language learning using VEC3D. J. Educ. Technol. Soc. **11**(1), 56–68 (2008)
9. Laffey, J., Schmidt, M., Galyen, K., et al.: Smart 3D collaborative virtual learning environments: a preliminary framework. J. Ambient Intell. Smart Environ. **4**(1), 49–66 (2012)

Multi-channel Scene Synchronization Strategy in Real Time Rendering

Xiaofen Li[(✉)]

School of Information Technology Engineering,
Taizhou Vocational and Technical College, Taizhou 318000, Zhejiang, China
2636369@qq.com

Abstract. This paper introduces a new synchronization method in real-time multichannel scene rendering, which is based on global time stamps, and collects and updates sync data in an adaptive way. Our method can reduce the times of sending acknowledge data between network server and each client node, thus keeps enough network bandwidth for use. It also handles slow or invalid network nodes and avoids the entire system to wait inefficiently, and can be used widely in interactive projects and researches.

Keywords: Multichannel rendering · Real time rendering ·
Software synchronization

1 Introduction

In modern virtual reality and system simulation field, when we meet rendering of large-scale real time scene and immersion type virtual reality experience needs, it can not do without auxiliary of multichannel display. Using multichannel display technology can break through resolution ratio of single display terminal and realize scene expression and interaction of ultrahigh resolution ratio.

What is said multichannel display technology here includes situation of using multiple windows, multiple displays even multiple computers to work together and render same big-scale scene.

Content of multichannel display commonly is an enact scene picture. If the picture is got by real time system rendering, then it will change with the input of user interaction event; or it can also be a continuous prerecorded video. Every channel used by multichannel display is one part of this picture and it changes synchronously, or it will make the whole scene to be torn, which will affect impression effect very much.

A simple multichannel display scheme is to use a set of graphic workstation of high property as main engine and at the same time output the display picture to multiple display terminals, for example display or projector, then it fuses and matches into a complete picture. But it has very high requirement to hardware equipment and if the channel numbers are too many (bigger than 4), generally speaking it is hard to find the

Fund Project: general project fund from education department of Zhejiang province (Y201738405).

Z. Pan et al. (Eds.): Transactions on Edutainment XV, LNCS 11345, pp. 246–255, 2019.
https://doi.org/10.1007/978-3-662-59351-6_17

commonly used display card matching with it, whose making and purchasing cost will also sharply increased because of this.

Method that possesses more universality is to use multiple computers or workstations to conduct distributed rendering work. In a local area network, every set of computer that participating in rendering work can be regarded as a node. This node is responsible for rendering one or multiple contents of large-scale scene, however after all nodes renders out scene concurrently, it then synchronously updates onto display terminal. Normal components of this system are shown as Fig. 1.

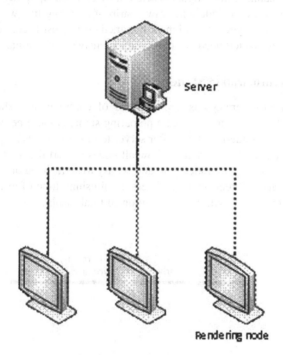

Fig. 1. Component of distributed multichannel system

Such method has high flexibility, which is suitable for multichannel rendering needs of any scenes. But because configuration environment and operation condition of all nodes hardware equipment can not be completely same, therefore we must conduct accurate control and management to process of synchronizing picture to avoid discontinuity feeling and tearing feeling of picture.

2 Traditional Synchronization Strategy

Scene synchronization strategy of multichannel display already has had some researches, including international famous manufacturer product like NVIDIA Quadro, Equalizer, VRJugger, for this they all have their own realization schemes. Traditional synchronization strategy includes Genlock, Fram Sync and SwapBufferSync. The article will successively state characteristic and existing problems of these methods and extend to get a new synchronization strategy of universality, the article will also state advantage of this new strategy comparing to traditional methods.

2.1   Genlock

Genlock is the most traditional and strict multichannel synchronization strategy. It requires to conduct one time signal synchronization when display output terminal start to generate every scanning line. Signal is sent out by external equipment in unification, display equipment of every node will draw a strip of scanning line when they receive every signal. Although synchronization of this method is most accurate, it can not be realized on software, which needs to purchase expensive professional equipment.

2.2   Frame Synchronization Strategy

Frame synchronization strategy is another kind of common multichannel synchronization method. It requires to send out a preparing signal at the time that every frame of all nodes real time rendering starts, after server terminal receives preparing signal of all nodes, it send a launching signal to allow all nodes to start the rendering of current frame. This strategy is easy to understand and is easy to be realized on software. But as different nodes bears different rendering pressure, finishing time of every frame is not confirmed, therefore it still will cause deviation of final display result. This process is shown as Fig. 2.

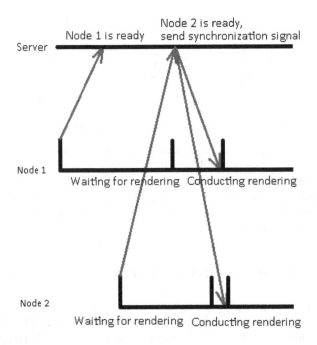

Fig. 2. Realization process of frame synchronization strategy

2.3 Swap Buffer Synchronization Strategy

Swap buffer synchronization strategy is an updation of Frame Synchronization, which is also the most widely applied multichannel display synchronization scheme. Standard drawing process of modern graph API (including OpenGL and DirectX) always firstly draw all image results of current frame into backstage buffer, then exchange to front desk to conduct display; next frame rubs off backstage buffer and newly draws image, constant recycles form continuous scene. However synchronization opportunity of swap buffer synchronization strategy is just selected before exchange of front and back stage, its realization process is shown as Fig. 3.

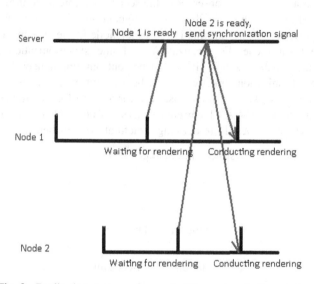

Fig. 3. Realization process of swap buffer synchronization strategy

Advantage of this method lies in: for similar computer equipment, time for exchanging front and back stage buffer is always consistent. Therefore, no matter drawing process of current frame is long or short, it can guarantee all pictures appear on the display terminal simultaneously as long as compulsorily conduct synchronization of all nodes before swap buffer, there fore integrity of scene picture is also guaranteed.

However, biggest problem of swap buffer synchronization is: if one node of multichannel system has problem (for example software or hardware failure), or drawing pressure of one frame is very big, which causes synchronization signal is delayed. Then the overall system will generate serious delaying because of this, even deadlocked. Although synchronization server terminal can adopt method of sending heartbeat signal, etc. to confirm failure node and repair or remove it, because failure is uncertain, therefore it must exist several seconds delaying and abnormal status before repairing problem, which causes the overall system can not be used within this time.

3 Synchronization Strategy Basing on Time Stamp

Integrating characteristic and problem of above strategy, we put forward a kind of new synchronization strategy basing on time stamp. The method will not cause the overall system to be sluggish or deadlock because of abnormal condition, therefore it efficiently enhances stability and practical value of the overall multichannel system.

3.1 Time Stamp

After interaction event of user is transmitted to synchronization server, calculate out current position and posture of observer in the scene, therefore to confirm content that display terminal should show in this frame. Synchronization server later needs to transmit this position posture information to every node in the system to respectively render different sub-scene. For realization of frame synchronization, information transmission and synchronization signal can be sent out simultaneously; however to swap buffer synchronization strategy, it must be sent out in two times.

In our strategy, we seal position posture information of every frame into a time stamp, i.e., simultaneously send current rendering frame ID and position posture information to all sub nodes. Here defining structural body as below:

```
struct TimeStamp

{

    long frameID;

    double referencedTime;

    Matrix4x4 viewMatrix;

};
```

Synchronization server does not need to consider sending opportunity, it only needs to guarantee to send out latest time stamp according to enough high frequency (such as 60 Hz, that is vertical synchronization frequency of general display).

3.2 Realization Process of Synchronization Strategy

First step to realize synchronization strategy is every node client terminal uses an independent line to always read and record time stamp sending from server terminal and store into a list. Because the using of independent uninterrupted line, this process has no relation with current rendering status of node, under condition that network delaying is very small, it can be regarded that time stamp server terminal sends out can always reach every set of node computer in the first time.

When client machine starts to render a new frame, it will check itself time stamp list and find out time stamp object No. N position at the end of distance list, transfer its content as current position and posture of scene.

The N here is a alterable parameter, it decides ability of node synchronization self-adapting. As list significant end always stores latest data (or has a little deviation of 1–2 frames) coming from server, therefore lists stored by different nodes, time stamp of No. N position distance end can also be regarded as the same. But if the N value is bigger, it means content that node machine renders has extent delaying compared to practical status of server terminal. Nevertheless, this delaying is integrity, that is to say image display of the overall system has some delaying, not behavior of one node. Therefore, more reasonable setting of N value will not have too much effect to actual sight and interaction of scene.

Realization process of this procedure is shown as Fig. 4.

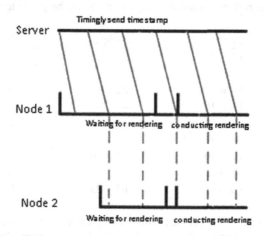

Fig. 4. Realization process of time stamp synchronization strategy

3.3 Adaptive Process of Node Synchronization

Biggest character of synchronization strategy based on time stamp is its dealing to abnormal node, it can self-adaptively adjust status of abnormal node to make it keep maximum synchronization with its other nodes at the same time of ensuring overall system will be affected. When abnormal node already can not guarantee normal synchronization, it also can select to quit by itself; or new normal node joins in at any time to replace it. The synchronization strategy described by this article can ensure these behaviors will not generate adverse impacts to overall system.

If frequency that server terminal sends time stamp is S, spending time that client machine node renders one frame is T, its selected time stamp object is F0, then when this frame rendering completes, the next time stamp object it selects will be:

$$F_1 = F_0 + T * S$$

We assume that sending frequency of server terminal is 60 Hz, there are three rendering nodes in the system, the time they renders a frame respectively is 1/20 s, 1/10 s and 1/15 s, then according to the above formula, it has:

$$Node1 : Fn = F_{n-1} + 3$$
$$Node2 : Fn = F_{n-1} + 6$$
$$Node3 : Fn = F_{n-1} + 12$$

Actual time stamp they render at every moment can be predicted as below table:

Moment	Node 1	Node 2	Node 3
0.0 s	F1 = 1	F1 = 1	F1 = 1
0.05 s	F2 = 4	–	–
0.1 s	F3 = 7	F2 = 7	–
0.15 s	F4 = 10	–	–
0.2 s	F5 = 13	F3 = 13	F2 = 13
0.25 s	F6 = 16	–	–
0.3 s	F7 = 19	F4 = 19	–
0.35 s	F8 = 22	–	–
0.4 s	F9 = 25	F5 = 25	F3 = 25

From the above table we can see, although rendering rate of all nodes are dominantly different, the time stamp they render are always consistent. Thus although node image of slow speed generates discontinuity feeling, synchronization strategy is still valid under this relatively extreme condition.

If one client terminal node loses response, then it means only itself does not accept time stamp signal of server any more, it will not affect operation of the overall system. However after a new node joins in the system, when total length of its time stamp list is under N, it does not render, when it exceeds N, it starts to render time stamp content at No. N position of distance list end and at this time it has already self guarantees synchronization relation with its other nodes.

4   Computational Results Test

Our using real time graphic rendering engine OpenSceneGraph as main multichannel system developing environment and realizes interactive synchronization real time rendering based on above synchronization strategy. Figure 5 shows six channel liquid crystal TV-wall display effect, the digital city scene it undertakes exceeds 20 GB.

Fig. 5. Multi-channel liquid crystal TV-wall display system

Figure 6 shows a three channels semi-immersion type projection display environment.

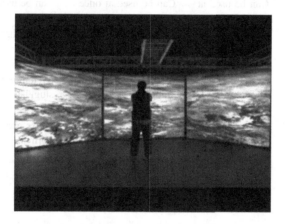

Fig. 6. Multi-channel arc projection display system

The below table conducts transverse comparison to Frame synchronization, exchange cache synchronization and synchronization strategy basing on time stamp.

Event	Frame synchronization	Exchange cache synchronization	Time stamp synchronization
Transmission position posture information	When every frame starts	When every frame starts	Independent thread
Execution synchronization	When every frame starts	When exchanges cache	When every frame starts
Synchronization accuracy	Medium	High	Medium

(continued)

(continued)

Event	Frame synchronization	Exchange cache synchronization	Time stamp synchronization
Transmission times of every frame network	1 time	2 times	Independent thread
Communication mode	Questions and answers	Notify when transmitting, ask and answer when it synchronizes	Notify
Condition of bad network environment	System is temporarily sluggish or deadlock	System is temporarily sluggish or deadlock	The system will not happen Deadlock, but the synchronization is not correct
Client machine enters	Can be used at once	Can be used at once	Can be used after queue is full
Client machine is lost	System is temporarily sluggish	System is temporarily sluggish	System has no influence
Client machine is delayed	System is temporarily sluggish	System is temporarily sluggish	System is temporarily sluggish
Client machine is in failure	System is temporarily sluggish	System is temporarily sluggish	Other parts of system is normal
Reliability of long time operation	Low	Low	High

In column of communication mode, "questions and answers" shows that it needs client terminal to feedback information to server terminal, at this time it will cause long time no answer or deadlock because of network or client machine failure; "Notify" shows client terminal does not need feedback, therefore client machine failure will not affect system itself.

From comparing results we can see, although a little inferior to method of swap buffer in synchronization accuracy, synchronization strategy basing on time stamp described by this article has very high system stability property, fault-tolerant rate of network transmission is very high, losing or failure of single client machine node has no effect to overall system, therefore it suits to be used in multichannel system of cluster-type, large-scale, high reliability very much.

5   Conclusion

Multichannel rendering synchronization strategy basing on time stamp described by this article has characteristic of high reliability, high fault-tolerant rate compared to existing schemes, it will not cause "cask effect" that overall system is sluggish because of fault in one client machine node. At the same time client machine node possesses self-adapting ability, which can ignore current rendering pressure problem, always keep synchronization with overall progress. Therefore it possesses high engineering feasibility.

This strategy not only can be used into real time large-scale multichannel expression, but also can be used in broadcasting of high definition film, or immersion system consisting of multiple distortion display screen.

However, synchronization accuracy of strategy described by this article appears a little not enough, which is possible to cause slight tearing feeling and discontinuity feeling when sighting, in the later research process, we can consider to combine this scheme with strategy of swap buffer synchronization, improve and optimize this synchronization strategy in further, enhance its engineering application value.

References

1. Wang, H.: Large Screen Projection and Intelligent System Integration Technique, 1st edn. National Defense Industry Press, Beijing (2010)
2. Eilemann, S., Makhinya, M., Pajarola, R.: Equalizer: a scalable parallel rendering framework. IEEE Trans. Vis. Comput. Graph. **15**(3), 436–452 (2009)
3. Ball, R., North, C.: Analysis of user behavior on high-resolution tiled displays. In: Costabile, M.F., Paternò, F. (eds.) INTERACT 2005. LNCS, vol. 3585, pp. 350–363. Springer, Heidelberg (2005). https://doi.org/10.1007/11555261_30
4. Equalizer: Video and Swap Synchronization. http://www.equalizergraphics.com/documentation/user/synchronization.html
5. Nvidia Quadro G-Sync. http://www.nvidia.com/page/quadrofx_gsync.html

On the Characteristics of Mise-en-scène in Animated Audio-Visual Language

Lingling Cui[✉]

Jilin Animation Institute, Changchun 130000, China
94640400@qq.com

Abstract. Animation mise-en-scène is in the system of animated audio-visual language, but it has its own characteristics in the process of expressing meanings and information. Though the form of animation mise-en-scène is pictorial, it also has its own features on the mind of constructing film space and scene. All these characteristics mentioned above are the key points of this paper. Whether it is the motility, subjectivity, description, spatiality, symbolism, contrast or economy, it reflects the unique charm of animation mise-en-scène. This paper focuses on concluding the characteristics of animation mise-en-scène, the thinking way that animations are different from other film, and the unique rule of animated audio-visual language in order to create more fantastic domestic animation films.

Keywords: Animation mise-en-scène · Characteristics · Animated audio-visual language

1   Introduction

Animations are drawn films that belong to the category of film art, and have their own characteristics. The thinking way of animation mise-en-scène learns from film art, but it differs in terms of process and performance due to the characteristics of its craftsmanship's features. Animation mise-en-scene takes the form of painting; however, it possesses unique method on film-space construction and scenes. The conclusion is developed from the deep discussion about its form and characteristics. Its distinctive characteristics release special charm in animation audio-visual language. The summery to animation mise-en-scene is the way to find out the animation method and the rules of animation audio-visual language and is benefit to produce widely welcomed animation products.

2   The Composition of Animation Mise-en-scène

In the course of animation creation, various meaningful elements in the screen space need to be combined and arranged, so the term animation mise-en-scène is introduced. It has some similarities with the mise-en-scène of stage plays as well as film and

---

This paper is the research result of the "13th Five-Year" Social Science Research Project of Education Department of Jilin Province, "Study on the Law of Animated Audio-visual Language". Project No.: JJKH20170991SK.

Z. Pan et al. (Eds.): Transactions on Edutainment XV, LNCS 11345, pp. 256–264, 2019.
https://doi.org/10.1007/978-3-662-59351-6_18

television works, for example, there is a sense of space; there are roles performing, however, it also has big differences, such as: the appearance and movement routes of the characters, the angle position of the cameras and the camera's movement routes, etc., so the director must be aware of them, and even in the early phase of the script, the careful arrangements or presentations should be considered. Only in this way can the movement of the characters themselves or the movement of the lens be fully coordinated and controlled in the filming and post-production processes of animations, which is called "animation mise-en-scène".

As the name suggests, the basic element of an animation is the mise-en-scène of an animated film, which should cover two art forms that are animated character scheduling and internal scheduling of animated shots.

In an animated film, there are no real cameras in most cases, but a software-simulated camera needs to implement the motion of the camera, or the motion of the camera is implemented by the animation creator's hand-drawn images. In animation production, the creator must shape the role through the reasonable movement of the lens according to the plot or the subjects' personality. For example, in the animated short film "Peter and Wolf", the cat is going to attack the crow, so it enters the frame from the foreground, and attack the crow with the blue balloon on the background. Here, how the cat appears and how the crow reacts, etc., which are all Character movement, while where the camera shots and what angles the camera adopts, which are the shot scheduling.

3 The Characteristics of Animation Mise-en-scène

Animated audio-visual language is a means of telling a story and expressing information and emotions in film and television animation, and is also a symbol system for animation creators to communicate with the audiences. Animation mise-en-scène belongs to the system of animated audio-visual language, but it has its own characteristics in the process of expressing meanings and information [1]. The characteristics of animation mise-en-scène determine its existing form (Table 1).

Table 1. Content overview of the characteristics of animation mise-en-scène

	Content overview	Function
Motility	• Camera displacement • Shooting angle change • Shooting focal length change	• Promoting the plot • Shocking visual effects • Describing character relations
Subjectivity	• Subjectivity of theme • Subjectivity of subject	• Highlighting key roles • Promoting the plot
Description	• Scenario • Artistic conception • Atmosphere	Artistic effect with imagination
Spatiality	Character movement	Strengthening the effect of spatiality

(continued)

Table 1. (*continued*)

	Content overview	Function
Symbolism	Add meaning	The effect of symbolic metaphor
Contrast	• Comparing actions of the characters • Comparing the utilization of space composition	Prominent theme
Economy	• Lens adjustment • Character movement	• Cost savings • Innovative shooting effect

The characteristics of animation mise-en-scène are discussed in details below.

3.1   Motility

The most eye-catching feature of animations is its mobility. First, the motility of animation mise-en-scène is presented on the "displacement" of the camera position while shooting. In addition to the continuous motion shooting methods of pushing, pulling, shaking, moving, raising, descending, etc., there are also "following", "swinging", "vibrating" and so forth. Second, the motility of animations is also reflected in the different shooting angles such as high angle, low angle, eye-level angle, oblique angle, etc. Third, there will be many unpredictable motion shots in the focal length of the shooting. This kind of frame is best at displaying and describing various characters' relationships, changes of the atmosphere and the way to follow up the progress of the incident. In the three-dimensional animated feature film "Ice Age", there is a long shot, followed by the single close-up of the "unlucky squirrel", gradually pulling up to the panoramic view of the entire migratory animal team, achieving a perfect transition between the prelude and the plot, and at the same time portraying the squirrels' running, bad luck and facetiosity, which also explained the background of the story - the big migration. The skillful lens scheduling, while effectively promoting the plot and guiding the next entry role (various migratory animals), also created a powerful visual effect. The virtual lens realizes the lens scheduling by motion. In this lens, all the scene changes from close-up to large panorama and distant view can be found, and the frames of each scene play corresponding roles; the virtual lens uses shaking, pulling and other. Scheduling techniques enable rich visual changes from eye-level to low to high angle and from telephoto to wide angle. In order to attract the attention of the audiences, the director of the real-life stop-motion animated film "The Mysterious Adventures of Thumb Fairy" adopts the "main body concentration" method as role scheduling. Through the internal focus shifting of the lens, it explains the environment around the main character and the state of other characters, and also maintains the focus on the main character as well as advancing the narrative process.

3.2 Subjectivity

In fact, animations, like any works of art, cannot completely avoid the subjectivity of the creative staff. For example, why does the film choose a certain type of picture, character or theme instead of another theme, picture or character? This explains that creative staff already has some subjective decisions and choices; you can imagine that if the creative staff does not make this decision, then nothing will happen. The animation mise-en-scène has strong subjectivity. Any scene scheduling is the creator's re-reconstruction of the script, expressing the author's viewpoint, attitude and aesthetic level. A very important part of the scene scheduling is the scheduling of the animated character. It can more effectively reflect the subjective strength of the creators and the level of design.

In the animation works, because the role modeling is more flexible and exaggerated than the real person performance, the scheduling of the subject shot in the frame often requires a key link to add more subjective design [2]. Role scheduling is an important part of animation mise-en-scène. The director changes the position and movement direction of the character, or uses the dynamic and static changes, which generate between the communicating characters in action and emotions. Then, adopting different frames or modeling to reveal the changes between roles' relationships and emotions, the more excellent screen effect could be obtained.

Every appearance of the character should be particular. Is it a bright and beautiful appearance, or a wretched appearance; is it to appear in a sunny place, or in a dark and terrifying place, which has deep meaning and plays a key role in portraying characters, so the animated role scheduling has a strong subjective, and it always conveys the careful design and ingenious arrangement of the animation director. In "Kung Fu Panda", a series of shots of the wolf's appearance, the background of the environment is particularly significant. This part is based on the subjective perspective of the messenger-duck, which has paved the way for the emergence of the wolf: the lens begins with a lot of high and low angles, which bring a huge sense of oppression; the next shot, a large number of long and wide shots of the prison, the director reduces the color of the frames in the mise-en-scène, and carefully creates an artistic effect that reflects the panic and serious atmosphere of the prison, successfully highlighting the relationship between the role and the environment, and laying a solid foundation to portray the inner world and personality of the characters. In this shot, in order to make a psychological preparation for the appearance of the wolf, the director adopted the subjective perspective of the duck. Before the wolf was seen, he used a lot of far, panoramic, high and low angles to let audiences expect the character to appear as early as possible.

In "Ice Age", the appearance of Mammoth Manny is a good example of a character mise-en-scène: in order to reflect its huge size, a low-angle looking lens is used, from the point of the bug to the eye-level, from the close-up of its sole to the back and to the panoramic view of the whole body; in order to highlight the direction of movement of the mammoth, in the mise-en-scène, it is designed to let the mammoth enter the screen separately from the right side of the screen, and let other animals enter the screen from the left side of the screen. The mammoth walks out of the frame from the left side, while the other animals leave the frame from the opposite direction, which forms the reverse motion of them, so the consequence is that the huge body of mammoth occupies the majority of the frame from the perspective of visual effect. Therefore, we say that the subjectivity of animation mise-en-scène is not only to highlight the main characters, and to portray the characters' personality, but also to promote the plot development of animation works and complete the wonderful narrative structure service.

3.3   Description

The description of animation mise-en-scène is reflected in the characteristics of a certain scene, mood and atmosphere. In the animation "Spirit", there is a stunning shot of the Spirit Leaping canyon. This shot is difficult to express in reality while shooting movies, but in order to create an amazing artistic effect the director uses the animation mise-en-scène to fully show it out, under the grand panoramic view and with the majestic momentum to show the Spirit's courage and freedom as well as arrogant and confident temperament. In this footage, when the Spirit destroyed the rails and was chased by the colonel and the cavalry, it fled all the way, but the chains on the body were stuck by the branches. In this critical moment, Crick rescued Spirit and he is temporarily out of danger. However, the cavalry regiment led by the colonel once again found the Crick and Spirit pushing them to the cliff. In this critical moment, Spirit took Crick to the other side of the cliff. The virtual camera uses multiple angles such as roll, slap, horizontal, overhead, bird's eye view, medium shot, and close-up to make the clip reach the ultimate effects in aesthetics and audiovisual. In particular, the high and distant shot of the pony king and Crick flying above the canyon shows the direction of Spirit's flight, and on the other hand shows the graceful posture of the Spirit leapfrog, and also reflects the depth of canyon and the steep cliff. The description and flexibility of the animation mise-en-scène are reflected in the enthusiasm, allowing the audiences to once again appreciate the audio-visual feast that everything can be done in the world of animation [3].

3.4   Spatiality

The spatiality of animation mise-en-scène is reflected in the character movement. The character's entry and exit should conform to the character's personality, emotions and thoughts. The character's action routes must have its logic and purpose. This process can be connected with different scenes, position of camera, or use a long shot to express. In animation "Wall • E", the roles are changed by long shots, using the intersection of the character's motion routes, and the different positional relationships of the character in the front background to change the subject of the frames. In the panoramic shot one, the robot that is cleaning the ground is fully represented. Panoramic shot two, in the cross road, numerous robots appear in the background. Panoramic shot three, the background of the Wall • E and Eva moved to the fore-ground. Panoramic shot four, the main body of the frame is changed, the cleaning robot exits the frame from the right, and the Wall • E and Eva become the main body of the frame. This group of shots realizes the spatial scheduling effect of the character object through the intersection of the character motion and the vertical motion of the subject.

In the "Ice Age", in order to express the encounter between Manny, Sid and the child's mother, and show the whole process of entrusting the baby, which can be seen according to the logical layout and scheduling of the role's actions in space, namely, the layout of the screen space outlines the approximate characters' relationships, and the basic characters' relationship corresponds to the next character motion trace. This group of shots achieves the effect of role scheduling in a specific space through the action of the child's mother and the changes of the composition.

3.5 Symbolism

Symbolism means that the viewer does not fully understand its meaning in the juxtaposition or contrast of the two shots. Instead, we understand its meaning in the juxtaposition of the objects in the same shot. The symbolism of animation mise-en-scène is to use the scheduling of the scene to give the shot space a certain meaning, showing the emotion in the film. In the famous animation "Lion King II", in order to express two protagonists, who have gone through all the hardships and finally came together, a symbolic approach was adopted: the grass on the ground sprouted and grew, and the full moon was hung in the sky, all symbolizing the coming of hope and the beauty of love. The animation "Corpse Bride" also uses the symbolic method to express the nobility and pureness of the bride and the happy ending of the two couples. In the last shot, the two couples hug each other and look at the moon in the night sky, and here the moon is endowed with a lot of symbolic meanings.

When some kind of profound meanings in the animations, the spiritual world of the character and meaningful frames should be expressed, the director often needs to use the intensity of the mise-en-scène. In the animation "Kung Fu Panda", the symbolism of the animation mise-en-scène is closely linked to the spiritual world of the characters. When the master and the turtle are talking about Tao, the flowers and fruits symbolizes Tao. Panoramic shot one, the foreground is flowers, and the background is the turtle, as for flowers, fruits and trees, which are the carrier of their talking, and also a symbol of their spiritual world; panoramic shot two, foreground is the master, medium-view is fruit, and the background is turtle; panoramic three, foreground is fruit, and the background is the master; panoramic four, foreground is fruit, and the background is the turtle; panoramic five, there is the turtle and the master under the tree; medium shot

Fig. 1. Kung Fu Panda

six, the turtle give the stick to the master, and the wooden stick is the symbol of the mission; panoramic seven, blossoms are the symbol of the turtle's spiritual world; far shot eight, the blossoms are gone and the trees wither, symbolizing the death of the turtle. In this group of shots, the talking of the master and the turtle is compared with the relationship between the flowers and the fruit through the slitting of the shots, to achieve a symbolic metaphor effect (Fig. 1).

3.6   Contrast

Contrast is one of the oldest and most effective means of artistic expression used in a variety of arts, and animations are no exception. Therefore, contrast is the most unique feature of animation mise-en-scène. Animated films often use different shots contrast to express the director's vision in the action of the character or the space of the frame so that the audiences can obtain the contrast effect from the self-psychological experience, and they can psychologically have their own conclusion to use their own feelings to understand the inner meaning of the animation itself.

In the animation "Ice Age", the mise-en-scène of Diego and the little girl's mother reflects the contrast. Diego takes up two-thirds of the space in the frame, and is in the upper part with a sense of control. The little girl's mother appears in a top-down posture, from the small part of the whole frame, overlooking the lower part of the frame, which naturally forms a strong contrast and the consequences of the strength of the two are self-evident. In the animation "Wall • E", a series of shots contrast the deserted earth with the bustling scenes of the past, reflecting the desolate scene of environmental pollution and garbage all around. Far shot one, deserted city; far shot two, huge billboards and empty shops; close-up shot three, money everywhere; close-up shot four, shaking to the panorama of bank building; close-up shot five, Wall • E is walking across the street; panoramic shot six, lively sounds, dazzling billboards and deserted cities, contrasting elements appear in the same frame. This group of shots reflects the environment in which Wall • E lives through the contrasts between the past and the present, desolation and prosperity. The contrast of the animation mise-en-scène is to highlight the theme of the animation work, playing an important role in revealing the essence of the problem (Fig. 2).

Fig. 2. Wall • E

3.7   Economy

Starting from the production cost of animated films, in order to save huge investment, animation directors often resort to the animation mise-en-scène. As mentioned earlier, it is the combination of animation shot scheduling and role scheduling, so in order to achieve and achieve the goal of saving huge costs, you must start from this source. The animated characters are hand-painted by the creators, or they are modeled and designed in software. The real characters in the TV dramas require expensive appearance fee, if they invite the popular stars to appear. The animation shots are generally the virtual shots made by software and the virtual shot can not only simulate the camera position and lens of the real camera, but also reduce the cost of equipment purchase and lease, and is not limited by the weather conditions when shooting outside. Therefore, the animation mise-en-scène itself is economical. The economy of animation mise-en-scène is reflected in the less waste of resources and the high quality of the works. For example, a film about the theme of the car, the animation "Cars", the protagonist red car called Lightning while racing in the field, many cars colliding, and finally lightning jumps up from the crashed cars and flies over. When the lightning is flying over the cars with an exaggerated and confident expression, the mise-en-scène is tight and the frame is stunning. Imagine if the cost of shooting this shot with a real car would increase rapidly, even with a real car, it would be difficult to shot the scene of flying from crashed cars, let alone a real car with a close-up shot of virtual cameras to show exaggerated and confident expression. This fully embodies the economy of animation mise-en-scène, creating high value with as few resources as possible. It can not only achieve the effect that the real film cannot realize, but also save costs and reduce investment, fully presenting the superiority of animation mise-en-scène and highlighting the advantages of animated audio-visual language (Fig. 3).

Fig. 3. Spirit

4   Conclusion

In the pre-production, the animation establishes the overall space through the drawing of the main scene. On this basis, the director combines the narrative main line design of the script to design the sub-lens. At this point, all the contents of the animation mise-en-scène from the animation role scheduling to the shot scheduling are basically determined. In these two projects, although the main scenes are virtual, the space of its expression is real. The form of animation mise-en-scène is pictorial, but its thinking of constructing film space and shot contents has its own characteristics. These characteristics are the key points of this paper. Whether it is the motility, subjectivity, description, spatiality, symbolism, contrast or economy, it reflects the unique charm of animation mise-en-scène. In summary, in order to better promote the narrative function of animated films, to make the animation more attractive to the audiences, and to make the theme of the animation more vivid, we must strengthen the understanding of the concept of animation mise-en-scène. This paper summarizes the characteristics of animation mise-en-scène in order to generalize the thinking way of animation, straighten out the rules of animated audio-visual language, and finally create more excellent animations.

References

1. Lei, Y.: On the Characteristics of Animated Audio-Visual Feelings. Chongqing University, Chongqing (2014)
2. Pan, J.: Subjective Study of TV News Program Narration. D. Yangzhou University, Jiangsu (2012)
3. Geng, M.: Appreciation of Animated Audio-Visual Language. China Labor and Social Security Publishing Press, Beijing (2010)

Human Eye Tracking Based on CNN and Kalman Filtering

Zhigeng Pan[1,2(✉)], Rongfei Liu[2], and Mingmin Zhang[3]

[1] China Academy of Art, Hangzhou, China
zgpan@hznu.edu.cn
[2] Digital Media & HCI Center, Hangzhou Normal University, Hangzhou, China
[3] Institute of VR, NINED LLC, Guangzhou, China

Abstract. The driver fatigue detection method based on human eye feature information has the advantages, such as non-invasion, low cost, natural interaction and so on, which has been widely favored. However, in the actual detection process, the driver's face will be shaken due to various factors, and there will be motion blur, which will cause misjudgment and missed judgment on the fatigue driving detection. Therefore, this paper designs a method based on CNN convolutional neural network to detect human key points, then uses Kalman filter to track human eyes, eliminates jitter interference, and greatly improves the accuracy of fatigue detection. The experimental results show that the proposed method can track the human eyes in real time and has high accuracy and robustness.

Keywords: Key point detection · Human eye tracking · DCNN · CNN · Kalman filter

1 Introduction

Human eye tracking has a wide range of applications in the fields of pattern recognition, human-computer interaction, and intelligent transportation. It is a hot issue in the field of computer vision [1]. Non-contact human eye tracking based on image processing has important research significance in driver fatigue detection and expression recognition [2–4]. Dong et al. [5] used the skin color model in the YCbCr space to segment the skin color, and then used the Kalman filter method to track the human eye, but this method is greatly affected by the skin color and illumination; Cheng of Central South University and others proposed a human eye tracking algorithm based on kalman filtering and meanshift algorithm [6]. Although the accuracy of eye tracking algorithm is relatively high, the real-time performance is poor. Comaniciu. D et al. proposed a new one. The color-based motion camera target tracking model uses the mean shift analysis method to derive the candidate target that is most similar to the given target model [7]. Finally, the target tracking is performed. This method has large system overhead and limited practicality.

In summary, the existing human eye tracking methods are performed using conventional methods using skin color, pixel features [8], and the like. This type of method is susceptible to external environmental interference, such as light, glasses and other

Z. Pan et al. (Eds.): Transactions on Edutainment XV, LNCS 11345, pp. 265–273, 2019.
https://doi.org/10.1007/978-3-662-59351-6_19

factors, high false positive rate, has certain limitations [9]. This paper proposes a human eye tracking based on CNN and Kalman filter. Firstly, the improved convolutional neural network is used to detect the key points of the human eye, and then the key points detected by the CNN are combined with the actual error sources and conditions. Tracking modeling, using the Kalman filter to track the human eye in real time, and finally analyzing and explaining the tracking results. Compared with traditional methods, this paper combines deep learning with traditional machine vision tracking methods for human eye tracking. This method has high practicability and robustness.

2   Convolution Neural Network

Convolutional neural network (CNN) is the most commonly used model structure in the field of deep learning. It is a multi-layer artificial neural network [10–12], which is widely used in pattern recognition and artificial intelligence. More network models. The hierarchical structure of CNN is mainly composed of input layer, convolution layer, excitation layer, pooling layer and fully connected layer. The following describes the convolutional layer and pooling layer operations:

(1) Convolution layer operation. As the name suggests, the convolution layer is a convolution operation on the input image. Each convolution is the extraction of image features. Figure 1 shows the convolution calculation process. In addition to the convolution kernel, the convolution operation has several important parameters, namely padding and step size. The padding is mainly to add some values to the input image when the convolution kernel exceeds the image during convolution, to ensure that the extracted edge information is complete. The step size is that the convolution kernel slides to the length once, and its size has an important influence on the output characteristic map.

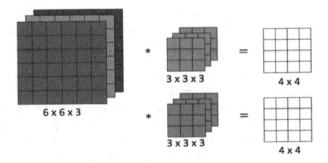

Fig. 1. Convolution calculation diagram

(2) Pooling layer operation. In order to reduce the data dimension and over-fitting, the downsampling and pooling operations are usually performed after the convolution operation is completed. At present, the most common pooling operations have two

forms, one is Max-Pooling, the filter core takes the maximum value at the corresponding position, and the other is Mean-Pooling, which is filtered. The kernel is averaged for the corresponding position. Take the maximum pooling as an example. The pooling operation is shown in Fig. 2. The Max-pooling core size is 2×2, and the step size is 2.

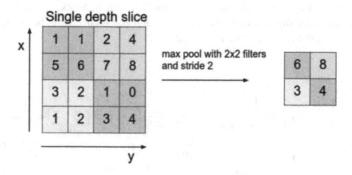

Fig. 2. Schematic diagram of pooling process

3 Human Eye Tracking Algorithm

3.1 Human Eye Key Detection

The key point detection of the human eye is to detect the two-dimensional coordinate information of the human eye feature point in the face image containing the eye, and is also a solution process for a regression problem. This paper is based on the DCNN network proposed by Sun et al. [13] for face key detection. DCNN is a three-level convolutional neural network, which mainly realizes the detection of five key points of the face: left and right eyes, nose, left and right corners. In each cascade, different network structures correspond to different detection sites, and finally merged to achieve precise positioning of these five key points. Its specific structure is shown in Fig. 3.

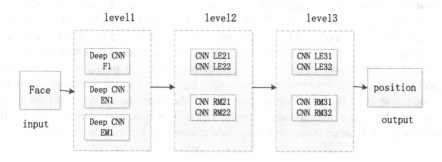

Fig. 3. DCNN network structure

Considering the real-time requirements of fatigue detection, and only need to detect a few key points in the eye for later target tracking, we modified and redesigned the EN1 network in the first phase of the above DCNN network, only for eyes. Key point detection of the part. Its network structure is shown in Fig. 4, which includes 3 convolution layers and 2 maximum pooling layers. The initial input image is a cropped image containing only two eyes, with a size of 40×20, and then an 8-dimensional feature vector is output through the convolutional neural network. It can be seen that the feature map after the first convolution is 20, and the second time becomes 40. The parameters of each layer are shown in Table 1.

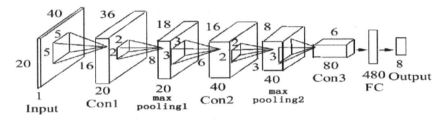

Fig. 4. Human eye key point detection CNN network structure diagram

Since the human eye area is relatively concentrated and the features are similar, we use a local shared convolution kernel in the network, which effectively reduces the number of parameters. At the same time, according to the regression idea, the parameter model we trained can be expressed as:

$$\text{Loss} = \frac{1}{n} \sum_{i=1}^{n} ((x_i - x_i')^2 + (y_i - y_i')^2) \tag{1}$$

Where (x_i, y_i) is the location detected by the network, (x', y') defines the key point location for the calibration. In the experiment, in order to reduce the human interference factor, we defined n = 4, that is, we calibrated the positions of the key points of the four human eyes, which are the middle positions of the upper, lower, left and right edges of the human eye, as shown in Fig. 5. Finally, according to the principle of Loss minimization, the position of the key point of the human eye detected by the convolutional neural network designed in this paper is also near the intersection of the four calibration points. The experiment finds that by setting the calibration point, not only in the detection accuracy. It has been improved and it has saved a lot of time costs. Overall, the detection efficiency is greatly improved, and the experimental results of the final human eye key point detection are shown in Fig. 6. The figure shows the test results of the human eye in three states: full open, half closed, and completely closed.

Table 1. Network parameters for each layer

Layer 0	Layer 1	Layer 2	...	Layer 5	Layer 6	Layer 7
I (40, 20)	CR (5, 20, 2, 2)	P (2)	...	CR (3, 80, 1, 1)	F (480)	F (8)

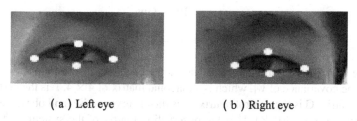

(a) Left eye   (b) Right eye

Fig. 5. Four calibration point locations

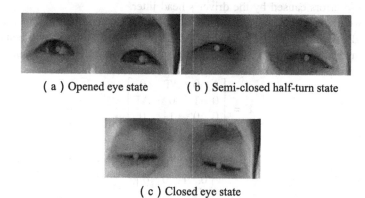

(a) Opened eye state   (b) Semi-closed half-turn state

(c) Closed eye state

Fig. 6. Human eye key detection results under different conditions

3.2 Kalman Filtering Algorithm

The Kalman filter is an optimal autoregressive data processing algorithm [14]. From a group of interferences containing various noises, the position coordinates and velocity of the object can be accurately and quickly predicted, which can effectively resist the observation error and ensure a smooth change of the output state. It can be found in many engineering applications, such as target tracking, radar positioning, etc. Based on the key point information of the human eye detected by the previous CNN, we establish a Kalman filter target tracking model:

First, in each video sequence, the convolutional neural network is used to detect the position of the key point of the human eye. The coordinates of the point are $(x(t), y(t))$, $(v_x(t), v_y(t))$ is the velocity in the x direction and the y direction at this point t, so that the state vector of the Kalman filter can be defined as

$$x_t = (x(t), y(t), v_x(t), v_y(t)) \tag{2}$$

Similarly, the observation vector is defined as $y_t = (x(t), y(t))$ that is, the observation vector represents the two-dimensional coordinates of the key point in each frame, and the Kalman system equation is obtained according to the state transition relationship above.

$$x_{t+1} = Fx_t + Gw_t \tag{3}$$

$$y_t = Hx_t + v_t \tag{4}$$

Where w_t is the system noise and satisfies the Gaussian distribution $w_t \sim N(0, Q_t)$, and Q_t is the covariance of w_t, which is a diagonal matrix of 4×4. F is the system state transition matrix, G is the control matrix, v_t is the observed noise, and obeys the normal distribution, i.e. $v_t \sim N(0, R)$, H is the observation matrix of the system, and R is the covariance of v_t, which is 2×2 diagonal matrix. In this paper, it is mainly caused by various noise errors caused by the driver's head jitter.

Here, we made a reasonable assumption: in the case where the time interval ΔT is small, the displacement of the key points of the human eye between two consecutive frames of images is small, and is regarded as a uniform motion. Then F, H can be set to:

$$F = \begin{bmatrix} 1 & 0 & \Delta T & 0 \\ 0 & 1 & 0 & \Delta T \\ 0 & 0 & 1 & 0 \\ 0 & 0 & 0 & 1 \end{bmatrix} \tag{5}$$

$$H = \begin{bmatrix} 1 & 0 & 0 & 0 \\ 0 & 1 & 0 & 0 \end{bmatrix} \tag{6}$$

According to the above relational definition, the time update equation and the state update equation of the Kalman filter can be obtained. Among them, the time update equation is:

(1) State prediction: $x_t^- = Fx_{t-1} + Gw_{t-1}$, x_t^- is an a priori state estimate.
(2) Error covariance prediction: $P_t^- = FP_{t-1}F^T + Q_{t-1}$, P_t^- is the a priori error covariance.
    The state update equation is:
(3) Filter gain matrix: $K_t = P_t^- H_t^T (H_t P_t^- H_t^T + R_t)^{-1}$.
(4) State estimation correction: $x_t = x_t^- + K_t(y_t - H_t x_t^-)$, and x_t is a posteriori state estimation.
(5) Covariance update: $P_t = (I - K_t H)P_k^-$, P_t is the posterior error covariance.

In the actual human eye tracking experiment, the initial position error of the human eye key point in the two-dimensional plane coordinate system is ± 10 pixels, the speed error is ± 6 pixels, and we are for each detected human eye. The key points define a Kalman filter for tracking. Therefore, in each frame, the position of the human eye key point at the t frame can be predicted by the position of the human eye key point at the t frame, thereby realizing the real-time tracking of the human eye.

4   Experimental Results and Analysis

The experimental environment of this paper is a general laboratory environment. In order to test the effect and performance of the Kalman filter to track the human eye, this paper tests the video sequence captured by the camera on a PC, as shown in Fig. 7. In the green rectangular human eye area, the red point is the key point of the human eye detected by the CNN, and the blue point is the prediction of the position of the red point at the next moment by the Kalman filter. The graph shown in Fig. 8 is a random sample of 300 frames of continuous image sequence. The image size of each frame is 640×480 pixels, and the tracking result of Kalman filter at each frame is recorded. The blue curve is the actual data of the key points of the human eye. The red curve is the tracking result for this point. It can be seen that the method of this paper can effectively predict the position of the human eye at the next moment and achieve a good tracking effect.

Fig. 7. Human eye tracking results (Color figure online)

At the same time, we simulated the car driving environment in the laboratory for 5 users, and the normal movement and shaking of the face in front of the camera, simulating the driver's various possible face poses, and setting all the frames to F_a the tracking failed. If the number of frames is F_e, the number of frames successfully tracked is $F_s = F_a - F_e$. The test results are shown in Table 2. User 1 is the author himself. Due to the familiarity with the experimental requirements, the number of frames for tracking errors is relatively small, while others have a large deviation from the face when they first started testing, even leaving the camera's capture area due to Kalman. The filter predicts the state at this moment based on the previous state, which causes the Kalman filter to be terminated and started repeatedly, consuming a large amount of system resources, resulting in a lower accuracy of the experiment. After several repeated exercises, the test basically stabilized, and the correct rate was basically around 95%–97%, indicating that the method has certain reliability.

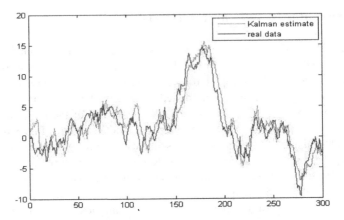

Fig. 8. Kalman filter tracking effect chart (Color figure online)

Table 2. Human eye tracking experiment result table

	F_a	F_e	F_s	Accuracy
User 1	340	8	332	97.6%
User 2	330	12	318	96.3%
User 3	300	10	290	96.7%
User 4	320	10	310	96.9%
User 5	350	16	334	95.4%

5 Conclusion

In the course of the experiment, we have re-modified the EN1 part of the DCNN network and designed the CNN network structure, which reduces the complex layers of the network and detects the key points of the human eye. Then based on the key points detected by this CNN and combined with the actual error source, the Kalman filter is used to track the human eye in real time. Finally, we carried out experimental verification and analysis, and the results show that the proposed human eye tracking method can achieve high accuracy and practicability.

At the same time, we can also see that the algorithm proposed in this paper faces an unavoidable problem, that is, when performing human eye tracking, if there is missed detection and misdetection of the key points of the human eye in a certain frame, it will affect the next frame. Predict the result, at this time kalman filtering will be invalid. We are currently considering adding the Mean Shift algorithm for comprehensive tracking. There is still a long way to go in the tracking of visual human eyes, and more excellent algorithms are needed to solve practical engineering problems.

Acknowledgments. We would like to acknowledge the support of the Guangzhou Innovation and Entrepreneurship Leading Team Project under grant CXLJTD-201609.

References

1. Cristinacce, D., Cootes, T.: Feature detection and tracking with constrained local models. In: Proceedings of the British Machine Vision Conference. BMVA, Edinburgh, UK, pp. 929–938 (2006)
2. Peng, N.S., Yang, J., Zhou, D.K.: Study on Bhattacharyya coefficients within mean-shift framework and its application. Soft Comput. Fusion Found. Methodol. Appl. **10**(12), 1127–1134 (2006)
3. Shi, H.W., Xia, L.M.: Human eye tracking based on Mean Shift algorithm and particle filter. Comput. Eng. Appl. **42**(19), 26–28 (2006)
4. Zhang, Y.Y., Wang, H.J., Huang, Y.D., et al.: Pedestrian target tracking method based on Meanshift and particle filter. Comput. Modernization **3**, 40–43 (2012)
5. Dong, W.H., Wu, X.J., Qu, P.S.: Human eye tracking based on rule and Kalman filter. Comput. Eng. Sci. **28**(11), 27–29 (2006)
6. Chen, Y.Q., Luo, D.Y.: Real-time tracking of human eyes based on Kalman filtering and Mean Shift algorithm. Pattern Recog. Artif. Intell. **17**(2), 173–177 (2004)
7. Comaniciu, D., Ramesh, V.: Mean shift and optimal prediction for efficient object tracking. In: International Conference on Image Processing. CiteSeer (2000). https://doi.org/10.1109/ICIP.2000.899297
8. Breitbart, Y., Garofalakis, M., Martin, C., et al.: Topology discovery in heterogeneous IP networks. In: Proceedings of IEEE INFOCOM, vol. 1, pp. 265–274 (2000)
9. Deng, Y.H.: Multi-target tracking based on decoupled de-biasing measurement Kalman filter algorithm. In: Proceedings of 2016 IEEE Chinese Guidance, Navigation and Control Conference (IEEE CGNCC 2016). China Aviation Society Guidance, Navigation and Control Branch Key Laboratory of Integrated Aircraft Control Technology, Nanjing Branch of IEEE Control System Association: China Aviation Society, no. 6, pp. 2859–2864 (2016)
10. Singh, A., Minsker, B.S., Bajcsy, P.: Image-based machine learning for reduction of user fatigue in an interactive model calibration system. J. Comput. Civ. Eng. **24**(3), 241–251 (2010)
11. Jiang, T.: An image classification algorithm based on multidomain convolution neural network. In: Science and Engineering Research Center. Proceedings of 2017 2nd International Conference on Wireless Communication and Network Engineering (WCNE 2017), no. 6, pp. 370–375 (2017)
12. Li, X.: Airplane detection using convolutional neural networks in a coarse-to-fine manner. In: IEEE Beijing Section, Global Union Academy of Science and Technology, Chongqing Global Union Academy of Science and Technology. Proceedings of 2017 IEEE 2nd Information Technology, Networking, Electronic and Automation Control Conference (ITNEC 2017), no. 5, pp. 270–274 (2017)
13. Sun, Y., Wang, X., Tang, X.: Deep convolutional network cascade for facial point detection. In: Proceedings of IEEE Conference on Computer Vision and Pattern Recognition (CVPR), vol. 9, no. 13, pp. 3476–3483 (2013)
14. Khashirunnisa, S., Chand, B.K., Kumari, B.L.: Performance analysis of Kalman filter, fuzzy Kalman filter and wind driven optimized Kalman filter for tracking applications. In: 2nd International Conference on Communication Control and Intelligent Systems (CCIS), Mathura, pp. 170–174 (2016)

Author Index

Printed in the United States
By Bookmasters